To all people of goodwill

THE PATHOLOGICAL MANIFESTATIONS OF CONTEMPORARY SOCIETIES: A PSYCHOLOGICAL STUDY ON IMMATURITY AND ITS SOCIAL IMPLICATIONS.

First edition. May 6, 2024.

ISBN: 979-8224317158

Written by Laurent Sueur.

Table of contents

Introduction.

1: The weakness of the French intellectuals.

    A. Paul-Michel Foucault.
    B. Jean-Paul Sartre.
    C. Albert Camus.
    D. The relation between their mind and their political actions and opinions.

2: Forever young and immature.

    A. The young savages.
    B. The adolescent liar.
    C. Violent youth.
    D. The borderline school.
    E. Joie de vivre.

3: The mousetrap.

    A. Main Street.
    B. Wall Street.
    C. Bernard Madoff.
    D. Jérôme Kerviel.

4: The rictus of the doll.

    A. This is not really entertainment.

      a. Tennessee Williams.
      b. Baby Jane Hudson.

    A. When girls cannot grow up.

> a. *An immature mother.*
> b. *Two absent fathers.*
> c. *I need to grow up.*

A. *Homicidal mothers.*
> a. *A rough woman.*
> b. *A monster or a lunatic?*
> c. *This flesh is my flesh.*

5: *A hive full of drones.*

A. *What is a man?*
B. *The equivocal function of sport.*
C. *The psychological importance of football for the immature man.*
D. *The structural answer of unstructured minds.*
E. *When the most dangerous drones escape from the hive.*

6: *Do not ease the pain.*

A. *The meaning of the figures.*
B. *Anaclitic addictions.*
C. *The Virgin Mary will save mankind.*
D. *A feeble social reaction.*

7: *Anaclitic racism.*

A. *Modern racism.*
> a. *The American Civil War.*
> b. *The French racists.*

A. *The Norwegian knight.*
> a. *Paranoid schizophrenia!*

b. *A man-child who does not ignore reality.*
c. *Light racism.*

8: *Islamic terrorism.*

A. *Al Qaeda.*
  a. *Osama Bin Laden.*
  b. *Mohamed Atta.*

A. *The French Jihad.*
  a. *Khaled Kelkal.*
  b. *The suburbs are burning.*
  c. *Violence against the Jews.*
  d. *Mohamed Merah.*

9: *The American psychopaths.*

A. *Trauma or interruption in the development of the ego?*
B. *The signs of antisocial personality disorder.*
C. *Them and the others.*
D. *The last journey.*

10: *Hell.*

A. *Adolf Hitler.*
B. *The courtiers.*
C. *The Four Horsemen of the Apocalypse.*
D. *Primal violence.*

Conclusion.

The history of mankind is an endless Greek tragedy. Does it mean that man's soul is as black as Hell, which always leads to massacres when humans are put together and interact? Each generation seams wilder than the one before. The Garden of Eden, this terrestrial peace, is a reality that is out of reach now. The 20th century set foot in Tartarus. Will the future be even worse? Does conscience exist? Is reason a pure speculation of philosophers who dare not look at the human animal anymore? Is not there anyone to hold the mirror of truth so that the narcissistic sorcerer may see his evilness? The mirror must not be broken: it is the only thing that can connect him to reality, and it could cure him, for he is ill.

Human nature cannot be that bad, for mankind sometimes stood on the side of creation. Hence, this human fury could be the result of an accumulation of social dysfunctions that transform good men and women into ogres. Jean Jacques Rousseau would not have made a mistake: nature (man) would be good, whereas culture (society) would be really evil. Actually, when Hannah Arendt tried to understand World War II, she almost shared the latter's opinion: Eichmann was a normal person obeying orders coming from a social hierarchy. She was obviously confused, and she stubbornly refused to take into consideration the harsh reality of pathological normalcy. Normal people put together would engender a social frenzy! What is normalcy? We can easily understand that it is not psychosis, but it is not reason either! Normalcy would be an intermediate state, a kind of unstable average of beliefs, opinions, and individual and social behaviors. Being here and forever the advocate of pure reason, I would easily point out the conceptual imperfections of such a definition. I would even emphasize the barbarity of this view since the cruelty of human organizations would inscribe crime on the marble of normalcy. Hence, normal people, by nature, would logically commit extraordinary massacres exhibiting their bottomless inhumanity.

Other people tried to find a more psychiatric explanation for mankind's curse. In fact, manslaughter was an idea that would only germinate in the mind of some sick people. For instance, Hitler was called a schizophrenic many times, schizophrenia being the most primitive form of human intelligence. Consequently, the most horrific crimes ever perpetrated had been committed by the maddest kind of person. The idea was not convincing; at least the academics who have studied this disease are dubious about it. Personally, I very much questioned the competence of people who shared this opinion and just let my mind remember Leni Riefenstahl's *Triumph of the Will*, more precisely the moment when Hitler walks through perfect lines of perfectly immobile soldiers. The smoothness of his walk contrasts with the rigidity of the men around him. He is almost as light on his feet as a male ballet dancer. At first glance one can understand there is not such a mental illness here: a schizophrenic does not walk, he jumps! Schizophrenia is palpable, silent substantiation, a disease inscribed on the skeleton of mankind and its fearful eyes.

In 1941, Hervey Cleckley, who was a psychiatrist, was less adamant. In his *Mask of sanity* (1), he emphasized the problematic behaviour of borderline patients who were not technically insane, but not sane either. We must notice that the European psychopathic blast of that time had moved some Austrian and German psychoanalysts and psychiatrists to immigrate to the United States. So, it is not a coincidence that the concepts of psychopathic personalities and personality disorders gained ground in the United State: experts, who had observed and understood the phenomenon because of the horror engendered by the connection between unbalanced people and dysfunctional societies, had contributed to scientific progress. In this connection, Cleckley portrayed an individual who looked like a reasonable person, but was not: the psychopath became the gravedigger of humanity. He was dangerous, not only because he could conceal his mental disorders but also because there were lots of people of that kind who were prone to violence. Cleckley was not a sociologist, and, once the danger was identified, he did not really try to find a social mechanism that explained the proliferation of this type of individual or described the conditions that were required to turn his personality traits into harmful weapons to human organizations. The culprit had been discovered, the social solution was clear: the psychopath had to read the *Mask of sanity*, understand that he was insane and undergo psychoanalysis, or be incarcerated in a psychiatric hospital if he did not want to make progress without anybody's help. He did not speak of the link between the level of decompensation and his dangerousness, nor did he say anything about the connection between him and the rest of society. A psychopath was dangerous by nature.

In 1974, something important happened, something that has not had a significant impact yet. Jean Bergeret (2) published *Normal and pathological personality*. For the first time, readers learned what normalcy was and they had a clear vision of the different levels of consciousness and of the limit between reason and madness and mental functioning and decompensation. The borderline cases were very well studied. Bergeret was very meticulous about terminology: he preferred to name them "immature" or "anaclitic" people. All of them were not considered to be dangerous; only "perverts of character", whom Americans would certainly call psychopaths. They were a threat which he portrayed using Shakespeare's character Iago. He even went further and depicted Maximilien de Robespierre as a "psychosis of character", an immature man who was not that stupid, but whose superego was quite ineffective, which would lead him to kill people remorselessly. Later in his career, he very much focused on anaclitic individuals (3), but he did not analyse the link between the intelligence of people and society. He was not a sociologist, and like all his predecessors, he described the pathological manifestations of the "disease" in order to cure the patient; he took care of individuals: sick human organizations did not fall within his competence.

However, thanks to the conceptual analysis of the psychologists, it's high time that we made progress with this topic, tried to link the facts together and placed the individual in a world of interactions, which is his world, no man being an island! Actually, it's easy because the observer does not really need to be very knowledgeable about psychiatry in order to achieve this goal. I would even say that history and literature are much more useful. Nevertheless, psychological obviousness obtrudes; I mean that human intelligence must be divided into three groups: psychotics at the bottom, neurotics on top, and immature people between them.

Psychosis is characterized by a loss of contact with reality and by its recreation. It's easy to recognize it in everyday life since there are numerous hallucinations, the discourse is absurd and in a worst-case scenario there is a lexical chaos. I have always enjoyed watching the handwriting of schizophrenics: it is as weird and beautiful as a medieval Irish manuscript. It is always interesting to see the articles and some words vanish into thin air. The individual plunges into an inner monologue that resembles a linguistic prison. I will not speak a lot of psychotics in this book for a simple reason: the loss of contact with reality implies that they can hardly interact with it, even when they want to destroy it. Consequently, they are not a real danger to society.

Higher, we find the gigantic group of immature persons (the borderline cases of the Americans, the anaclitic people of the French), which is a problematic lot that perplexed psychiatrists and psychoanalysts. In fact, they used to regard them as psychotics or neurotics and did not define a psychological entity. The mistake is understandable: very immature people have psychotic traits, whereas slightly immature people exhibit neurotic features. The level of intelligence, their inner equilibrium, their socialization process, and their behavioral disorders are not homogeneous at all. Besides, Bergeret worked so much on the issue and for such a long time that he tried to subdivide the group. I will not follow in his footsteps because the information is not reliable enough. Moreover, the most unbalanced immature people, namely the most brutal psychopaths, commit crimes when an external factor moves them to do so. In other words, they are not the only reason why there are dysfunctional societies. One of these conditions is the circumstances; another one is the level of decompensation (the severity of psychiatric disorders): we will analyse this in chapter 9. Hence, I preferred to separate the very immature people from the slightly immature ones. That being said, those people share some features: when they decompensate (lose their grip), they are depressed, they exhibit narcissistic traits and their superego becomes quite inoperative. Hence, it's easy to identify them. Of course, they are the main characters in this book since we will see that they compose the largest part of society and are the most active elements.

The third group, the people with a neurotic personality, advocate reason. They went through the Oedipus complex and did not fail, even though the result was not always brilliant. For instance, people with an obsessional personality have an inner superego that is not as unwavering as that of persons with Hysterical Personality Organization. In this connection, the man with an obsessional personality remains the son of his father because the resolution of the Oedipus complex is incomplete, whereas the man with Hysterical Personality Organization takes the place of his father and easily becomes the father of his own father. From a psychological point of view, this means that the result is quite different: the level of morality, consciousness and reason is much higher. When a person with Hysterical Personality Organization decompensates, reason remains intact and it is the body that goes mad: the mind cannot because it must not. It is rare to find neurotics, and they have not the amount of influence over society which they should have. They will appear here, especially in chapter 10.

Besides, this study exists because I am a person with Hysterical Personality Organization, which means that I can easily identify more primitive mental structures. For instance, I compared my perception of things with that of people with an obsessional personality and each time the result was the same: I immediately notice what does not fit, the element that renders things illogical, whereas the others put great emphasis on the ideas they share. Moreover, anaclitic individuals and people with an obsessional personality display characteristics which I don't. For instance, the oral and narcissistic features that make them look alike do not affect me, which leads to a strange result: my world and the anaclitic one are so different that it seems that we do not speak the same language. Furthermore, in chapter 10, we will meet another person with Hysterical Personality Organization; we must acknowledge that only people of that kind can recognize such individuals and understand them.

The aim of this book is to shed light on a huge problem so that the future of mankind may be less awful: awareness is the only path to peace and pure reason, which are the essential requirements for man's survival. The function of any serious academic research, whatever the subject, is to achieve this objective. So that this study may be understandable, I have chosen not to invent causalities. Hence, the chapters are structured in such a way that they do not exhibit the definitive determinism that might lead us to believe that each one is the logical consequence of what was said before. However, the organization of the chapters shows that barbarity spreads. In fact, I did not enjoy writing this book, which is why it took me many years to do so. On the other hand, new elements, dreadful ones, compelled me to act and write it. I chose to lay out the most sordid facts in the last two chapters in order to ease the pain felt by the readers. Although I did not describe the most barbaric ones, everybody will be able to understand what happened.

Is there a thesis here? At least one can say that there is an obsession: to redefine madness in order to include a part of normalcy. We will see that very immature people are quite insane and that some of them don't know what death means. Madness cannot only be characterized by hallucinations. The psychiatric definition does not really accord with psychiatric reality and its social consequences. The second point, the most important one, is aimed at explaining the role played by the anaclitic nebula in the high level of social dysfunctions. In fact, I want and need to know whether madness kills itself, impotent reason hides itself and normalcy devours itself and the whole universe.

1. Cleckley, Hervey, *The mask of sanity. An attempt to reinterpret some issues about the so-called psychopathic personality*, St Louis, 1941.
2. Bergeret, Jean, *La personnalité normale et pathologique*, Paris, 1974.
3. Bergeret, Jean, *La depression et les états limites*, Paris, 1975. Bergeret, Jean, *L'érotisme narcissique. Homosexualité et homoérotisme*, Paris, 1999.

Chapter 1

The weaknesses of the French intellectuals.

Philosophers and then psychiatrists and psychologists have been trying to perceive and define reason for the last 2500 years. Whatever their ideologies, they all failed because they did not put emphasis on the different levels of consciousness. The only one who understood that and who systematized the approach is Jean Bergeret, a French psychiatrist and psychoanalyst.

His work is immense; he had the strength to study and identify the missing link between reason (neuroticism) and madness (psychoticism): what he calls the anaclitic organizations and what we will call immaturity. According to him, most societies are mainly immature since between 33 to 50% of the population (1) can be regarded as immature. These statistics must be questioned because the mental health of populations varies a lot and cannot be reduced to numbers which are only partial inquiries. In a sense, qualitative approaches relying on cultural and political manifestations with a psychological meaning are to be analyzed and used in order to define personality traits en psychological features.

However, it is clear that he subtly described the anaclitic world, trying to build a kind of hierarchy that ranged from mild psychological disorders to pure reason. Actually, according to him, perverts, who do not acknowledge the existence of the female sexual organs, are almost mad, whereas the "perverts of character (the psychopaths)" (2) are not. Then there are the "psychotics and neurotics of character": the former are quite immature, whereas the latter are not that immature. We must not take this for granted, for we may have doubts about the place of perverts in the mental pyramid: they are already in the process of identifying with the phallic mother (3), whereas the perverts of character, especially the unbalanced psychopaths, are not and fight against their instincts and nervous breakdown. Hence, I will only refer to very immature people, putting great emphasis on the role of the superego in a problematic approach to the Oedipus complex.

The sources are silent about sexuality, which does not enable us to recognize the perverts. This difficulty can be overcome only if the writer speaks of his mother in laudatory terms. That's not the case here, which means that neither Michel Foucault, nor Jean-Paul Sartre, nor Albert Camus were perverts, which is already an important piece of information. Moreover, I was very cautious about the Oedipal characteristics because immature people went through that process; even though it was not completed, the incomplete Oedipal psychological features give much information about the level of consciousness.

Many things have been written and said about the Oedipus complex, but ordinary people do not really know what this means. Let us dot the i's and cross the t's: when, in a symbolic way, the boy is about to kill his father in order to make love to his mother, he suddenly understands that his behaviour would condemn him to insanity. Actually, he cannot destroy the image of his father because he is also his ego ideal, a role model he needs to protect: if a man with a neurotic personality decompensates (goes mad) and brakes the mirror, he will destroy a part of himself and almost prevent any return to the reassuring origin of his superego. The superego opens the eyes of the child: the understanding of the difference between good and evil is what will enable the individual to control his or her instincts, which gives birth to the kingdom of peace, grace, life and acute perception of reality. On the other hand, improbable sexual intercourse with the mother looks like a Greek drama, for it would lead to psychosis. In fact, it would be an awkward attempt to recreate the umbilical impulsive connection between them, and the child would not be a distinct person anymore.

In other respects, it has to be borne in mind that post-war France is a sick country. The Second World War and the Military Administration in France were a kind of psychopathic earthquake. This apocalypse engendered incomprehension, all the more so because the French did not do what the Germans did: a kind of mea culpa, which led them to put on trial and punish the culprits and to redefine the meanings of good and evil. The French purged many institutions and punished some Nazi collaborators, but it was a meaningless, inadequate response. Most criminals were not penalized, namely the French police officers who persecuted and deported so many Jews. After the war, the monsters remained in the same place and occupied the same positions. Some victims returned and tried to forget their journey to Hell, even though the scars kept reminded them of the fact that they had been treated like flesh, the flesh on which psychopathy lives and which enables it to survive and destroy everything. We will see that in the last chapter.

Is post-war France a psychotic country? No, but the war acted as a trauma. Hence, French society was quite psychopathic, and the "committed intellectuals" (*intellectuels engagés*) played the part of the lost consciousness of a society that was completely unable to think well, understand the problems, and address them. However, many of these intellectuals were not persons with neurotic personalities, but immature men who misjudged situations. This chapter is aimed at showing the level of understanding of three famous "philosophers", their adaptability to reality and their ability to give an appropriate answer to a disabled society looking for the truth.

A- Paul-Michel Foucault.

Paul-Michel Foucault did not leave us an autobiography in order to help us to know the genesis of his "self". However, we must not glorify that sort of document, since the author usually tries to conceal many things, often forgets others, or explains in a certain way a behaviour, although he or she does not understand it very well. Such a distorted testimony is less useful than an intelligent description by a friend or an acquaintance. In this connection, in 1989, Didier Eribon (3) published a book in which he portrayed him thanks to some of his friends and schoolmates, whom he did not name, which prevents us from checking the information. Nevertheless, the vividness of Didier Eribon's description allows us to perceive Foucault's personality.

The young Paul-Michel Foucault had a high conflict personality and behaved in a strange manner. First of all, he hated his father: later he preferred to be called Michel, not Paul-Michel, since Paul was also the first name of his father. At school, he had great difficulty making friends and worked a lot, probably in order to fight against depression and suicide. He was a megalomaniac who was so antisocial that he kept on fighting and quarreling with the others; he could hardly bear living with them: he preferred to stay in the sickbay, where a physician looked after him so that he might not commit suicide, which he had already done in 1948.

In spite of this, one day a teacher found him lying on the floor; his body showed signs of laceration. Another day, he ran after a schoolmate holding a knife in his hand. This behaviour was so dangerous and unusual at the *Ecole normale supérieure* that the students thought that he was quite unbalanced; they all hated him. An acquaintance of his stated that he fought against madness his whole life. According to Didier Eribon's book, Foucault must be a psychopath, but let us crosscheck the data.

The first information of quality we have is the way he used to think and write.

He wrote essays in philosophy and history using the same philosophical jargon. It may work in philosophy, but it is completely inappropriate in history. Actually, it is clear that his mind needed this psychological crutch to work. In history, the understanding of facts comes from the document itself. Most of the time, and even all the time, historians just verify that it is reliable; then they cite it providing almost no additional information, which makes the historic discourse rather flat, quite inexpressive and very monotonous because of these endless lists of events. It is very effective and the readers can always understand the facts, read the documents and form their own opinions if necessary. Foucault distorted reality by means of a lot of empty rhetoric. But why did he express himself in that fashion? Actually, his level of consciousness and his ability to perceive the outer world did not allow him to accept reality ant its logic as they were. Very immature people don't really like plain speaking: there is always a double meaning, a kind of ugly, threatening explanation behind the beautiful façade. This led Ernst Kretschemer to classify this level of intelligence into the paranoid delusions (4) because, according him, there was already a paralogical discourse. Even though this is not absolutely true, we notice that Foucault's primitive mind is full of preconceived ideas. In *Mental illness and personality* (5), lunatics are the victims of psychiatrists' omnipotence (6). In *History of madness during the classical age* (7), his view is less extreme: physicians are but jailers. Of course, he does not deny the reality of insanity: he knows it too well and he is fighting against it. Nonetheless, one could argue that he might have told the truth, for the "general hospital" looked like a prison, not a place where scientists used to cure and help patients. In fact, there are very few documents that can support his argument, and the more he expresses his opinion, the less he gives evidence on the subject. Besides, in these two books, and some others, there are many strange opinions, especially about the image of the father and the anaclitic group.

According to Didier Eribon, Foucault hated his father. This is an enormous problem because a boy needs to like his father so that he may try to identify with him and build up his superego in that way. Foucault's failure is very visible in his 1954 essay on madness. He is 28 when he publishes it and adolescence is already ancient history, but his hatred of the father figure is tangible.

In the first pages (8), the physician, the father figure, is compared not only with an omnipotent creature but also with God himself. Actually, he refers to the famous psychiatrist Babinski, whom he regards as a man who controls the mind of his hysterical patients: poor insane people who just have to "rise and walk" if Babinski asks them to do so.

His hatred of psychiatry was even more visible when he tried to explain Freud's little Hans's case (9). Here he understood nothing. For instance, he did have very little Oedipal mental material and transformed the Freudian explanation of the Oedipus complex into something very different.

According to him, Hans is fighting against his fear and the phobic symptom is therefore considered as the child's desire to see his father die; in this way, he destroys the fence between him and his mother. Freud and his followers immediately explained the ambiguity of the phobic symptom: they stated that Hans's father was a sexual rival and also a model he liked, all the more so because he was close to his son and sometimes acted as a friend when he played with the little boy. Foucault's point of view is twisted, whereas the Freudians' is not; he adds (10): "... without doubt, he fears that he is going to be bitten by the horse, which proves that he fears castration: this symbolizes the paternal prohibition on intercourse. ...". We may say that there are not many Oedipal characteristics here because, according to him, the father prohibits his son from having sex with his mother in order to avoid incest. So Foucault's idea about castration is not a vague Oedipal anxiety, but something more primitive, excessive and anaclitic: he believes that the father does not forbid the expression of the desire to have sex with the image of the mother, but that in fact he forbids any sexual intercourse. Besides, nothing is said about his role in the psychological identification. Hence, the father becomes an archenemy.

In this connection, Foucault does not understand the role plaid by morality because his superego is inoperative. Consequently, any social responsibility or restraint is viewed as a punishment. For instance, in his *History of madness* (11), the General Hospital is but a prison where patients are compelled to work for an institution whose aim is to impose its morality on amoral people. The physicians are transformed into the accomplices of such morals. Must we think that this echoes his visit to Doctor Delay (Sainte Anne Hospital, in Paris) after his suicide attempt? Is he blaming his father, who was the man – the physician should I say since he was a doctor by profession – who asked one of his colleagues to cure his son of his mental disorders? Maybe, but here, more than a short episode in a young adult's life, there is psychological resistance, which shows that his father was not a role model for his son and that he did not enable him to achieve a higher level of consciousness.

In the case of such personalities, some circumstances can improve things; in other words, did Foucault find a reassuring father figure around him, which enabled him to start building a superego? It is not that easy to answer this question, but, at the end of his life, in *The use of pleasure* (12), he defined morality with less anger, even though there was no trace whatsoever of morals! Hence, Foucault's personality had changed, but, of course, it was not organized at the neurotic level yet.

On the other hand, in his work, we also find the classical anaclitic argument about the exclusion from the group. In his 1954

Mental illness and personality (13), the insane are separated from the group in order to be send to a mental asylum. There is no information about the threat they represent to themselves and the others. In 1964 (14), he still shares this opinion. So we must admit that even though his personality had slightly improved, at the end of his life, he remained an immature person: what Bergeret would have called a "pervert of character with a psychopathic character".

B- Jean-Paul Sartre.

Sartre was less unbalanced since he was not a person with antisocial personality disorder. Nevertheless, it is clear that, at least when he was young, he used to fight against depression. In his almost autobiographical novel *Nausea*, Antoine Roquentin, the main character, divides his personality into two entities; the sane and objective part looks at the inner one and describes it (15) as follows: "... He says he is afraid of going mad... he says he is disgusted with existence... He runs in order to flee and to throw himself into the lake...". Is it already a psychotic scission of the self? Maybe, because very immature people can use the weapons used by psychotics; they can even experience hallucinations and reshape reality. However, these depressive episodes do not last that long and Roquentin comes to his senses. That being said, he lives in a parallel universe and strives hard to unite his mind and his body and perceive reality (16).

So that we may apprehend this low level of consciousness, we must read very carefully *The words* (17), which is a genuine autobiography.

He published it in 1964: he was 59. It is a well-written book, and the French is absolutely tip-top. It is so well-written that we understand that what he says can be really artificial, but it remains a good source of information.

The young Jean-Paul has no father, for he died during the First World War. He is raised by his mother, who is an immature girl, at least it is how Sartre sees her; he regards her as his older sister. He spent the first part of his childhood with her, in the house of his maternal grand-parents. His grand-father venerates his grand-son, whereas his grand-mother immediately knows that he is but a grinning little monkey. However, Jean-Paul is the typical spoiled brat. Nonetheless, many years after the facts and his childhood, he is aware that his family was dysfunctional, which had psychological repercussions for his personality, especially his superego. One could even regard this book as a kind of deliberate attempt to analyse his childhood, which obsesses him, so that he may acknowledge the most important problems, solve them and act.

The 59-year-old Sartre knows that the most important factor is his dead father. A child needs to identify with a real person whom he admires, or at least likes. He cannot identify with a ghost; life cannot look like death, or else you go crazy, insanity being death, mental death in the midst of life. It is self-evident that he showed a reckless disregard for the role played by the father in a family, but one does wonder where such an opinion comes from since he never knew his own father. Is it an opinion he formed after having seen his uncles interact with his grand-father? It is impossible to give an answer. Does he reproach in this manner his father for being dead? It may not be the correct answer either, for he thinks that his absence made him a free little boy who did not have to obey a cumbersome father. However, his situation was quite difficult because he lived with an immature woman who used to tell all her problems to her son; his grand-father used to consider him as a marvelous creature; his grand-mother might have been quite critical of that situation: Sartre says that she was the "spirit" that always said no. He had an unhappy childhood, which moved him to think and write that he hated it.

Furthermore, he is aware that he has a problem with his superego. He even writes that, according to a famous psychiatrist, he has no superego, and he accepts this opinion, which is not completely true. Actually, he did have a superego, even though it was not his main trait. First of all, we must say that the popular novels he read had an influence on him (17). He often spoke of this kind of literature and stated that the books he used to read were really decent since the good guys always killed the bad ones.

Besides, his teachers usually said that the young Sartre was a moderately intelligent child but a righteous one. I think that sometimes he might have considered his grand-father as a father figure: we must note that he obeyed his grand-father, especially when he was speaking of literature. Aged 59, he even said that he had probably chosen to become a writer in order to please him.

To corroborate the presence of a superego, we can even refer to his essay entitled *Reflections on the Jewish problem* (18). In this book, he is preoccupied with good and evil, and he does fashion the image of a bad anti-Semite facing an innocent Jew. Hence, Jean-Paul Sartre, without a doubt, is a bit more reasonable than Foucault.

C- Albert Camus.

As for Albert Camus, fortunately, he left an autobiographical novel, *The first man* (19), which was published many years after his death. Some people could argue that *Wedding* (20) has some biographical data, which is true, but it is not as introspective as *The first man*. Actually, both *The stranger* (21) and *The rebel* (22) are much more helpful than *Wedding* (23); they enable us to discover Camus's self and state of mind.

Like Sartre, Camus lost his father in World War One, but unlike him, he looked for a father figure, at least during his childhood. His book, *The first man*, is dedicated to him, a ghost haunting the pages of this novel. I even think that most of his work, which deals with insanity, destruction and rebellion against massacres, has a lot do with the understanding of the disaster that turned his father into an ever-present shadow, a distressing absence. Of course, this search has many connections with the history of a blood-stained century, but his personal history and the general evolution of humanity during the 20th century are strictly mingled, which prevents us sometimes from separating easily what comes from a state of mind from what relies on a fair reaction to a historical apocalypse.

However, in *The first man*, Jacques – Albert in reality, who is the main character – tries to find information about his father. For instance, one day he asks his uncle whether his father was intelligent or not. Nevertheless, very few people can give him the information he needs so that he may imagine or even fashion a consistent father image. Fortunately, the main character considers his primary school teacher as a helpful substitute. One must realize that a boy who lives with a stupid woman who has poor interpersonal skills can regard Monsieur Bernard as a very important man. Jacques even considered that his teacher was a wise man, the only man who schooled him and helped him to become a man. It is very touching to see a famous writer, the winner of the Nobel prize of literature, reveal so many years later what he owes to the teacher who taught the little "Jacques-Albert" not only to be a human and a man but also to think clearly by means of a good understanding of the language (French here) and the way one must read a problem in order to get information and solve it more easily.

Logically, the superego of Camus is stronger; it is not as strong or operative as those of people with an obsessional personality (which is the personality organization that follows his), but it allows the individual to perceive reality much better ant to interact more easily with people. This Oedipal characteristic enabled him to be quite stable and to strengthen his personality organization his whole life long. Furthermore, without undergoing psychoanalysis, sometimes people can achieve a higher level of consciousness and become persons whose personality is organized at the neurotic level.

We can perceive Camus's moral sense thanks to his opinion about the moral sense he had when he was a child. In this manner, we can see what changes and understand that his mind was not motionless and that he grew mentally. In that respect, he writes that at home nobody but his teacher had taught him how to differentiate good form evil. Nonetheless, the little Albert knows that to steal is wrong, whereas it is right that women and mothers should be protected. Hence, without doubt Camus is slightly immature and quite rational, which enables him to understand himself.

For instance, *The rebel* could be considered as the reaction of a psychopathic mind struggling against a paternal superego. This would give birth to the image of a persecuting father trying to devalue his son's weak self. However, his rebellion is much different, for it is legitimate if the rebel fights against madness (24). He adds that Sade used to follow his feelings (let's say his instincts); he declares (25): "... He did not invented a philosophy but followed the monstrous dream of a persecuted man. ...". Hence, since he rejects God and thinks that Nature is a destructive factor (26), Sade creates a chaotic world.

Camus is more intelligent than Sade since he admits that human feelings must follow rules and then give up a part of their subjectivity, selfishness and, in a way, liberty.

D- The relation between their mind and their political actions and opinions.

In the late 70s, Michel Foucault was sent, by the Italian newspaper *Corriere della Sera*, to Iran, in order to describe and explain what was taking place there: a revolution that led to a theocracy. His mental peculiarities had already moved him to write books based on the rejection of any kind of power, which he regarded as an instrument used by fathers to forbid their sons to unleash their desire for life or murder. However, a book rarely enables its author to perceive reality as it is. In Iran, Foucault was confronted with real life. One may believe that this could lead daydreamers to have their feet on the ground.

In his case, we immediately realize that he distorts reality so that it may fit his preconceived ideas, which engenders a paralogical discourse that is considered as quite strange by sane people. Moreover, he is only interested by the acting out (the revolution): timewise, there is no past and no future, just the present. He lives in the moment, and he is fascinated by it (27); he does not try to conduct an analysis of the historical background or the plausible political consequences. In this connection, Foucault is convinced that the King of Iran is an armed despot facing a defenseless Saint called Ayatollah Khomeini (28).

His conception of religion is not psychotic but psychopathic. Islam is a force that allows people to resist any government (29); it is not a compromise, but a force (30) that moves nations to rebel against a king, his police, and any regime; it is a way of life, a whole universe. The rebel without a cause devotes himself to a cause in order to rebel against something external. He is the good guy; the outside is bad; the relation between both is a battle he must win. The only difference between psychopathy and psychosis is that very immature people can easily see the difference between them and the others, even though the ongoing psychological identification can sometimes make it unintelligible.

The way Foucault looks upon Islam is peculiar. His ignorance about it is bottomless, and it is clear that he did not read the Quran, which is a compilation of normative principles. More than the Bible, the Quran imposes rules on the believers; there is no need to interpret them; everything is quite clear; its logic is almost juridical: some things are allowed, some others are forbidden, and the believer must accept this and obey. Actually, Islam is the exact opposite of what Foucault wants. However, in his mind, it turns into a non-hierarchical structure where submission disappears so that faithfulness may become the real nature of the dogma. Once again, his state of mind erects an impassable wall between him and reality.

As for Sartre, he was more intelligent than he, and he did not have a high-conflict personality, which allowed him to understand reality better. For instance, in his 1954 lecture on the atomic bomb (31), he understands immediately that the hydrogen bomb is not only the image of the most abominable threat to humanity but also the expression of pure violence. Nonetheless, there is also a significant blindness, especially to Marxism and communism. One could claim that a lack of knowledge can also lead intelligent, sane people to misunderstand reality, which is true. But Sartre did know the texts and even went to the Soviet Union in order to see the application of Marxism in a country.

In 1954, he stayed in the USSR and wrote articles that were published in the French newspaper *Libération*. Like so many visitors, he was escorted by an official guide and interpreter, his visits had been arranged by the KGB, and he met people whose loyalty towards the regime had been verified by the authorities. However, since he had lost his ability to think critically, he described a kind of paradise. Some months before, Pierre and Hélène Lazareff (32) had portrayed a world over which fear and suspicion reigned even though Stalin was dead. Sartre seemed almost mesmerized. Was it because the USSR was a part of his ego ideal? I can't prove it. Nonetheless, he faced the communist reality and did not notice, for example, the economic problems, especially the role plaid by the concentration camps (gulags) and slavery in the production of the goods which the population needed.

Besides, he writes (33) that people can speak freely and criticize the government. According to him, fear has disappeared and the educational system is very intelligent. Sartre completely misunderstands the situation. Since he is not a person whose personality is organized at the neurotic level, he lacks the concepts that would allow him to understand what he sees. Consequently, the immature man who always privileges the group of people over the individual extols the youth organizations (the pioneers), which are based on brainwashing. He states that there is a lot of competition between the Young Pioneers, who are children and adolescents who live together in order to perform the same activities. The courageous, honorable children can display their competences so that they may rise through the communist social hierarchy. These pioneers are deemed to be hard workers, whereas the young capitalists are called lazy people.

In 1960 (34), during his Araquara lecture in Brazil, his faith in Marxism and in the Russian communist regime is still great; he even says that it cannot be surpassed. Is his idea about a perfect communist society an expression of his hatred of his middle-class childhood? It is self-evident that he did not like his youth and that, from a mental point of view, he was still fighting against the feelings he had had during this part of his life, but the way he admired Marxism and complied with it is not a clue. Obviously, he had not overcome his childhood. In 1973 (35), he even thinks that a revolution can happen in France because capitalism and its institutions are deeply dysfunctional. Hence, he tries to be on friendly terms with the French "Maoists", for the French Communist Party is not a revolutionary force anymore. Nonetheless, in 1975, he declares (36): "... Marxists explain that man is the product of his economic system, which does not correspond with what I believe.

...". He is not a Marxist anymore! Many people criticized him for vacillating over politics. What does this drastic change mean? A better perception and understanding of reality? In other words, did he mature? No, he did not. Actually, he is still unable to perceive what is true or false. He is entangled in an archaic unsolved problem. Many years later, what he considers to be the root of the problem (a middle-class lifestyle that is aimed at earning money in order to buy goods) helps him to explore reality by putting forward the so-called communist solution. Hence, his whole life long, he tried to understand reality in this manner, but he kept missing the point. At last he realized that he was wrong, and he looked for another concept that helped him to comprehend his own self and reality, with which he was not well acquainted.

It can otherwise be verified thanks to his article on the 1972 rebellion in the prison of Toul (37); he writes: "... What is a prisoner? It is a man who is held against his will. Why is he there? Because he dared to rebel individually against our sinister society. ... It is the government and its obedient justice that transform these men into prisoners, and most of them are our brothers. ... We could say (38): they are ourselves, it is our brother, our son, who was unlucky. ... The director of the prison is the king. Everything depends on his whims. It is he who interprets the law and nobody else. At Toul, the director is a wicked man (39) who regards all the prisoners as obedient slaves...". It is a very important document because, in literature, we almost never have data on immature people's psychological identification, perhaps because writers are often more intelligent. Here it is not really literature, since it is a speech. Consequently, there is no more rhetoric: the true self speaks a language that comes directly from the mind.

Identification is a common anaclitic habit. It occurs in different circumstances. It allows the individual to consider that other humans, animals, or things are like him or her and as good as him or her. Then, since others are good and look like oneself, one can defend them and oneself. Here, Sartre identifies with victims and legitimizes their rebellion. Sometimes that mental process is linked to psychological projection; it is often a tool used to build the self, and it is not only used during the Oedipus complex. We should add that his vocabulary is childish; for instance, a person whose personality is organized at the neurotic level would never ever use bad (39) in such circumstances. Moreover, there is a classic anaclitic argument contrasting the powerful, a threatening paternal superego, with the weak, the memory of these "children", an inefficient superego which states that they exist, that they must be respected (even though they are dangerous), and that the individual is more important than society. Sartre did display antisocial tendencies; at the end of his life, he was still an immature person who understood neither himself nor others.

Unlike him, Camus is highly adaptive, and it is very difficult to find evidence of a mental disorder, which proves that slightly immature people are almost sane. Even though he lived in a tormented century and wrote *The rebel*, we don't observe symptoms of psychosis, or psychopathy, or any behavioral disorder, which would justify a rebellion.

He was born in Algeria; his father was killed during World War One; he faced World War Two and the "Algerian events". He was very attached to this part of the world: in his published work, we find some beautiful descriptions of that region. During the Algerian War of Independence, he was very concerned about what was happening. On the 22nd of January 1956, being in Algiers, he speaks to the members of a committee whose aim is to find solutions or at least to try to declare a ceasefire so that the population may continue living normally (40).

Is there a link between empathy, humanity and the level of intelligence of people? In other words, is a person with Neurotic

Personality Organization more humane than someone with Psychotic Personality Organization? We must think so because a person with Psychotic Personality Organization is only preoccupied with his or her survival; others are regarded as enemies and therefore they must be killed. Moreover, there are not intelligent enough to understand what compassion is. People whose personality is organized at the neurotic level control their instincts and thus know how fragile a human's life is. When they think of death, they are overwhelmed and try to conceal their feelings, whereas people with Hysterical Personality Organization do not. Between both, we find the mood swings of immature people; the very immature ones are in survival mode, which always upsets people with Neurotic Personality Organization, all the more so because the former do not seem insane or at least not completely. They cannot be forgiven when they belittle or mistreat people: they are immediately regarded as monsters, not as insane men or women.

But Camus is not very immature, and his righteousness compels him to give an answer that fits reality and which a person with Neurotic Personality Organization could have given. Of course, his speech shows a utopian anaclitic argument about the need for the Arabs and the French to get together, even though the ones are fighting the others (the war began in November 1954). He immediately calls for a truce so that the innocent civilians may be spared (41). Then he explains why saying (42): "... nothing can justify the death of innocent people. ...". A person with an obsessional personality could have said the same thing, using the same words. We immediately realize that Camus's political believes did not rely only on a preconception based on an altered perception of reality. The presence of an efficacious superego enabled him to have free will and, sometimes, to discover the truth.

Consequently, people who had to enlighten the dysfunctional post-war French society were not the most intelligent minds (persons with Hysterical Personality Organization). Moreover, two of them had great difficulty perceiving reality. Of course, they were not really influential, for they were not powerful politicians, and in democracies, it is almost impossible to convince many people when the ideas are obscure and when other intellectuals and journalists write and say things that are very different. Obviously, French society allowed them to exist, but because of its weakness, they were not in the right place: they were unable to fulfill their obligations, and therefore they did not help it to work better. Whatever the society, each time intellectuals do not or cannot get closer to reality and the truth, the rest of it stands still.

1. Bergeret, Jean, *La personnalité normale et pathologique*, Paris, Dunod, 1996, p.33.
2. The individual tries to destroy the narcissism of the people around him so that he may build his personality more easily.
3. Eribon, Didier, *Michel Foucault (1926-1984)*, Paris, 1989.
4. In chapter 9, the description of psychopathy is an interesting benchmark.
5. Foucault, Michel, *Maladie mentale et* personnalité, Paris, Puf, 1954.
6. Op. cit., p. 15.
7. Foucault, Michel, *Histoire de la folie à l'âge classique*, Paris, Gallimard. 1964.
8. Op. cit., p. 15 and 16.
9. Op. cit., p. 42.
10. Op. cit., p. 42.
11. *Histoire de la folie*, Op. Cit.
12. Foucault, Michel, *The use of pleasure*, New-York, Random inc., 1985, p.25, first edition by Gallimard, Paris, 1984.
13. Op. cit., p. 75 and 79.
14. *Histoire de la folie...*

15. Sartre, Jean-Paul, *La Nausée*, Paris, Gallimard, 1938; *Nausea*, New directions, New York, 1969, p. 52 and 53.

16. Op. cit., p.65.

17. He really liked the chevalier de Pardaillan, the hero created by Michel Zévaco. Pardaillan fights against Princess Fausta, a beautiful women who wants to lay down the rules in a chaotic country (16th c. France).

18. Sartre, Jean-Paul, *Réflexions sur la question juive*, Paris, Morihien, 1946.

19. Camus, Albert, *Le premier homme*, Paris, Gallimard, 1994.

20. Camus, Albert, *Noces*, Paris, Gallimard, 1959, first edition Algiers, 1938.

21. Camus, Albert, *L'étranger*, Paris, Gallimard, 1942.

22. Camus, Albert, *L'homme révolté*, Paris, Gallimard, 1951

23. Op. cit.

24. Op. cit., p.18.

25. Op. cit., p. 44.

26. Op. cit., p. 46.

27. Foucault, Michel, "Une poudrière appelée Islam", French version of an article translated into Italian and published in the *Corriere della Sera*, 13th of February 1979: "... this movement that has attained an objective so rare in the 20th century: an unarmed nation which stands and crushes with its hands an "almighty" regime. ...".

28. Foucault, Michel, "A quoi rêvent les Iraniens", *Le nouvel observateur*, 16th to 22nd of October 1978.

29. Foucault, "A quoi rêvent les Iraniens"...

30. Foucault, "Une poudrière appelée Islam"...

31. Sartre, Jean-Paul, "La bombe H, une arme contre l'histoire", *Discours*, Berlin 1954. He is invited by the World Committee for Peace.

32. Lazareff, Hélène and Pierre, *L'URSS à l'heure de Malenkow*, Paris, La table ronde, 1954.

33. Sartre, Jean-Paul, *Libération*, 15th of July 1954.

34. Sartre, Jean-Paul, *Sartre no Brasil, A conferencia de Araquara*, Sao Paolo, Editora Unesp, 2005; first edition 1986.

35. Brunier, Michel-Antoine, "Sartre parle des maos", *Actuel*, n° 28, February 1973.

36. Friedman, Jane, "Terrorism can be justified", interview of Sartre in *Newsweek*, European edition, 10th of November 1975.

37. Sartre, Jean-Paul, "Déclaration de Jean-Paul Sartre à la conférence de presse du comité vérité Toul du mercredi 5 janvier 1972", *La cause du peuple-J'accuse*, n° 15, 7th of January 1972.

38. Speaking of them.

39. He uses "méchant" which is much more childish than bad.

40. Camus, Albert, *Actuelles III: chroniques algériennes, 1938-1958*, Paris, Gallimard, 1958; "Appel pour une trêve civile en Algérie", speech, Algiers, 22nd of January 1956.

41. Op. cit., p. 116.

42. Op. cit., p. 118.

Chapter 2

Forever young and immature.

Societies are mainly composed of immature people; we will see this in chapter 6. Consequently, all the cultural manifestations might be related to immaturity. Logically, literature and filmmaking should show a lot of narcissistic and psychopathic traits. Nonetheless, when we analyse, for instance, what, by nature, is the most psychopathic genre, namely action movies, we immediately realize that it is not the product of a single mind, but the direct result of the interaction of different factors: the psychotic (paranoid) characteristics are sometimes so predominant that one wonders whether the film director is an immature person who is becoming psychotic or not. It is clear that sometimes people who compose society agree to watch paranoid movies in order to keep on believing that they are persecuted by so-called enemies whom they would like to persecute and kill. In that regard, some American science fiction movies of the 50s and the 60s are quite paranoid and full of hallucinations (*The Invaders* being one of them).

If we want to better understand the problem of immaturity, we must therefore analyse a recurrent anaclitic theme in filmmaking rather than a movie, a famous one, made by an immature director because the writer, or the screenwriter, or the producer could have spoiled the borderline essence of the work. From a scientific point of view, would the theme of narcissism be interesting? It depends on what we mean by narcissism: if it is the futile contemplation of oneself, its study would not provide information about the apocalyptic social implications we want to point out here. If we believe that it is a regression to a primitive position that compels the individual to destroy what he or she regards as a danger to his or her survival, it can be interesting indeed, for we may certainly discover some psychopathic fears in contemporary art, which might lead some of the older readers to speak of decadency: art, half a century ago, might have been beauteous and less violent!

As for me, I have decided to adopt a more sophisticated approach so that we may understand more easily what will follow and may become aware of the extent of social problems. So I will examine here the vision of immaturity by contemporary societies through literature and movies. I will dissect famous works dealing with childhood and youth in order to see whether society regards this stage as the golden age of unconsciousness or a return to primal violence and madness.

A- The young savages.

In 1954, William Golding, the winner of the Nobel prize of literature, published the famous novel *Lord of the flies* (1). The theme may resemble a classic Robinson-like adventure, but, this time, the main characters are disconcerted children, not adults who perceive reality better than they. It is said that they are schoolboys evacuated from an unknown place during a war. Their ship ran aground on a deserted tropical island where there is water and plenty of food but no adult who could tell them how to behave.

The novel deals with human nature and the author's poor opinion of it (2). In this connection, we cannot really contrast good with evil because if we can find evil characters like Jack Merridew, the ones who are less evil, like Piggy, have sometimes reprehensible weaknesses (3). All the children are actually spied on by the devil, the lord of the flies, the evil that dwells in their inhumane hearts.

The older boys spontaneously establish democracy. Their republic does not ape that of the grown-ups; it just shows the limits of that kind of regime: its constitutional and organizational restrictions, which mirror the mental boundaries of man. Ralph, aged 12 and a few months, is the oldest of them. He is a kind of link between childhood and adulthood; they may have elected him as their chief because of this (4). His vision of democracy shows that he often experiences cognitive distortion. In fact, he does not have a clear idea of what to do so that they may live on the island or even be rescued. He needs the group in order to be more reasonable and to establish rules that will civilize this pack of wild children.

Their democracy is influenced by religion. The conch Ralph has found on the beach is used as a bell: he blows into it in order to summon the assembly. When the children ear the sound of this bell, they stop doing what they are doing and, mesmerized by its sound, they gather like the believers in a church. The conch is a magical object they must hold if they want to speak and be heard during the meetings.

However, there are disruptive forces in their attempt to organize themselves. The major problem is the difference in age between the children. The younger ones, who are six years old, live a primitive life (5): they eat fruit and play the whole day long. They are subhuman creatures who live in a magical world which they neither really understanding nor control. They are so preoccupied with their unfounded fears that one may consider them to be lunatics. The other factor is Jack Merridew; he wants to seize power in order to assert himself and compel the smaller boys to join his tribe of hunters. In the end, it is Ralph's absence of leadership that facilitates the collapse of this little world.

In the book, the evil that destroys everything is mainly incarnated in Jack Merridew. He is the chief of the choirboys, who then became the pack leader of the hunters who provide meat (pork) to the community. He is a kind of fallen angel, and he becomes wicked progressively. We might believe that he signed a pact with the devil when he dared to cut the throat of a wild pig. When he relates the scene to the others, his savagery is palpable. When he sees the blood flowing from the animal, his true nature appears and his joy leaves the others open-mouthed (6). The rules of civilization are therefore abolished (7). The new Eucharist is the flesh of the pig, and each time they hunt and eat the fruit of their devilish action, they become more ruthless. Jack Merridew's choir boys, who are clad in ecclesiastical robes, turn progressively into half-naked savages covered with war paint: God and civilization have failed!

Merridew is a proselyte; he wants his devilish tribe to increase. The younger souls are easy to convert. The arguments he supports are simple and plain: he tells them that he will feed and soothe them (8). Actually, these little boys are fearful creatures; at night, the sounds of the forest and the mysterious deformed shadows of nature easily exacerbate their irrational anxiety. What they call the beast is the dead body of a parachutist they barely see because of the entwined branches and the faint light; it is also their fear of a world they do not understand and thus regard as dangerous.

Two children oppose Merridew: the immature Ralph (10) and the reasonable asthmatic Piggy, whose reason is unable to pacify this primitive society. He is the impotent conscience that tries to protect the good part of mankind. Unfortunately, on the island, he is one of a kind, and his scientific, reasonable arguments fall flat in front of a sea of illusions. He is the reason that is everlastingly tormented by the wickedness of mankind. He is the one in the group who always refers to the consoling image of a humane, reasonable adult: his aunt. Logically, like the others, he is saved by adults: a warship lands on the island and rescue them. The naval officer who finds the boys keeps things in perspective: the devilish small human animals become children again. Nonetheless, he is surprised to discover that British children can regress to such a level of cruelty (11): British civilization cannot tame human nature, which is pure evil. William Golding's opinion about childhood and mankind is much different from that of the naive Jean-Jacques Rousseau.

B- The adolescent liar.

François Truffaut's opinion is less pessimistic, probably because his view of childhood has to do with his life and the problem he had with his own family. According to him, children and adolescents are not sane mature individuals, but the fault is not theirs: parents are the real culprits.

In the *400 blows* (12), he recounts the history of Antoine Doinel, a 12 or 13-year-old boy living in Paris, at the end of the 1950s. His mother is cool towards him. He is the fruit of a liaison she certainly wants to forget. His stepfather adopted Antoine so that he might bear his name, which would prevent his neighbors, the teachers, the civil servants and his wife from backbiting him. Antoine has not always lived with them. At the beginning, he was raised by his grand-mother, who insisted that her daughter should not abort. After his birth, Antoine's mother changed lives and left the bothersome child with her mother; she almost forgot him until her ageing mother was too old to keep on rearing him.

Antoine discovered the truth about him and his mother later in life. The movie does not move us to say that he considers her to be dangerous. She is not a loving mother and she regards her son as an intruder. Of course, Antoine knows that he intrudes into the lives of his mother and his stepfather, which moves him to live his own life, the life of a brainless kid who does not like school very much and prefers going to the cinema to attending classes. He often steals money from his parents and commits petty crimes with the help of his friend René, someone who is also a member of a problem family. However, all his actions lead him to be confronted with his mother's demeanor. For instance, while he was skipping class, he caught her kissing a man in front of the Wepler café (*Place Clichy*). A movie is not a book, and the interpretation of pictures is tricky, especially

Truffaut's, who used to put in double meanings. That being said, Antoine's obsession with the sea is a bit odd. It is almost a geographic absurdity in a very Parisian story. Hence, we may regard the sea as a metaphor, all the more so because in French *the sea* and *mother* are feminine homophones (*la mer, la mère*). Antoine would certainly like to leave his bad mother behind in order to get closer to a more gracious, peaceful image of creation. In the last scene, he is running on a beach in the direction of the water: Mother Nature is always kind, and she gives birth to wonderful creatures. She does not ask for anything in return. The movie ends with a picture of Antoine, who silently looks at the camera. What a mysterious ending; the mother-son relationship is less mysterious!

To survive and have a kind of control over objects and the world, Antoine lies. His parents know this, which is why they tell a psychologist that he keeps lying. The psychologist asks the boy why. His answer is not really convincing: he asserts that his lies seem more real than reality. He also minimizes the importance of his hypocrisy. In fact, he may lie about his lies!

One must say that Antoine's excuses are wishes. When his teacher asks him why he did not go to school the day before, he answers spontaneously that the reason for his absence is that his mother died. This lie is not aimed at reinventing reality but at curing it. Unfortunately, reality is unkind to him: his secrets make matters worse because they are always discovered. So his parents learn that he did not attend classes, that he plagiarized a passage from a book by Balzac instead of writing an original essay and that he stole a typewriter. Since they are fed up with him, with the help of the police and the judge, they send him away to a youth facility, where he feels more out of place and rejected than ever. Truffaut's opinion about childhood is not pure veneration of innocence! The sad life of his autobiographical Antoine contrasts with the glamorous black and white Paris of the late 50's: his unhappiness is therefore more perceptible.

C- Violent youth.

Americans also had a bad opinion of youth. In *Rebel without a cause* (13), James Dean's acting is much more excessive than what is described in the original script. The scriptwriters did not want to portray a psychopathic teenager but a problem child begotten by a problem family.

In fact, James is a seventeen-year-old student who lives with a toxic mother (14) and a vapid father. He regards all women as Gorgons. His father is not a good role model, which is why he does not know how to become a man. As for Judy, she is sixteen and does not get along with her father, who does not really take care of his daughter. The third character, Plato, is almost an abandoned adolescent: his father is absent and his mother is always on the road. He longs for a stable, protective family. His friends, even if they are as young as he, could become substitute parents, from a psychological point of view.

In the movie, the most immature and unbalanced adult is certainly Jim's mother. She ignores reality when it is unpleasant, which moves her to deny his son's involvement in the death of a youngster. Jim, who is more intelligent and realistic than she, opposes his mother's denial. He declares that he is involved in the accident. The teenager was killed because he raced against him. Unfortunately, he lost control of his car and died.

In *High school confidential* (15), the parents of the students are also unbalanced people. For instance, the main character lives with his aunt, who is a well-endowed peroxide blonde, and the parents of the leading lady take to drink. Drug addiction would therefore be the direct result of a dysfunctional family.

In the history of filmmaking, the late 50s are a key moment. The glamour and glitter of Hollywood give way to a more realistic approach. Of course, there are gangsters, social problems and historical disasters prior to that time, but there is always enough artistry to erase the sordidness of the facts. Everything may not be extraordinary, but everything is not ordinary. In *High school confidential*, art disappears: it is a kind of documentary that is aimed at showing that drug addiction in American high schools is a growing problem. In that regard, on the street, one may encounter Tony, who is the main character, a rude drug dealer who uses a lot of slang terms. He prefigures the indecent 1967 *Valley of the Dolls* (16), which dealt with a similar subject.

In that movie, youngsters are a fragile population that is sometimes seduced by cannabis, which is a gateway to hard drugs and a classic issue. The film director even portrays a junkie who has all the symptoms of drug withdrawal. Since it is a propaganda film, it is clear that the idealistic world of beauty queens and handsome quarterbacks is not depicted. Nevertheless, in 1971 (17), Stanley Kubrick goes further by choosing to adapt Anthony Burgess's *Clockwork Orange* (18) for the big screen; that book is an apocalyptic vision of adolescence and mankind.

Alec is clearly a psychopath. He is aged 15 at the beginning of the novel, 18 at the end. Burgess's aim is to show the passage from youth to adulthood, which is why he wrote 21 chapters, 21 being the age of majority (and maturity) in the United Kingdom in the 60s. Alec is a violent teenager, but we do not know why. The reader or spectator can only acknowledge this and watch him committing violent crimes.

The near future in which he lives cannot tolerate that kind of behaviour, for if it did, it would lead to societal collapse.

Consequently, he is put in jail and has rehabilitation therapy so that he may be allowed to live in society again and may become, at last, a peaceful citizen. The medical treatment he undergoes is called the Ludovico technique. It is a kind of aversion therapy: the patient is injected with a product so that he may feel nauseous each time he sees violent movies and deeds. The treatment works very well, but Burgess has a poor opinion of this conditioning.

The main point relates to the origin of man's kindness. According to the author, goodness comes from within; it is a way of behaving that a man adopts out of his own volition (19). If an individual is compelled to obey, he ceases to be a man or a women and becomes a soulless robot. However, he does not write what goodness is. We can easily understand that it is related to violence and that it could therefore mean peace. Dr. Brodsky's opinion about good might be Burgess's point of view too (20). For the dedicated physician, the very model of righteousness is the Christ: instead of answering his assailants roughly, he preferred to be beaten, and he turned to them the other cheek also. Instead of persecuting his enemies, he chose to be crucified. From a social point of view, the victim is the only decent individual; the assailant embodies the end of society, which is why he must be reformed or killed. The author even goes further by making the physician who rehabilitated Alex say that soon he won't be able to kill a fly: the Buddhist argument transforms his opinion into the definition of life of a person whose personality is organized at the neurotic level.

However, Burgess's democratic ideals are profoundly vitiated: he believes that an idea, even a good one, cannot be imposed on people. According to him, since freedom and free will characterize mankind, nothing can be compulsory. There is an enormous conceptual error here since there is nothing in his novel about the way to engender goodness and to move each member of the group to approve of it. Good would be a natural feeling that would characterize maturity, which is true, but he does not say anything about the social or psychological process that transforms a wild infant into a wise adult. Besides, he is silent about insanity and lifelong immaturity: do they exist or not?

On the other hand, there is nothing about consciousness or freedom of conscience. In other words, is Kant's moral limitation of freedom a manifestation of conscience that compels each individual to respect anybody's existence? Besides, he does not define liberty. A good definition would emphasize the ability of the individual to repress his or her own feelings. He or she would be so sane that he or she would always behave reasonably, even though he or she would not want to act responsibly; this conduct would redound to society. Burgess was not a philosopher, but he was a citizen, and, as a member of society, he should have defined those essential concepts accurately. He did transform the reality of youth into an infernal fear.

D- The borderline school.

The film industry has also tackled the problem of schooling. French speakers may remember *Zero for Conduct* (21) and *Diabolique* (22), which are not masterpieces. Lindsay Anderson's *If...* (23) is much more interesting and famous: it won the *Grand Prix* at the 1969 Cannes Film Festival.

The story takes place in a "public" school. The building and setting are really old-fashioned: the Gothic church overshadows the other buildings, pupils are grouped according to age and the prefects keep order. This is a real community since, most of the time, pupils pull together. Women are rare; there are only two of them: the matron and Mrs. Kemp, the housemaster's wife. Like many boarding schools around the world, it is not an Oedipal organization: the triadic structure of the family is completely absent and gender parity does not exist. It is very anaclitic because parenting is delegated to the cane of adolescent prefects.

Travis does not fit this world of academic conventions, but he is not a complete psychopath. He is something of an eccentric (one of the prefects called him a degenerate). He probably does not stand the atmosphere of the school and one must admit that the very goal of school, which is science and truth discovery through science, is omitted. We may share Forster's view that nothing is taught and learned in boarding schools, except sport and esprit de corps! Their existence is therefore illegitimate.

In such a world, sexuality is a problem. The way it is depicted in the movie is quite obsessional: there is not the vulgar description of the act but evocations of it. Besides, there is a scene in which a student tells the priest about his impure thoughts; the combination of sex, dirtiness, vice and misconduct is a classic obsessional characteristic. In this connection, the libido is repressed, not by the group but the conscience of some pupils. For instance, one of the prefects, who is very strict, represses his own homosexual impulses in a neurotic manner: his morals compel him to sublimate the impulse. This well-portrayed character with an obsessional personality does not fear narcissistic erosion; he just refuses any kind of sexuality: the mind replaces libido. Consequently, when the film director deals with the anaclitic sexuality of Travis, the result is not completely anaclitic, all the more so because the movie would have been censored. For example, there is a flamboyant desexualized scene in which Travis tries to kiss a girl; she slaps his face; then, to the sound of an African arrangement of a religious tune, the two of them, naked, mimic what could be interpreted as the courtship display of a lion and a lioness on the African steppes.

The aim of the movie is also to show students rebelling against the establishment, which is symbolized by the parents, the director, the staff and, of course, the prefects. It is tempting to acknowledge here Travis's anaclitic struggle to overthrow the obsessional prefects. Actually, when he says (24) "you expect us to lick your frigid fingers for the rest of your frigid life", libido, if it is present, gives way to a Marxist class struggle, an updated version of King Richard's "villains you are, villains you shall remain". Hence, the establishment would be the obsessional upper part of society and the rebellious youngsters the psychopathic foundations. This movie echoes the events of May 1968, when French immature students defeated the neurotic *Général de Gaulle*.

The movie ends with a massacre. Travis, a friend of his, and his girlfriend discover weapons while they are cleaning a part of the school. They decide to destroy the establishment. They wait for the best moment. At the end of the academic year, the parents, a famous general, a prince, and some personages gather in the church. Standing on the roof of a building overlooking the church, they are expecting these people to exit from it. Then, they start shooting them. The establishment (commanded by the general) counterattacks with guns. The director uses demagogy: he declares that he understands them, asks them to trust him and tells them to be reasonable. The girl blows his head off. No doubt the last scene is a psychopathic massacre. If the first title of the film was *The Crusaders*, Anderson chose Rudyard Kipling's poem *If* (25), which describes the transition from childhood to manhood; it is certain that Travis did not learn to become a man in Lindsay Anderson's boarding school: he remained a dangerous, angry old little boy.

The British have never questioned these institutions, even though they are not always impressed by their pedagogical efficacy. Moreover, in the United Kingdom, there is a place that is the exact opposite: it is Summerhill School.

The school was founded by Alexander Sutherland Neill. His philosophy is not original; it is the modernization of Jean-Jacques Rousseau's opinion about childhood and human nature: the child is naturally good and wise (26), and it is society and civilization that corrupt his or her mind. This institution is composed of children, teachers and other adults who advocate self-government; it is a kind of anaclitic democracy where each person, in spite of his age, knowledge and intelligence has the right to express his opinion and vote. The aim is not knowledge but the welfare of children through freedom. The concept of authority does not exist, since there is no real *patrum auctoritas*: the director does not establish the rules, nor does he organize the curriculum. Actually, adults express less concern about learning than those who live in Anderson's public school!

In this connection, the pupils are not obliged to attend the classes or even work in the workshop or the garden. They must choose their life freely. Neill writes that some children preferred to play for months rather than attend the classes. Besides, when they have decided to work, they can choose their subjects. Neill did not have strong opinions on subjects and he did not care about what to teach and which way to teach it. In his book, we notice that he is more interested in handicrafts and gardening than in mathematics and literature. His aim is to make children happy so that they may become happy adults. In order to achieve that goal, love is the only manner since children "react to love with love" (27). His naive point of view emphasizes the narcissistic component of human interactions, which is the negation of the existence of other ways to interact with people.

One wonders whether this place is quiet. The answer is yes because problem children are not accepted or are excluded (28). So that peace may reign in the school, the director must enroll "good" boys and girls in it, not bullies. Nonetheless, good children do not always agree with a director who is not regarded as a valid superego: Neill writes that his views were rarely shared by the community.

Summerhill, which still exists, is just a school among many others. It may look like the absurd response, an isolated one, to the rigidity and inefficiency of ordinary schools. It is more than that since it influenced many progressive schools and enticed immature teachers and even state organizations into sharing Neill's views. If the British do not know that Summerhill School exists, the French education system has been deeply affected by the naive ideas of Neill. Hence, the academic reality may appear to be less realistic and much more immature than fictional films. The motion picture industry is much more aware of the numerous problems inherent in childhood, immaturity and mankind.

E- Joie de vivre.

Filmmaking considered, at last, the problem of the evolution of immature adolescents. The movie *Harold and Maud* (29) is a comedy that shows a young adult (probably aged 20) who makes the acquaintance of an old lady (aged 79) in a funeral. Harold is depressive. He has no father and lives with his rich mother. He has great difficulty catching her attention, which leads him to invent and stage sophisticated suicide attempts. The movie starts with one of them, and his mother hardly notices what he is doing. She just exits the room telling him: "dinner at 8"!

The following day, Harold is more persuasive: he covers himself and the whole bathroom with red paint looking like blood. His mother enters the room and is shocked; she bursts into tears and sends him to see a psychoanalyst. It has to be said that the sessions are quite inefficient: Harold does not verbalize his feelings and the psychoanalyst is not perspicacious. On the other hand, in order to transform her son into a real man, she decides to find him a suitable wife. Marriage is the logical condition which guarantees that family will continue to exist and it is also a pathway from childhood to adulthood: a way to take on responsibilities. In order to achieve that goal, she chooses the efficiency of science: a computer selects the suitable candidates according to a personality test Harold has also passed. Soon afterwards young ladies come to the mansion to meet him. He tries his very best to frighten them. The discouraged mother believes that the military could be the solution, but Harold's uncle also fails to turn his nephew into a man.

As for Maud, she represents the immature maturity. She is an eternal adolescent, who sits for artists and lives in a railroad car as if it had to leave at any moment, but it always stays alongside the platform. She is a bit crazy or weird. She is also very childish: once she saw a tree, in a pot, in a city, and she took it in order to set it free and plant it in a nearby forest. She is quite irresponsible: she often steals cars and has major issues with the police, but she does not care.

Maud usually attends funerals of people whom she does not know. We do not really know why: is it to steal the cars of the relatives or to be confronted with her own death? Aged 79, she must now face the cruel reality of ageing and nature's decision. Since she is aware of her own death, she may mature and become at last an adult, but it seems that, at the beginning of the movie, her anxiety over her death is not detectable. She knows that it will happen, for she is not a psychopath who denies it, but she is not a person whose personality is organized at the neurotic level, which is why she is not afraid and does not feel the need to be at peace with the world. Maud is a daydreamer who is not completely in tune with reality.

Maud and Harold met at a funeral. They got to know each other better when she invited him over at tea time. There is, of course, a marked contrast between the baby-faced Harold and the old Maud, but they communicate easily because they think in the same was. Actually, they understand each other and fall in love soon. Harold is so excited that he proposes to her and tells his mother that he is going to marry Maud. His mother is appalled; the psychoanalyst is not that shocked by the age gap. However, Maud chooses to take some pills in order to hasten her death. Why did she commit suicide? Did she want to bring with her the everlasting image of love? Obviously, she refuses earthly happiness and forbids him to live with her and be happy, though this may no last long.

Harold is so sad that he takes his car and drives to the cliff. A scene shows his hearse falling into the sea. He is not inside. He is playing Maud's favorite tune on the banjo she had offered him. He has chosen to live. Maud enabled him to have plenty of joie de vivre, but she did not do this in a neurotic way, for she did not act like the old king who sits his son on the throne of moral duties and of the triumphant logic of mankind's destiny, the aim of life being life itself. Maud just enabled a young man to fall in love. He could therefore keep on cherishing the memory of his first love and live. At long last a mother figure had looked at him and acknowledged his existence. At long last he was alive.

Hence, when we analyse the vision of immaturity of the film industry and literature, we realize that society does not ignore this issue. The situation is a bit weird, for authors and filmmakers are much more aware of the problem than the people whose duty is to raise children and teach them how to become adults, namely parents and teachers. Some authors even have a low opinion of it: children and adolescents are therefore regarded as monsters. In fact, they are neither good nor evil, since goodness and badness can only be characteristics of grownups, that is to say people who are supposed to be mature and who have a strong superego. Youth is a changing state; it is a world in the making that cannot be condemned since nature, human nature, has not finished its work. This poor opinion may have something to do with the cataclysmic World War Two, a moment in the history of the mind and of mankind we will examine in chapter 10.

1. Golding, William, *Lord of the flies*, London, 1954,

electronic edition, Global village contemporary classics. Movie by Peter Brook, Janus films, USA and UK, 1963.

2. *Lord of the flies*, p. 290: "... the darkness of man's heart...".

3. *Lord of the flies*, p. 225: Piggy excuses the murder of a boy saying that it was just an accident.

4. *Lord of the flies*, p. 29: the author declares that he is larger than life, which moves the little boys to regard him as a kind of hero; see also p. 83.

5. *Lord of the flies*, p. 82, 83.

6. *Lord of the flies*, p. 97 to 99.

7. *Lord of the flies*, p. 130.

8. *Lord of the flies*, p. 216.

9. *Lord of the flies*, p. 83.

10. *Lord of the flies*, p. 47: "... Until the grownups come and fetch us we'll have fun...".

11. *Lord of the flies*, p. 290.

12. Truffaut, François, *Les 400 coups*, Les films du carosse, movie, France, 1959. Scenario by François Truffaut and Marcel Moussy.

13. Ray, Nicholas, *Rebel without a cause*, Warner Bros., movie, USA, 1955. Script by Stewart Stern and Irving Shulman.

14. I am writing here what is exactly written in the script.

15. Arnold, Jack, *High school confidential*, Metro Godwin Mayer, movie, USA, 1958. Screenplay by Robert Blees and Lewis Meltzer.

16. Robson, Mark, *Valley of the Dolls*, 20th Century Fox, movie, USA, 1967.

17. Kubrick, Stanley, *A Clockwork Orange*, Warner Bros., movie, USA, 1971.

18. Burgess, Anthony, *A Clockwork Orange*, London, 1962, electronic edition, PDF pagination.

19. *A Clockwork Orange*, p. 82 and 83.

20. *A Clockwork Orange*, p. 123.

21. Vigo, Jean, *Zero de conduite*, Gaumont, movie, France, 1933.

22. Clouzot, Henri-Georges, *Les Diaboliques*, Cinédis, movie, France, 1955.

23. Anderson, Lindsay, *If...*, Paramount pictures, movie, U.K, 1968. Screenplay by David Sherwin.

24. Second part of the movie.

25. Rudyard, Kipling, *Rewards and Fairies*, New York, 1910, p. 181-182: "If".

26. Neill, Alexander Sutherland, *Summerhill: a radical approach to child rearing*, New York, 1960, electronic edition, PDF pagination, p. 14.

27. *Summerhill*, p. 107.

28. *Summerhill*, p. 45.

29. Ashby, Hal, *Harold and Maude*, Paramount Pictures, movie, USA, 1971. Screenplay by Colin Higgins. Published as a novel in 1971.

Chapter 3

The mousetrap.

Economy is but a codification of the interactions between the members of society. Consequently, if society is mainly psychotic, its economy will display psychotic characteristics and will thus be dysfunctional. If society is organized at the neurotic level, its economy will be balanced and the economic growth will be sustainable in the long-term. Of course, there are many factors and economy is not only characterized by the main social component, all the more so because exchanges can be problematic and ecological and demographic elements interfere with the data and results.

The least I can say is that world economy is neither efficient nor well organized. The 2007 crisis, I should say the 2000-2030 crisis, proves it and will move me here to determine whether societies are mature and sane or immature and thus dysfunctional. It must be said that the world knows that Marxism and its socialist variant proved a complete failure where they were implemented. In the Soviet Union, for instance, it harmed the economy, to the extent that the government was unable to produce the goods its population needed to survive, although it was helped by myriads of enslaved workers detained in the Siberian concentration camps. On the other hand, one wonders whether capitalism is, by nature, an appropriate system. Actually, the cycles described by Nikolai Kondratiev show periods of expansion and contraction, whereas people and economists wish the economy were in equilibrium. The accumulation phases (phase A) and repayment ones (phase B) could be regarded as the major symptoms of an immature economy that first dreams that it will make big profits thanks to new products; then, confronting reality, it discovers that dreams were but illusions: the loans taken out during the accumulation phase (which lasts 25 or 30 years) are repaid after 15 or 20 years (monetary inflation helps the customers who have a fixed-rate mortgage to do so). However, capitalism is not a dysfunctional system per se. I would even say that it is the only way to counterbalance the psychotic omnipotence of some parts of society. Actually, the right to property is, historically and humanly, the most efficient counterpower to any authoritarian regime that is economically linked to them. Moreover, competition between companies of the same size, or almost, can improve the quality of the goods and exchanges if most customers behave rationally thanks to the analysis of objective pieces of information. Hence, in the first two chapters, I will study the level of maturity and rationality of today's economy. Then, in this macroeconomic approach, I will include two individuals who severely damaged the system (I mean Bernard Madoff and Jérôme Kerviel). Hence, I will try to find whether they are the product of a system, a kind of autoimmune disease, or an accident that only questions its soundness, not its validity.

A- Main Street.

Has entrepreneurial capitalism been enslaved by financial capitalism? Has creation been subdued by the vicious whims of lazy gamblers? Since the beginning of industrialization, Return on Capital Employed has been trying to supplant man's intelligence and his legitimate desire to build a better world.

Since the beginning of the 19th century, this kind of capitalism has been lessening the importance of man, man being an outlay in the production system. The docile machine (the spinning mule for instance) has progressively taken the place of workers and transformed our modern factories into robotized spacecrafts where humans are almost completely absent. From 1811 to 1813, some British workers tried to reverse the process: they destroyed the machines that were stealing their jobs; the owners of the factories complained to the authorities, and 17 men were hanged. The connection between the old-fashioned aristocracy and the upper middle class was so strong that politics and money united their efforts to defeat the proletariat: in 1812, the law provided that workers would be sentenced to death if they destroyed the machines. Machines had won, for profitability was the ultimate goal.

In the United States, the process was less violent and the result more acceptable. Man was first included in the semi-automated assembly line and then excluded: the robots rapidly learned to mimic the awkward movements of human beings thanks to artificial intelligence. Since Americans did not resemble Europeans, they did not exclude mankind from the production system. They cherished work and thus never dared to enter the insane world of suicidal capitalism. The Europeans dared! They might have been more irrational than the Americans since they easily crossed the Rubicon and overcapitalized their companies: thanks to that money, they replaced the human workforce with robots. A European factory, nowadays, especially in France, is a deserted island full of restless automatons: man has completely disappeared. They have reached the point of no return: robots produce goods which unemployed workers cannot afford to buy. This situation engenders gigantic social disorders and pits work (or rather lack of work) against capital even more. They must rethink the role of man in the economy. This time, they must not forget to transform workers into capitalists, that is to say a logical, efficient counterpower: a part of the salary must be paid in shares.

On the other hand, the system is quite insane and immoral. Actually, many products that are sold are not only useless but also harmful to customers and the planet. Profitability implies that goods which slowly kill consumers cannot exist: for instance, in a civilized world, it is illogical to sell tobacco or alcohol. In fact, like the drug dealer who kills his client (or at least ruins his health), which leads him to earn less income, tobacco and alcohol producers damage people's health and engender social problems: the social cost is enormous, and they spend millions on trials.

The subprime mortgage crisis followed the same shortsighted logic. A bank can advance people some money if the latter can give the money back. If they cannot, lenders get into trouble: since the customer cannot pay, the bank forecloses on the house and tries to sell it in order to get its money back. It does work when there are very few foreclosures. During the subprime crisis, bankers (mainly the American ones, but the Spanish did the same) agreed to lend money to low-income people. The risks being high, they demanded high interest rate. In order to turn a high-yield, high-risk investment into a safer operation, they restructured the debts, which transferred the risks to banks and financial institutions all around the world. It is hard to believe that all the persons involved in that drama were not aware of the potentially catastrophic consequences. Did the opacity of these financial products deceive everyone, including smart people? Wasn't it self-evident that the absurd yield was a warning? It seems that nobody wanted to acknowledge reality, and when it surfaced, as usual, the short-sighted banks disappeared, their clients went bankrupt and the world abandoned its idea of endless prosperity.

This logic of depredation is not new; it represents the psychopathic root of unbalanced economies, a kind of primitive approach to nature. For thousands of years, man has stolen his food and clothes from nature; he never gave anything in return. With eight billion people on the planet, such behaviour is just unacceptable, but it is the rule. Consequently, natural resources like coal, petroleum and shale gas are plundered and wasted. Toxic components are released into the atmosphere, which changes the climates and causes the sea level to rise: islands are submerged, their inhabitants flee and the world looks like the Danaides' barrel. Nature is not only a contributing factor in mankind's survival, it is also a source of wealth. Each time a flower or an animal disappears, man makes his life more unbearable, his survival more hypothetical and poverty his ineluctable fate.

From a microeconomic point of view, we must question the pertinence of hierarchies in companies. An efficient hierarchy takes into consideration the level of awareness of people. Since its aim is to develop strategies, the top of the pyramid must be composed of reasonable, knowledgeable and educated people. Their goal cannot be to get richer; their ambition must be to search for the products that will enable humanity to survive and prosper in accordance with the ecological requirements. In order to take account of all kinds of personalities, below them we should find people who are less intelligent and insightful. Since they are not stupid, they can also invent plans and ideas. Persons whose personality is organized at the schizophrenic level cannot do so, which is why they are to obey sane senior executives.

Unfortunately, it's very rare to see such an organization. It seems that anaclitic pride is the main characteristic of corporate hierarchies. This is a serious dysfunction since the level of awareness is so low that they will not be able to react efficiently to external stimuli. There is much immorality too, which suggests that larcenies and other internal risks will not be easily identified. The problem will have to be significant so that it will be identified, regarded as a danger and solved.

These anaclitic hierarchies are produced by academicism and conformism. Since the establishment do not know what truth is, they hire people who resemble them, which creates an impression of harmless normality. The French are highly conformist. Their inefficient educational system is dominated by what they call *Grandes Ecoles*. These schools (like the *Ecole normale supérieure* we saw in chapter 1) compel students to take a competitive examination that is aimed at identifying the best ones. Candidates memorize information, official information about various subjects, and write essays that will fit in with the jury's preconceived ideas. The candidates who share the examiners' views or at least pretend to do so get good marks. The French believe that parrots are intelligent students! Actually, it is very easy to select conventional people thanks to the stubbornness of mathematics, physics and chemistry (subjects which form part of the entrance examination for *Polytechnique*, *Ponts et chaussées* and *Ecole des mines*), but law, economics and literature can also serve that purpose. When we examine the subjects which students must study in order to take the entrance examination for the most famous school (ENA), even what they call "general knowledge" (*culture générale*) is a meaningless ballet routine: entrechats and jeté battu jumps must be done at the right moment. Nonetheless, the summary of administrative data is probably the most grotesque exercise a teacher's mind ever invented (1): formalism led to political doublespeak and the result is a two-part composition full of gibberish. Needless to say, this French elite is narrow-minded. Later on, the result of such a state of mind will be revealed thanks to the analysis of Jérôme Kerviel's case.

Besides, in world economy, there are not many counterpowers. Of course, the Americans have long understood that the system could not work without limiting the size of companies: their antitrust laws date back to the 19th century. However, if the whole planet implemented them, they would reduce the danger, but the system would not be more reasonable. No regulation can boost the economic agents' intellectual capacity; only education can do so, I mean compulsory education through intelligent media.

In this field, there are many newspapers, books and academic studies, but today television is the spontaneous answer to eternal questions. *Bloomberg television* and *CNBC* are thus lighthouses whose flickering flames enlighten unbalanced economic agents. It's very difficult and almost impossible to measure their impact, but, at least, we can say that their journalists give the most intelligent viewers valuable information which they can check, evaluate and use, which must somehow have a beneficial influence on the stock markets.

B- Wall Street.

If we now look at the little world of the financial products and stock markets (the tip of the iceberg), it does not seem really sound either. In fact, the stock market, especially since the year 2000, is a world of fear. It even was in panic mode in 2008. A stock market crash is by no means unusual; it is always caused by the discovery of the fact that valuations and expected returns are false, which leads to an immediate correction. In 2008, it was neither a stock market crash nor a bear market, but something new: stocks used to tumble, but they also used to recover after the slumps. Prices were extremely volatile. Fear reigned: it was contagious, insane and desperate. The NYSE floor brokers were tired, depressed and confused: were these shores those of the Styx or did they forecast the Apocalypse? No blue chip or defensive stock could limit the damage. The brokers just sold everything they could and kept their assets liquid. There was no safe haven but ready money.

The bond market was a mirror of the panic that was spreading through investors. In order to ease the pain and prevent a chain reaction leading to the collapse of the global financial system, the Federal Reserve Bank of New York cut its rates to an incredible 0-0.25%. Because of inflation, the return was negative, but the whole planet bought massive amounts of American treasury bonds in order to lose a bit of money, not all the money! The stock and treasury markets were therefore places where capital was destroyed! They were not aimed at producing wealth anymore.

As a matter of fact, the fearful financial world viewed the United States as necessary purgatory. Investors withdrew their money from Europe, regardless of the soundness of the companies. In 2023, the situation is still unstable: the European multinationals that operate all around the world are undervalued, whereas the American ones are overpriced. The Dow Jones industrial and the Standard and Poor 500 are higher than ever, and the European indexes are not that high, even though they are not really exposed to their depressed internal market. Is fear still sneaking around?

Besides, entrepreneurial capitalism has been replaced by speculative capitalism. The stock and financial markets are the masters of the world; investors are under the illusion that they will strike gold in two shakes of a lamb's tail. When people invest in stocks, the time horizon must be long so that entrepreneurs may choose a strategy, implement it and make profits. Scalping and day trading are completely absurd when we take into consideration what such techniques return. Of course, it does not produce wealth; it is not an investment either. It is just the manifestation of the anxiety of daydreamers who are not even able to support the system which enables them to live. That's the very definition of parasitism. Moreover, it is the symbol of people who do not have the courage to choose a stock (which is an idea), defend a point of view, implement a strategy, get information about a company's performance, stand to lose money, and change tactics, when necessary. It is a kind of archaic thinking, the conditioned reflex of an individual who stammers.

One must acknowledge that people who work in trading rooms are not always intellectuals. Jérôme Kerviel described the mood of the *Société Générale*'s employees (2), and the childish behaviour of some of his co-workers is almost shocking. They look like small children in front of a video game console. They even named their mainframe computer Game Boy! The reality of trade and amounts vanishes in front of this larger-than-life video game. As if they were in a casino, they aim to win the jackpot, and the most thrilling way to win it is to play with dangerous toys: derivatives.

An old-fashioned capitalist cannot regard them as investment products. It is said that they allow people to stay invested in a bear market: warrants, turbo warrants, index-trackers and ETFs protect their investments. If these products did not exist, they would sell their stocks and things would go south. When we compare the 2000-2002 bear market with the Stock Market Crash of 1929, the trends are very much alike. During the decade 2000-2010, European indexes experienced negative returns. We can therefore have doubts about their so-called positive influence, all the more so because in 2008 the hedge funds sold their stocks and bought derivatives with the money.

Warrants are one of these extraordinary products: they are call or put options on indexes or stocks. Needless to say, this is not investment anymore but pure speculation. These warrants have a multiplying factor, which means that when the underlying asset goes up or down, the profit or loss, according to the warrants' volatility and maturity, will be multiplied with a coefficient. One invests little money, but one can rapidly earn much more money than with shares. Of course, if the investor misinterprets the trend indicators, he or she can lose what he or she has invested. Hedge funds use these products in order to make money in a bear market and to maximize profits. Unfortunately, when there is a lot of volatility, when the indexes go up and down at any moment because of hesitations on the part of the people who are involved in a credit crunch, the investor ends up swimming against the tide. He or she loses touch with reality; he or she alternates between cheerfulness and deep despair: probabilities become improbable and psychology is therefore the key factor that protects he or she from insanity and poverty. The derivatives market is but a casino, a way to go over the top, to become a bipolar, adrenaline junkie and to feel alive in a virtual world. Sometimes the trader is a kind of Pluto winning virtual billions; sometimes he is a beggar losing a fortune: at the end of the year, profits are minimal (if there are some), although there was a lot of work and anxiety. Société Générale is a well-known warrant expert; the role it played in the virtualization of the financial markets is great, but many other financial institutions can also be blamed. They wanted to earn money as soon as possible, denying the existence of the investment rhythm and process; they refused to back real investors up and turned simple-minded traders into high rollers. Many of them were forced into bankruptcy: greed is dangerous when reality is ignored.

In this connection, the virtual intelligence of computers has replaced brainless traders and investors. Hence, mathematical models and electronic trading platforms are created by human minds in order to help man to decide. This is completely absurd since the stock markets are a darkroom full of human passions and illusions which no machine can copy. History shows that computers even made the situation worse in 1987 and on the 6th of May 2010 (3).

Individual and institutional investors programmed their computers to buy and sell financial products. It is not dangerous to use a limit order to make a purchase, but it is very dangerous to use stop-loss orders (4). Actually, if people are not in front of their computer monitors, even for a short while, the stocks are automatically sold, which accelerates the fall of their prices. The system has brakes, but they are weak. During the *May 6, 2010 flash crash*, it is clear that once the big fall had occurred, the market participants disengaged the autopilot and, after, behaved in a strange way. Some of them preferred to sell, which accelerated the fall and activated the stop-loss orders. Some others, who were happy to buy stocks at a lower price, bought lots of them, which engendered a reversal. Some participants reported that they sold because "they feared the occurrence of a cataclysmic event of which they were not yet aware" (5). In fact, some of them decided to do so, although they had no information whatsoever: they were losing touch with reality and were driven by fear, fear amplified by computers.

Hence, we realize that, because of them, the world was messier and madder. The financial markets and world economy are highly dysfunctional. They are not completely insane, but, according to the classical economists, they have not reached the nirvana of perfect equilibrium. Consequently, they are immature.

C- Bernard Madoff.

In this immature world, an immature man committed fraud. He destabilized the unbalanced economy a little more.

It's easy to sketch out the mind of Bernard Madoff, even though this man was discreet. First of all, we must say that he was quite immoral since he fooled many people for decades, including friends and members of his community. Remorse and apologies came too late: in front of the judge, when he pleaded guilty (6). One would even believe that his apologies were suggested, or even written, by his lawyers. Madoff was not a talkative man; his answers were always short and inexpressive, and suddenly, when he expressed regrets, the sentences were much longer, well constructed and emotionally charged. In that regard, his daughter-in-law declared that he was not an intellectual who would have elaborate conversations; he neither expressed complicated ideas nor used chichi words (7). She did not say that he used to keep to himself either. However, in her interview, she added a very important piece of information: "Bernie was a total need freak. Everything had to be perfect. Off his clothes were perfect shirts, colored-coordinated, perfect shoes, lined up. Everything had to be totally clean." Even in his early seventies, Bernard was still a dandy who was very preoccupied with his appearance and clothes. His vulnerable narcissism could not withstand too much imperfection, since it could have led to vulgarity. He was not a man with an obsessional personality because he was not afraid that people noticed that his clothes were dirty; he was an immature individual, for not looking good petrified him.

In his letter to his daughter-in-law, dated August 4, 2009 (8), many parts deal with his self-esteem. For instance, he asserts that the other inmates treat him with respect, like a crime boss. They call him Uncle Bernie or Mr. Madoff. Everybody, including the staff, cares about his well-being and tries to greet him. After all, prison was a place where his narcissism was not questioned, and he felt good there. Actually, he felt secure, all the more so because the inmates did not quarrel with one another; he could socialize with people and, most of all, he did not have to make decisions, since he was no longer in control of his own life. He was not afraid anymore to make mistakes or not to control the outside world; he was a child again; he was a boy who refused to have adult responsibilities (9). He could thus concentrate on his narcissism and had finally found the right place to do that.

In Fact, his whole life and his fraud were a quest for protection. Thanks to Diana Henriques (10), we realize that he did not really feel comfortable in the strange world of trading.

He started his career in the 60s. He traded OTC stocks, and he soon had issues. In 1962, the prices of the products he had sold plummeted (11); his clients faced substantial losses. He bought back their stocks in order to erase the losses and gain a reputation as a trading guru (12). He lost his money in the operation, not his reputation. His first job in the dangerous world of trading was a failure, and one wonders whether he already tried to reduce the risks (using a certain technique). Henriques does not really know when he transformed his business into a Ponzi scheme and what his motivations were. Nonetheless, she writes that, in 1987 (13), the fraud had started. Personally I think that his lack of success, the stagflation in the 1970s and the stock market crash of 1987 led him to invent a reliable method for investors to earn money. A Ponzi scheme is a simplistic way to get money without investing it. At least, there is no danger of losing it. The only problem is that the deceiver must find lots of new customers in order to pay the dividends. When the rate of return is 14%, the deceiver can give the dupe his or her money back for 7 years, but after that term, he must get funding and start using the money invested by new clients. Moreover, there's a high risk of customers asking for their money. In the case of Bernard Madoff, his fraud was well handled, but it is clear that it had reached a critical point, for much capital was needed, and thus the whole world had to be involved in that Ponzi scheme.

The people who gave him their money were attracted by a very high yield: 13.5 % (14). This rate is just absurd, and one has to question the intelligence of investors. Nonetheless, some people were doubtful. Victor Teicher and John Nash (15) were the first to be surprised. In 2001, Michael Ocrant (16), Erin Arvedlund (17) and Harry Markopolos (18) worried about the high rate of interest.

Markopolos even thought that it was a fraud. On the 25th of October 2005, after a third report to the SEC, he was questioned by the Boston Bureau of that institution. They were worried and told the New York unit to act (19). The latter did not believe that Madoff was guilty of such a crime. However, they met him in February and May 2006, but they neither decided nor discovered anything. By late spring 2007, some bankers were worried: on the 15th of June 2007, an e-mail from JP Morgan Chase (20) stated that he had executed a Ponzi scheme. It took people 20 years to understand that the return he promised was utterly absurd.

Madoff is not the product of the system, but his history shows that it is extremely fragile: a well-mannered man uttering honeyed words can persuade people who just want to believe in impossible dreams. Investing is like democracy: both can work only if participants are reasonable people, not dreamers.

D- Jérôme Kerviel.

As for Jérôme Kerviel, he is not an immature man but a person with an obsessional personality, which shows that the financial system is weak.

In 2010, he published a book on the case in which he is involved: the billions lost by Société Générale in 2008 (21). In the first pages, his personality shows through, for he sexualizes his speech, which is a neurotic trait. His world is not that of anaclitic narcissism but that of neurotic genitalization (22). Nonetheless, since he is a man with an obsessional personality, the resolution of the Oedipus complex is incomplete. So he cannot be regarded as a reasonable adult. He is not a person with Hysterical Personality Organization, which means that he knows what reason and truth are, but he does not always behave rationally. Besides, his morals do not have the marmoreal rigidity of that of hysterically organized persons. In fact, it is an operative characteristic (23) but not a constant obligation.

We also notice that he believes that the mind is superior to passions (24), which is a classic obsessional trait. For example, when he explains why he likes his job (25), one perceives signs of magical thinking (through mathematics, figures, trends and charts) and discovers how he understands the facts and acts. If his first trade was stressful (26), he soon learned to interpret the figures and act fast, which proves that he was not insane. People who suffer from obsessional neurosis hesitate a lot and regress to a stage where they keep reciting numbers or chanting incantations that are aimed at preventing action and sexual intercourse, which they fear. This is not the case here. Actually, he acknowledges deriving pleasure from trading: money and profit are obsessional banalities that represent libido.

There is also a primitive connection to the mother. In fact, we find a strange piece of information about the moral values his mother inculcated in her two sons, which shows that she is proud of their education (27). Here again, the obsessional traits are classic: the mother of a person with an obsessional personality fosters the intellectualization of impulses and is a key factor in the construction of the superego of her children. Hence, a man with an obsessional personality cannot have a purely masculine superego. We must now compare this with his opinion about his employer: Société Générale. He asserts that the bank is an omnipotent woman who protects and feeds her employees (28). Actually, it is not a woman but a mother: men with an obsessional personality do not master the concepts that turn a mother into a woman, which is her true nature. There is always little emotional distance between them and their mothers. This lack of objectivity leads people like me to regard them as immature people, for they are incomplete.

However, Kerviel is more intelligent than an ordinary immature man, all the more so because he is not a neurotic. Consequently, we must try to understand the process that turned a sane man with an operative superego into a danger to society. He is more than an ordinary criminal: his deeds and the billions he lost hit the system so hard that it nearly collapsed.

The first problem deals with his immoral behaviour and the necessity of supervision. In his book, he keeps saying (28) that the people who worked at Société Générale did not observe the rules, or rather, that their rules were immoral. He also asserts that the hierarchy (people who studied at the *Grandes Ecoles* mentioned above) knew that he was misbehaving, but they did not do anything to stop him. He even adds that his bosses were not righteous men (30), which may be true since they allowed him to behave as he did. He would have liked to be stopped and helped by one of them and writes that all this was really confusing (31). He had lost touch with reality, and like an immature man, he was asking for the help of a father figure, but he did not find any, since the hierarchy was unhealthy.

The other important point is his trading mistakes. Actually, he needed to invest a lot of money in order to make big profits. Hence, he invented a trick that was aimed at hiding the amounts he was investing. He writes that he spent 30 billion euros, but, in early 2008, the money he had spent might have amounted to 50 billion (32). The enormity of the sum is almost unreal. When people, even sane people, live in a world of numbers, which are by nature unreal, the unit of account disappears: euros, pounds and dollars do not make sense anymore. Besides, the money invested is not lost until the financial products are sold. Consequently, hope, which leads people to make lots of mistakes, moves them to wait for a better trend and spend a little more money. In the case of Kerviel, the phenomenon was aggravated by his complete ignorance of market psychology, economic realities and financial needs. In other words, he was neither knowledgeable nor competent enough to be a trader. Sometimes he invested well and earned money, but in 2007, when the direction of the markets was not clear and volatility increased, calm and steadiness were not sufficient. People needed to go back to the basics: the reality of the economy, the superficiality of the prices and the imperious tyranny of capital liquidity. Jérôme Kerviel, like his colleagues who studied at the *Grandes Ecoles* or not and most of the traders around the world who lost unimaginable amounts of money, was just irresponsible and incompetent.

The difference between him and them is the amounts spent and the solution imagined, not by him but by *Société Générale*: they panicked and sold his stocks, which caused chaos. On the 22nd of January 2008, the markets, especially the Cac 40, plummeted; the same thing happened the following days. The persons in charge closed Jérôme's positions within five days. At the end of the operation, they lost around 5 billion euros. This case is much more disturbing than that of Madoff since the protagonist is neither immature nor insane. In fact, sanity intended to destroy a part of the system! Does it mean that Kerviel considered that it was immoral or even insane? He was not politically engaged and cannot be regarded as a French Bolshevik attacking the Versailles of world finance. Nevertheless, this affair shows that a financial institution like *Société Générale* chooses its traders and employees according to subjective impressions. This means that objectivity, the objectivity of results, real competences, reason, intelligence, knowledge and morals is nonexistent. This world is therefore suicidal.

1. Students must read a dossier which includes lots of documents and sum it up. There are so many texts that, because of the lack of time, it is impossible to read them all. Hence, one must read the titles, try to understand them and just focus on the artificiality of the structure of the summary, not the very essence of the subject.
2. Kerviel, Jérôme, *L'engrenage: mémoires d'un trader*, J'ai Lu, Paris, 2010, p. 20, 90, 106, 107, 108, 122, 123.
3. Commodity Futures Trading Commission, Securities and Exchange Commission, *Findings regarding the market events of May 6, 2010*, Washington, 2010.
4. To protect one's capital, they place a sell order at -5/-10 %; when the price is reached, the stocks are sold automatically.
5. Commodity Futures, p. 5.

6. United States district court, southern district of New York, *Bernard Madoff's plea*, New York, the 12th of March 2009, p. 23, 24.

7. Druckerman, Shana, Rhee, Joseph, "Madoff family secret: Stephanie's story", *ABC news*, the 21st of October 2011.

8. Druckerman, Shana, Rhee, Joseph, "Like a mafia don: Bernie Madoff's boastful letter to angry daughter-in-law", *ABC news*, the 20th of October 2011.

9. Amiel and others, "Bernie Madoff can live with fraud victims' anger, but not family scorn. He tells Barbara Walters exclusively", *ABC news*, the 27th of October 2011.

10. Henriques, Diana B., *Bernie Madoff, the wizard of lies. Inside the infamous $ 65 billion swindle*, Oxford, 2011. Kindle pagination: l. means location.

11. Henriques, l. 839.

12. Henriques, l. 864.

13. Henriques, l. 1919.

14. Henriques, l. 2512: in 1992, the rate was even 14 % for people who had at least 2 million dollars.

15. Henriques, l. 2445.

16. Henriques, l. 2512.

17. Henriques, l. 2551.

18. Henriques, l. 2613.

19. Henriques, l. 3218.

20. Henriques, l. 3652.

21. Kerviel, Jérôme, *L'engrenage: mémoires d'un trader*, J'ai Lu, Paris, 2010.

22. Kerviel, p. 14.

23. Kerviel, p. 78.

24. Kerviel, p. 86, 96.

25. Kerviel, p. 155.

26. Kerviel, p. 102.

27. Kerviel, p. 67.

28. Kerviel, p. 21.

29. Kerviel, p. 13, 14, 18, 19, 20, 23, 28, 46, 47, 107, 127, 133, 134, 135, 136, 137, 199.

30. Kerviel, p. 107.

31. Kerviel, p. 136.

32. Kerviel, p. 125.

Chapter 4

The rictus of the doll.

To be or not to be a woman: this is a problem, all the more so because very few people know nowadays what a woman is exactly. Simone de Beauvoir (1) tried to define that, but, in spite of the success of the book, neither women nor men were really convinced by what she wrote. However, what is now an issue was regarded as a self-evident truth by our forebears: women were determined by biology and religion. Biology gave her a body, along with its procreative function, whereas religion compelled her to raise children until the end of time. An idea accepted by the majority of people does not transform it into an absolute truth; it may even be the opposite. Let us select a "neurotic" definition so that everybody may understand. A woman is the result of a biological sex which compels her to give birth. Hence, education must allow her to accept her gender and that someday she will have to bear children. Furthermore, she must realize that her children are also the children of a man whose duty is to separate them from their mother so that they may not remain the monstrous excrescences of an omnipotent mother: intense love is not love but the gateway to psychosis. Later she will have to value the role played by the father in raising their children and remain aloof. Obviously, her position is unpleasant since separation is her destiny. Moreover, men's view on her is, from a cultural point of view, quite uncomfortable. Nonetheless, nowadays she is not regarded anymore as a dangerous Athena whom men did not dare to look at for fear of petrifying, but there is still a certain distance between the sexes. We remember that, not so long ago, psychiatrists believed that she was an unquiet animal that was likely to develop a mental disorder. Hysteria was, by nature, a mental illness that struck mainly women. It was a dangerous illness since it was characterized by an accumulation of symptoms of immaturity and of psychosis sometimes. I let it be known that Charcot's hysteria has nothing to do with Bergeret's hysterical conversion. Nowadays, physicians do not regard her as a lunatic and womanhood is not a disease anymore! Nevertheless, when little girls cannot gain this enviable status, they become horrible monsters: old little girls are twisted and they do not behave themselves.

A- This is not really entertainment.

The media keep informing readers and viewers about all sorts of problems. When they do a good job, they enable people to understand the problems, which moves the voters to vote for politicians who can fix them. The media are the eyes of society, whereas politicians should be its conscience. This scheme works when most people are reasonable, which is rarely the case. Since journalists are ignorant about psychiatry, the information they give about some psychopathic killers do not allow the citizens to understand the facts or to address the issue. Are entertainers more competent than they? There is no doubt about it, and classic novels provide useful information about psychopathic killers. However, no book has ever led to collective action: did Shakespeare's description of Iago in *Othello* compelled James I to implement a policy aimed at curing the psychopaths of the kingdom? No, it did not; the political responses always came after the disasters, and the psychopathic killers were hanged after the crimes had been committed. Nowadays the film industry recycles classic novels and plays, and the number of spectators has never been so high. When the film is produced by the Americans, the whole planet watches it, but if individuals may be a bit influenced by it, there is no social impact, even when it is a documentary. When he started his career, Robert Redford believed that a movie could change society; some years later, he changed his mind, and he was wright. However, when a weirdo is portrayed in a play or in a movie, this means that its model exists in society. Artists rarely invent anything. Most of the time, they copy what they see: writers are academic painters, not avant-garde sculptors. Besides, the more the work of art is seen, the more society agrees to see the pathological reality, which may influence some people.

Like what we saw in chapter 2, the characters portrayed are not what society wants to see. Can we say that movies are a kind of "looking glass upon the wall" in which nations see themselves, which enables them to acknowledge their vices? In other words, are societies' dysfunctions immediately revealed by movies? Not exactly, since a work of art has something to do with the author's idiosyncrasies: he cannot portray reality as it is, and he often includes autobiographical elements. On the other hand, films are not always realistic: when societies are quite healthy, movies depict crude reality sometimes, but when they are sick, they transcend death and sorrows and plunge into technicolor idealism. In that regard, the Great Depression could only give birth to glamorous musicals. Let us check the information.

a- Tennessee Williams.

Tennessee Williams portrayed many women in his works, and many of them were distressed creatures. One could readily deduce that his mother and sister served as a template for most of his female characters. Personally, I think that he used to project his own anaclitic distress onto feminine characters since it is very difficult to perceive him when we analyse his male characters. Nonetheless, there is a way to get information about his personality: check whether his female characters are alcoholics or not. If they are, it is certain that he refers to his own alcoholism. We can also look for women who, at some point in the play or in the movie, try to seduce a man. Actually his female characters are so ambiguous that they do not exhibit the emotion felt by women with Neurotic Personality Organization but a passion that is not gender-specific, which means that he may have displayed his own feelings. Consequently, two women, I should say two girls, strand out: Catherine Holly and Blanche Dubois.

Catherine Holly (2) is an unbalanced young lady who has been suffering from an unidentified mental disorder since she witnessed the death of her cousin Sebastian Venable. In Mankiewicz's movie, Elisabeth Taylor's portrayal emphasizes the restlessness of the character, not her hypothetical insanity. Moreover, she speaks well, which suggests that she is not a psychotic. If she had lived in another age, she would have been called a hysteric; let us regard her as an impulsive girl whose equilibrium has been disturbed by an external event. She resides in a psychiatric hospital, but, in the movie, she stays at her aunts' house so that she may meet a psychiatrist who will decide whether he will lobotomize her in order to ameliorate her mind and mood. In the 1950s, American psychiatrists would lobotomize some of their patients, whereas Europeans did not dare to perform such operations: Freudian psychoanalysis had already defeated neuropsychiatry. Consequently, Catherine's rebellion against a world that wants to deprive her of a part of her mind is not the insane response of a raving lunatic. It is a logical fear of a dangerous operation that could lead to death, mental death. Besides, her family treats her badly. It seems that she is a hunted beast that must bite so that it may survive. Hence, she quarrels with the sister who looks after her. For instance, the nun does not want her to smoke and when she sees her holding a cigarette, she tells her that she will ask the physician to lock her in a calming room. Catherine retorts that she is not violent, but she burns the hand of the sister when she hands her the cigarette.

Catherine's discomfort increases when she sees the psychiatrist who wants to evaluate her condition. Her anxiety increases because her dysfunctional family worries her. She goes into the garden shouting "leave me alone", but the psychiatrist goes up to her and sedates her. More relaxed, she does not really try to seduce him, but she kisses him and asks him to hold her in his arms, which can be interpreted as a way to tell a father figure to protect her. It is clear that there are no father figures in the play, and the only available man is his brother: a rather truculent, inconsistent male. Tennessee Williams clearly portrays an immature woman on the verge of psychopathy, not psychosis, who is more mistreated by her family than by society. Hence, the schizophrenia of his sister – did she really suffer from this mental illness? – did not move him to depict Catherine as a psychotic. However, the prefrontal lobotomy his sister underwent, which left her in a docile, childlike state, is a drama he never forgot. It is a kind of threat to lunatics and to people who do not behave themselves or keep family secrets, like Catherine.

His most impressive description of an immature woman is of course that of Blanche Dubois (3) in a *Streetcar named desire*, a character who might have been inspired by his mother.

Blanche is a middle-aged southern lady who conceals a lot of things, especially her alcoholism. She comes to visit her sister Stella and lies about the reason for her journey to New Orleans. She declares that she was so tired that she took a leave of absence, which was suggested by the superintendent of the high school where she works. One can notice Blanche's vulnerable narcissism at the very beginning of the play; she asks her sister to turn the light off so that nobody may see her face, which is neither so pretty after a long trip nor so young-looking: wrinkles always need appropriate makeup and lighting. Stella knows Blanche very well, and she always communicate with her in the same way; she even asks Stanley, her husband, to behave like her and compliment her on many things, especially her dress. She is fully aware that ageing may harm Blanche's narcissism. In scene 3, for instance, she powders her face and asks

Stella how she looks; Stella does not forget to answer: "as fresh as a daisy".

As for Stanley, he does not really stand Blanche's narcissism; the play deals with the comparison between two touchy people who both try to question the other's pride. Stanley, for instance, makes fun of Blanche's snobbery, whereas she compares him to a monkey! In William's play, there is this argument which is supported by the southern racists (see chapter 7), but this time the ape is not black. However, Williams is much more aggressive, and this passage of scene 4 does not fit the character's demeanor; it is even illogical to have a poor little thing who wears fur clothes, a rhinestone tiara and too much makeup speak angrily. In Williams' Blanche, there is something so unfeminine. Actually, in some of the dialogues, he expresses his feelings, not those of an old little girl from Louisiana. The scene should have emphasized the narcissistic issues: Stanley should have been blamed for his rudeness and she, like a self-absorbed girl who is treated unfairly, should have recited a list of childish recriminations. Here, she calls him a wild beast, a sub-human, a brute and a prehistoric man.

In scene 5, the atmosphere is more feminine. Blanche tries to seduce Mitch. Her delusions of grandeur are perceivable; so is the way she interacts with people: she has lost touch with reality and she thus creates a fantastic world that resembles a play in which everything is larger than life. She identifies with Marguerite Gautier, *The Lady of the Camellias*, and tells Mitch that he is Armand now. She begins to speak French, and, after having checked that he does not understand this language, she asks him whether he wants to go to bed with her: she is coquettish mainly because she wishes to feel desired and important.

The reality she does not like reappears. Thanks to Stanley, who gathered information, Mitch discovers that Blanche is not a saint. In fact, she used to go with men, and in her hometown, nobody respected her. She even declares that she had an affair with a seventeen-year-old boy who was a student of hers. So she was dismissed from her job for inappropriate behaviour. Blanche is not a snobbish psychopathic southerner but a wild immature Jezebel. At the end of the play, Tennessee Williams sends her to a psychiatric hospital. Did he consider that Blanche's behavior was pathological or did he think that society used to regard it as such? It is impossible to give an answer, all the more so because movies and plays were censored back then.

b- Baby Jane Hudson.

Some years later, Robert Aldrich adapted Henry Farrell's novel for the screen. It portrays two elderly sisters. The part of Blanche is played by Joan Crawford. She is a disabled woman who is almost tortured throughout the film by Bette Davis, who plays Baby Jane Hudson. The character of Blanche is shallow; it is aimed at revealing Jane's cruelty. The movie focuses on Bette Davis, who was pleased to be cast in a lead role at a time when ageing movie stars had difficulty finding employment.

The character she plays is unusual in the history of literature and filmmaking. Men who wrote about women preferred to deal with femmes fatales, young innocent lovers, courageous mothers, saints, witches, and bad women; Henry Farrell did not portray a women but a child star who remained a child when stardom stopped. One may believe that he just looked around him and recorded the true history of an acquaintance of his or that of a person who epitomized a cultural phenomenon. Actually, vaudeville and Hollywood gave birth to child stars: we remember mainly Shirley Temple and Judy Garland. If Shirley Temple sank into oblivion when she grew old, Judy Garland kept on performing and remained famous until she died. None of them became monstrous old little girls. Actually, the description of the mental disorders is so accurate that we think that Farrell did not create the main character from the observation of different people. Bergeret would have described Jane as a "psychosis of character": a very immature person who hardly perceives reality. One must admit that Farrell's description is much more accurate than many of those given by talented psychiatrists. Of course, a good writer's speech is often flowery and a good director rarely forgets to highlight the plight of unbalanced characters, but Aldrich's baroque movie cannot be the mere observation of a narcissistic mother one can hear say to her daughter after a ballet lesson: "someday you will be a star, sweetie". In fact, very few dance moms create monsters.

Whatever the information they had, Farrell and Aldrich portrayed an alcoholic old little girl. When she was young, she was a vaudeville star mollycoddled by her father. Many years later, she still lives in the past and remains Baby Jane, a porcelain doll that displays a milky face covered with rice powder, smoky eyes and blond ringlets. She still sings the songs of her youth, especially *I've written a letter to daddy*. She lives in a world of puerile fantasy.

There is a direct link between Jane's narcissism and the image of her father: he used to tell her that she was a brilliant performer. We can even think that when she feels insecure or when she has low self-esteem, the memory of her father cheers her up; she declares: "Remember when daddy and I used to rehearse at the beach? I'd be dancing on the sand... and all the people would come and watch... all crowd around to see Baby Jane Hudson. ...". Unfortunately, reality resurfaces in a most cruel scene. In fact, she is in front of a doll that resembles her when she was young; she looks at the ribbon on the doll's head and sets it on hers. Then, she recites a poem ending with: "because I am much too young to know". She gets closer to an unflattering light that underlines her age; then, she sees her image in a mirror. She cannot deny reality, since the author chose to portray an immature person, not a lunatic. In art, mirrors are often seen as objects that foster vanity; sometimes they turn into devilish artifacts that deceive faded beauties who wear too much makeup. Thus, they rarely enable people to perceive reality as it is. In the history of filmmaking, the most famous mirror scene is in Walt Disney's *Snow White and the seven dwarfs*. We do remember the narcissistic queen asking the mirror on the wall who is the fairest one of all. The Evil Queen is more resilient than Baby Jane; when the mirror tells her the truth, she accepts it and intends to kill Snow White because this murder will allow her to remain the prettiest lady in the kingdom. Neither the Grimm brothers nor the Walt Disney studios considered madness to be an option. In *What ever happened to Baby Jane,* the same solution was chosen; reality was not denied, but Jane was turned into a victim of truth: when she sees her image in the looking glass, she discovers that she is a hag and screams. Bette Davis's hoarse voice injects drama and meaning into the scene: inside her, there is an immature adult who expresses her discomfort.

Jane does not like Blanche. The spectator does not really know why. The movie starts with the car accident in which Blanche was seriously wounded. Nevertheless, we learn at the end of the film that it is Blanche who wanted to kill her drunken sister. Actually, Jane is portrayed as a bad girl who enjoys mistreating people. Her sister is a frail creature who is the ideal victim. Mistreatment allows Jane to feel superior to her sister. In a scene, Blanche rings Jane; Jane retorts that her sister still believes that she is a movie star whose wishes must be fulfilled immediately. Hence, there is also a clash of enormous egos.

Jane knows how to torture Blanche. The option chosen by Farrell is logical: he puts great emphasis on Jane's oral sadism. So the drunkard uses food to engender suffering. It must be said that she does not give a lot of food to Blanche, who almost starves, but two scenes are even more disturbing. The first one deals with Blanche's bird. She keeps it in a cage. Jane knows that she likes it. She removes the cage from Blanche's room in order to wash it. Incidentally, she kills the bird and sets it on a plate, along with vegetables. The plate is concealed under a cloche. Blanche is devastated when she lifts the cloche and discovers the dead little bird. Some other day, following the same procedure, she serves her a rat and bursts into laughter.

Farrell and Aldrich did not forget the psychotic traits of very immature people. For instance, Jane feels paranoid when dealing with Edwin. She wishes to have him to herself and believes that her sister will try her very best to steal him: for instance, she may tell lies about her in order to scare him. Hence, Blanche is transformed into a persecutor, an anaclitic persecutor who does not want to destroy the subject (individuals) but strives to separate the subject from the object (the world in which individuals live).

On the other hand, Blanche knows that Jane is mentally unbalanced and dangerous. She tries to flee from her and calls her physician so that he may help her, but the plan fails: she is savagely beaten. At the end of the movie, Jane is livid. She ties Blanche to her bed; when the maid discovers her, Jane kills her with a hammer. Then she panics and takes her sister to the beach. She wants to go back to the good old days, when her father was alive. She reaches the beach, loses touch with reality and becomes a little girl again: she speaks and behaves like a child. She is serene, but she has lost her mind. In fact, it is a good description of an ageing immature person (5) going mad. The author has not chosen a curable nervous breakdown but an incurable unidentified mental illness. The wicked old little girl is a lunatic now.

B- When girls cannot grow up.

If persons like Baby Jane remained movie scarecrows, there would be no problem. Unfortunately, there are many immature women like her who give birth to girls who, in turn, become immature women! Although I am convinced that *birds of a feather don't flock together,* in the case of Isabelle Caro, I must admit that the proverb is right. Isabelle was a young woman who suffered from anorexia nervosa. She published her memoirs in order to help people like her. This is a very important document because she gives us a lot of information on her disease and on her family, especially her toxic mother (6).

a- An immature mother.

Magdeleine, Isabelle Caro's mother, was born in a family that might have been quite dysfunctional. In fact, her sister Jacqueline is an immature person who is described as a woman suffering from depression. Besides, Isabelle Caro declares that Magdeleine also suffered from depression. In her youth, she was an idealistic girl who used to listen to the songs of a famous singer she worshiped. She was a groupie who finally met her idol, was impregnated by him, although she was already married, and had a child (Isabelle). We assume that she concealed the fact from her husband. When Isabelle was born, she was just amazed by her: wasn't she her creation and the child of a man whom she idealized?

She soon became a possessive mother, who refused to send her daughter to school. When Isabelle was four, Magdeleine suffered from a serious nervous breakdown and focused her attention on her daughter, who became her raison d'être. Her behaviour became highly pathological: since she did not want her daughter to grow up, she hid the watches and clocks that were in her house in order to combat the passing of time. Isabelle had to remain an infant for the rest of her life, and statural growth became an obsession. She believed that fresh air made children grow faster. So she locked her daughter in her house (7) and used to put a scarf on her mouth and nose when she had to go outside (mainly in the garden). When she prayed, she would ask the Virgin Mary and God to keep her child from growing (8). Magdeleine resembled Baby Jane: she was the jailer of a defenseless individual. Since she was an ex primary school teacher, she homeschooled her. When she needed to go outside, Magdeleine was always close to her. For instance, when she went to the hospital, she slept in the same room. Later in life, when she moved to Paris in order to study, Magdeleine followed her and lived in the same flat.

However, Isabelle grew, and Magdeleine still needed to play with human dolls. When her child was eight, she put a four-year-old girl up for the summer holidays. She regarded the little girl as a real puppet: she enjoyed dressing her, for instance. When Isabelle was twelve, she put another four-year-old girl up; she ignored her daughter for the holidays, but she took care of her precious little new doll.

When she was thirteen, she still slept in the bed of her toxic mother, who did not consider puberty to be a catastrophe, which means that, little by little, she adapted to reality. Nevertheless, Isabelle told her that she wanted to undergo plastic surgery, which led her mother to oppose her: her creation had to remain as it was. She was gradually losing her grip on her daughter, yet she tried to manipulate her. When the latter settled in Marseilles, she agreed to leave her alone, but there was still a close bond between them.

b- Two absent fathers.

That toxic mother could prevent her daughter from growing up because there was no counterpower, namely an effective father. It has to be said that the father of Isabelle is not the husband of her mother. According to her, her biological father is her mother's idol: a pop singer. She had an affair with him while her husband worked for that man. She told it to her daughter eighteen years later (9), but she had always felt that her father was not Joseph.

This family secret might have been the very reason for Joseph's frequent absences and indifference to Isabelle's plight. According to her, he did not reject her when she was born. Nonetheless, she declared that she did not know whether he knew that he was not her biological father. It is clear that the relationship between him and her changed as time passed: he was close to her when she was young and became distant when she grew up. Perhaps he doubted his paternity or discovered that he was not her father. Perhaps he did not stand his life with a depressive and her excrescence-like child. Moreover, Magdeleine had a pretty bad opinion of men and of her husband. Shockingly, she did not call her husband Joseph but Le Gouen, which is his surname. This shows that they did not like each other, and it did not facilitate communication. Besides, she blamed him for her loneliness and problems; she was so weird and rude that it is she who was responsible for her husband's emotional coldness. Thanks to Isabelle's book, we find (10) the classic narcissistic logorrhea of the victimized woman who blames men for her situation. Even her idol, the real father of her child, was called a selfish man, whereas all men were considered to be wicked persons.

Moreover, there was rivalry between her and him (11), which did not make any sense: Isabelle was her mother's prisoner and would see her father on weekends only, which was too little time to bond with his daughter. Isabelle was her mother's doll, and the poor girl whom she regarded as a threat only represented the anxiety she felt about the possible loss of a part of herself. Her daughter was not seen as an individual but as a projection of her emotions. It was not a psychotic projection (one's negative emotions are projected onto another person) but an anaclitic one, since Magdeleine projected her hopes onto her in order to fortify her self and her self-esteem. Isabelle had to be the talented violinist who was supposed to entrance her and do her proud, for it was she who had born that genius.

On the other hand, Joseph was insipid. It is certain that he was an immature man. Isabelle wrote that he feared his own father (12) and did not take his job seriously (13): he was a braggart who lied about his competencies, who was often late for work, and who was careless. Joseph was a moaner who kept exhibiting his discomfort. According to her, he was an old hippie who was unable to save her from her mother. Isabelle expected him to be a supportive, caring father: a genuine father figure. Later in life, she tried to find it in the arms of a middle-aged paramour, but the damage was done: an immature couple had created an immature girl suffering from severe anorexia nervosa.

c- I need to grow up.

She cannot recall what happened to her before she was four. Fortunately, she remembers what has to be taken as a key moment. When she was four, her mother stopped seeing her lover and therefore had a serious nervous breakdown. She refused to go outside and stopped cleaning her house, which became a mess. Isabelle was disconcerted, all the more so because she was not allowed to go outside anymore; she believed that she had done something wrong, but she did not dare to ask her mother to tell her what was going on. She writes (14) that Magdeleine did not want her to grow up, which seems logical when we check the information contained in the book. Actually, Magdeleine threw away all the clocks in order to forget that time flies. At the end of her prayers, she would say (15): "Please, Virgin Mary, allow my daughter to remain a little girl". She always had her put on clothes that were too small. She compelled her to wear nappies until she was eight (16).

At an early age, Isabelle adopted her mother's fear, for, in this anaclitic relationship, she was the only adult. Hence, the only way to be loved, protected and educated was to fulfill that woman's weird wishes. Consequently, she obeyed her, even though her desires were absurd. She would have liked to stop time and even step back in time in order to be a little girl for the rest of her life (17). When she was height, in order to please her melancholic mother, she asked her if she could sleep in her old cradle again. It was too small, but Magdeleine bought a new one (a bigger one) and set some rattles on it (18).

The passing of time was ignored, but the biological clock compelled her to deal with a new reality: when she was twelve, she reached the age of puberty. Now she was petrified of looking in a mirror and discovering changes in her body (19). When she was fourteen, the female sex hormones turned the little girl into a woman. She could reduce the size of her breasts (20), but one noticed that she was becoming an adult because her face had changed and she had body hair. So she kept epilating her body. Later in life, she underwent plastic surgery (21) in order to have a babyface. We do not know whether she wanted to please her mother or herself, but it is certain that her mother's gerascophobia (fear of growing older) had become her main trait. As for her anorexia, even though we may find out several causes, one must admit that it correlated with the Peter Pan syndrome (people don't want to grow up).

In her book, she records that the first time she decided to stop eating was when she tried to free herself from her mother (22) and fled. We don't know her age, but we know that the trick to get sick failed: her mother went with her to the hospital and slept in her room. She felt as if she were a hamster in its cage: she was a little girl full of energy who would de-stress by running frantically in the house. Not only was she her mother's prisoner, but she feared that she did not love her anymore. Hence, she needed to put some distance between them, but she could not really flee.

When she was eleven, she followed a vegetarian diet, but she did not explain why she changed her eating habits (23). At the age of twelve, she saw a physician, who declared that she was neither tall (1.51 m.) nor skinny (39 kg.). She began to think that she was overweight(24). During the summer, they put a four-year-old girl up. She started to starve herself: she ate the same amount of food as the four-year-old girl, but she replaced the carbohydrates with low-calorie vegetables (25). Soon afterwards she refused to eat anything. This demeanor had a lot to do with the first physical changes induced by puberty. Moreover, we learn that after the age of sixteen, because of malnutrition, she stopped menstruating (26). She had subdued nature, for she was neither an adult nor a woman. In her book, she describes her food rituals, and one must admit that the traditional psychoanalytical explanations (rejection of the penetration of the external world and the control of oral sadism) do not fit. In fact, she used to buy the food she liked when she was very young. She would put it on a baby plate, along with a small fork and knife. She would put the food in her mouth, masticate it, spit out everything and wash her teeth with diet coke. From a psychological point of view, Isabelle was still a little girl: she lacked the concepts one grasps later in life. She was not intelligent enough to understand what was going on and react against this absurd situation. She was a person who could not resist her reflexes. She had become her own jailer. She died on the 17th of November 2010.

C- Homicidal mothers.

Some mothers are more dangerous than Isabelle's, for some mothers kill their own children! That's what did Véronique Courjault. On the 12th of October 2006, she confessed to having killed three of her newborn babies in 1999, 2002 and 2003. She burned the first one; the two others were put in a freezer. On the 18th of June 2009, she was sentenced to eight years in prison. She was released on parole in May 2010. This was neither the first case of homicidal mother in France nor the worst one: Dominique Cottrez had killed eight infants from 1989 to 2007. Nonetheless, this case is well-documented, which enables us to get a clearer idea of the problem.

a- A rough woman.

Véronique Courjault is not a feminine woman. She is described by the Public Prosecutor as a beefy woman, and police lieutenant Bejeau said that she was reserved, unemotional and dull. The psychiatrists and psychologists who examined her noted that she had difficulty expressing her feelings. I fact, she has great difficulty understanding reality, although she is not a psychotic; she is an unintelligent immature person who is faced with madness.

In Marie-Sophie Tellier's documentary (27), there is the testimony of Katy Lorenzo, a psychologist who met her. Thanks to her, we realize that she was raised in a dysfunctional family and that her mother did not take care of her. That woman did not want to have children, did not like them very much, and did not parent them very well, but she had many. She had issues with maternity, and she did not teach her daughter Véronique how to become a woman. She told Katy Lorenzo that she did not want to look like her mother, or be like her, or live like her. Such an opinion proves that her superego is not linked to her mother; I may add that if she has one, it must be at an embryonic stage, hence its inefficacy.

Her upbringing was so bad that she does not get hold of many important concepts. Above all, she is very cold. One would wonder whether she is a human being or not. When Fanny Puel, a psychiatrist, describes how she burned the body of the first child she killed, one notices that the murderess displayed no emotion: she was so disconnected from reality that she did not realize the enormity of the crime. She put the corpse into the fireplace, added some wood and watched it burn until the end. She did not cry; then she explained the situation with detachment.

On the other hand, Fanny Puel gives us some information about the absence of internalization of the social patterns. In fact, when she got married, she was clad in black, as if she were in mourning. When one asked her why she had done that, she answered that she was pregnant and that she could only fit into that black dress (which belonged to her sister-in-law). In France, since the Middle Ages, black has been associated with death, and she agreed to wear a black wedding dress! This demonstrates that she mixes life up with death and that she internalized neither the traditions of her country nor its taboos.

b- A monster or a lunatic?

The crimes were so shocking that the judge ordered eight experts to investigate them. French judges almost never do that. If the experts had said that she was insane, her case would not have come to trial. Some journalists resolved to regard her as a sane person who was a barbarian; *France-Soir*'s headline read "She is a monster". During the trial, other journalists, who were supported by a few obstetricians, pointed out that it was a case of pregnancy denial, which is temporary insanity, but the court-appointed experts stood their ground. Actually, they did not regard the immature woman as a schizophrenic (which is a common mistake).

It has to be said that there is a special connection between France and madness. The philosophers of the 18th century tried to enlighten a brainless king (Louis the 15th) and his subjects. Then Philippe Pinel, Emmanuel Esquirol and so many others systematized the approach and invented modern psychiatry (28). We may have forgotten that, not so long ago, there were lots of brilliant intellectuals in that country. Some years later, French psychiatrists and psychoanalysts, thanks to this impressive amount of knowledge,

cannot make the mistakes the others make. Moreover, since the 19th century, psychiatrists have carefully separated reason from madness: hallucinations and the re-creation of reality are common symptoms of psychosis which enable them to evaluate the sanity of a patient.

In fact, they did not notice any sign of psychosis in Véronique Courjault's speech, and they spoke to her as if she were a normal person. So they asked her rational questions and listened to her answers. They asked her why she had killed her babies. She answered that she did not want children anymore. Paul Bensussan asked her why she did not use contraceptives. She replied that she could not become pregnant again. He asked her if she had thought of getting an abortion while she was pregnant. She said that she hadn't. When he asked her how she believed it was going to end, she just cried and declared that she did not know. To the logical questions of the experts, Véronique gave illogical answers. During the trial, she interacted in the same way with the Court and the Jury. Moreover, she had great difficulty expressing herself. Neither the experts nor the uneducated people called her a lunatic, but all of them were aware that she was unable to explain her evil deeds. This time, the psychopathic characteristics did not deceive the spectators: they did not categorize her as sane or insane. Actually, they put her in an undefined category. There are many states between pure madness and reason but very few words to name this reality. Nineteenth-century psychiatrists would use lots of unpleasant names (like mental retardation, cretinism, idiotism and stupidity) to describe the level of intelligence. In this case, although they had a limited vocabulary, they realized that she was a rough woman who understood neither herself nor others and who was unable to verbalize her feelings: she was a kind of automaton.

c- This flesh is my flesh.

Although she was unintelligent, she could almost perceive the separation between her body and the outer world; since she was not a psychotic, she did not regard the outer world as a threat. However, pregnancy was a major challenge, for she had to realize that the baby who was growing in her womb was not a part of herself but a distinct object.

At the beginning of her pregnancy, she felt the three babies move in her womb. She did not give them names, nor did she pondered whether they were boys or girls. Fanny Puel declares that she forbade herself to bond with her future children. She did not realize that they were human beings. She said to the Jury: "I did not consider them to be babies: they were not human beings". As a matter of fact, she believed and told Fanny Puel that these infants were her body, a part of herself over which she had complete power.

Consequently, this belief and her immorality moved her to strangulate her newborn babies and to burn them or put them in a freezer. When they asked her why she had behaved in that way, she replied that, where she lived, the garbage was inspected every day, which had prevented her from finding another solution. In some other cases, mothers keep the corpses close to them, as if they did not want to lose this mummified part of themselves, but nothing indicates that Véronique shared this view.

However, immature women with symptoms of psychological distress can harm themselves and others: if Baby Jane Hudson killed a maid in a movie, Véronique Courjault really killed three of her children. Lots of books written by men and women deal with the nature of women; none of them states that they become human being only if their personality is organized at the neurotic level. If they remain old little girls, they soon become monsters.

1. Beauvoir, Simone de, *Le deuxième sexe*, Paris, Gallimard, 1949.

2. Mankiewicz, *Joseph L., Suddenly, last summer*, Columbia pictures, movie, USA, 1959. Original play by Tennessee Williams.

3. Kazan, Elia, *A streetcar named desire*, Warner Bros., movie, USA, 1951. Scenario by Tennessee Williams, Elia Kazan and Oscar Saul.

4. Aldrich, Robert, *What ever happened to Baby Jane?*, Warner Bros., movie, USA,1962. Adaptation of the novel by Henry Farrell, published by Rinchart and Company, New York, 1960.

5. Bergeret, Jean, *La personnalité normale et pathologique*, Dunod, Paris, 1996, p. 158-160. Description of Albertine, an immature person who became a psychotic. Bergeret does not write that she is a melancholic, but he describes some symptoms that are less severe than those that characterize paranoia, which are a bit dissimilar to those that characterize schizophrenia.

6. Caro, Isabelle, *La petite fille qui ne voulait pas grossir*, J'ai lu, Paris 2009.

7. *La petite fille...*, p. 47.

8. *La petite fille...*, p. 48.

9. *La petite fille...*, p. 37.

10. *La petite fille...*, p. 60-61.

11. *La petite fille...*, p. 68.

12. *La petite fille...*, p. 25.

13. *La petite fille...*, p. 23.

14. *La petite fille...*, p. 47.

15. *La petite fille...*, p. 48.

16. *La petite fille...*, p. 85.

17. *La petite fille...*, p. 83.

18. *La petite fille...*, p. 85.

19. *La petite fille...*, p. 123.

20. *La petite fille...*, p. 143.

21. *La petite fille...*, p. 175.

22. *La petite fille...*, p. 72.

23. *La petite fille...*, p. 97.

24. *La petite fille...*, p. 120.

25. *La petite fille...*, p. 123.

26. *La petite fille...*, p. 193.

27. Tellier, Marie-Sophie, *Véronique Courjault, l'affaire des bébés congelés,* 17 juin media/France televisions, movie, France, 2010.

28. Sueur, Laurent, *Le traitement de l'alienation mentale, en France, de la fin du XVIIIeme siecle au debut des années 60 du XIXeme siecle*, thesis, Paris, 1996.

Chapter 5

A hive full of drones.

The immature male is certainly more problematic for society than the immature female. I would not say that he is more violent, for, in the United States, for example, there are gangs of violent women. Nonetheless, because of his strength, he is always stronger than women and children. Consequently, the physical frailty of his two favorite prey moves him to become an ogre. This phenomenon, especially rape, has been well-documented by scientific literature.

We should try to discover if immature men and women with the same intelligence or mental impairment respond in the same way and if society is equally disrupted. When they describe mental illness, psychiatrists say peremptorily that men and women suffer from the same mental disorders. However, as to personality disorders, the answer isn't quite so obvious, for immature people are not that mad, and thus we have to take account of social and cultural factors. Of course, male and female individuals, for instance, suffer from anorexia nervosa or psychopathy, but there are nuances: society does affect the demeanor of people with personality disorders. Let's take an example: football. In fact, women's football is considered to be less prestigious than men's: sponsors give very little money to the ladies and their sport is almost never broadcast on television. This lack of visibility implies that psychopathic women do not form groups of violent football supporters who display the consolidation of their self-esteem on television each time their team score a goal. In this example, society facilitates the formation of anaclitic groups of violent male football supporters, whereas it prevents women from behaving in that fashion.

As a matter of fact, society is friendlier to men, who can easily form small groups. These gatherings of immature men could be regarded as a way to improve the social skills of the sociopaths who belong to these groups; one would wonder whether their anxiety lessens and their mental health improves. In other words, does the anaclitic group enable immature men to go through the Oedipus complex, resolve it, and become more adaptable and intelligent?

A- What is a man?

The definition of man is of course the complement to the definition of woman we have seen in chapter 4. Hence, man's duty is to have children. Like women, if he cannot have at least one, he cannot become a man; he remains a withered flower that will never fructify. But this is not enough. Actually, the main function of a real man is to separate the child from his mother so that the infant may realize that he is not a part of her. Later in life, the father raises his son: he teaches him how to recognize reality through science and enables him to develop his sense of right and wrong, which will soon turn him into a reasonable, righteous and wise man. This state is the resolution of the Oedipus complex; it is a stage which a man reaches if his father confers at least a part of his authority on him. So the boy becomes a man and the father of his own father. A man can and must create a man in this way if society wants to survive. This is the definition, of course, of a person with Hysterical Personality Organization; it is the most accurate one and could someday enable society to be reasonable and efficient.

As for a more ordinary definition of man and manhood, there is a very interesting study of a panel of around sixty young men (ranging from thirteen to nineteen) living in the Balkans. In fact, after a horrible war that displayed all the anaclitic characteristics we will analyse in chapter 10, the next generation, which was the result of a psychopathic turmoil, remained in the classrooms of Zagreb, Belgrade, Sarajevo, Podgorica and Banja Luka. The young male students who were interviewed were volunteers. So they were not the best students, but they were quite intelligent and cooperative (1).

They had to define what a man is and to describe the mind and body of their ideal man. The participants had Plasticine in order to enable them to illustrate their points, and one must admit that the result is more explicit than what they wrote. As a matter of fact, many of them modeled figurines that looked liked Hollywood warriors, but a bit more vulgar: they were muscular, some of them had body hair, especially on the chest, and some were well-endowed. One participant had even made a penis that was longer than the leg of his statuette (2); the size meant that he was always ready to have sex. This is a cartoonish image of manhood, an interpretation based on zoology. An adolescent with Neurotic Personality Organization would have removed the genitals of course. At least one of them modeled a fully clothed figurine depicting a muscular basketball player wearing trendy clothes; I am not sure that the young man who made it was an adolescent with Neurotic Personality Organization, for it is also a kind of caricature: a fashion victim, not a basketball player (3).

When we analyse now what they said about the moral qualities of a man, we notice that there is no information about genital love. For instance, none of them associate sexuality with procreation. It is self-evident that women have no role to play in their social organization. They do not even associate pleasure with women: their world is autoerotic and self-centered. Even when they speak of the protective role played by men, the latter protect their pride and reputation (4), not their wives or children. Womanhood is seen as a scarecrow: girls are regarded as narcissistic dolls who keep speaking of make-up and gossiping about everybody. Femininity is a poison that can dissolve their non-established gender identity. It seems that they consider femaleness to be the worst possible disgrace. Being seen behaving like a girl, like crying, is tolerated only if the man is drunk as a lord (5)! In this connection, homosexuality is regarded as a sign of femaleness, which is an inferior status. So a boy who becomes gay will suffer from low self-esteem (6). The anaclitic fight against homosexuality has nothing to do with Freud's description of President Schreber's delusion. It is not a struggle for psychological survival but a fight that enables a boy to be proud of himself.

On the other hand, their role models are problematic. In other words, the role played by their fathers appears to be insignificant. The authors do not say that they were killed during the war or that they were absent fathers. Nonetheless, they state that, for some reason, many fathers were not involved in their sons' upbringing (7). Hence, their role models cannot be found at home, and they do not say that a member of their families or acquaintances replaced them. No other man teaches them how to become a man, and the personal identity they are trying to build is a blend of social stereotypes and peer group interaction based on these stereotypes. So it is important for them to form a male anaclitic group (8) since they will not remain loners fighting against their natural inclinations and distorted perception of reality. The group enables them to befriend people, who may resemble them (9) since they are so narrow-minded that they don't stand persons who do not behave like them. Their rage is seen as a characteristic which all humans share. The only amiable human being is oneself or someone like oneself. Consequently, the heterogeneity of the outer world is regarded as a threat, which they avoid by living in a peer group that makes them feel secure and proud of themselves, which allows them to accustom themselves to heterogeneity without being unsettled (their fragile psychological equilibrium cannot withstand too much disorder). Nonetheless, their group is quite dysfunctional because nobody acts as a superego and no woman teaches them to accept differences, which are not a danger but an obligation to bring forth a sane society that will perpetuate itself. Instead, they ape manhood and challenge each other's so-called virility. They keep showing that they are strong and quarrelsome. They keep fighting so that they may be proud of themselves, violence being the only means of achieving that goal (10). Fortunately, some of them go to church and told the authors (11) that it is a place where they learn how to distinguish good from evil. They may be less stupid than their fathers, who committed those crimes during the Yugoslav wars. However, the study does not show that these young men are righteous. They will remain immature individuals if they continue living in such a suffocating system.

Moreover, social organizations do not enable immature men to discover what masculinity is because people disagree about genders and the role played by men and woman in society.

Some years ago (12), in a paper on homosexuality, bisexuality, intersex persons and transsexualism, I had demonstrated that psychiatrists had finally agreed to reject the gender beliefs by turning what was formerly seen as a symptom of mental disorder into a personality trait regarded as normal. The Americans followed a democratic procedure, whereas the French resisted, and they still do. Actually, thanks to the Americans, anaclitic homosexuality had been well categorized, for normalcy is not reason, and it can even be highly pathological! Nevertheless, they should have studied homosexuality in each personality organization in order to explain its genesis and function in each category. This might have enabled society to understand the phenomenon and to implement a policy aimed at improving the mental health of mankind.

In this connection, same-sex marriage is gaining ground. It endangers genitalization (psychosexual stage that characterizes a sexually mature adult personality). Children raised by same-sex parents may have difficulty accepting sexual and gender differentiation. They are unable to develop their gender identity by means of their parents' personality traits, for they are not gender-related. Their lives look like a quest for a gender grail they try to find at school or in a sports club, where role models are poor: teachers and coaches are not parents, and their effectiveness is inversely proportional to the number of students. Same-sex couples raising children create immature adults who are not really intelligent and who belong to "normal" societies that are quite problematic. If this androgynous situation were the rule, immature men would seek to destroy femaleness. It's not science fiction, for it already exists. In fact, when women are raped and killed during wartime, not only in the Balkans but also in Africa, the murderer is always a psychopathic man whose father was not a good role model and whose mother did not teach him to accept femininity. Thanks to morals (the father), heterogeneity (the mother) is regarded as a crucial factor in the perpetuation of life and civilization. These psychopathic rapists regress to primary narcissism, acknowledge their omnipotence and try to belittle and kill women. They failed to become men with Neurotic Personality Organization, but they succeeded in becoming monsters.

B- The equivocal function of sport.

Immature men join sports organizations. Their relationship with sport is highly equivocal because the relationship between society and sport is ambiguous. Actually, one practises a sport in order to enjoy it, but also for other reasons. Of course, some people practise for health reasons. I don't know the exact proportion of people, but I assume that they are not numerous. Nonetheless, this medical positivism, which dates back to the 19th century, exists, but is it always associated with health?

It is when it is related to orthopedics. After an accident, one must move in a certain way in order to improve the mechanical efficiency of the body. However, since the beginning of sports medicine, some people have misinterpreted it. For instance, Elisabeth of Austria practised gymnastics and horse riding in order to keep fit. Her dresses are quite interesting, especially the ones she would wear at the end of her life: she was as slim as when she was 20. She was obsessed with her image: she used to follow an extreme diet, spent much time plaiting her beautiful hair and refused to be portrayed by painters or photographed, although she was still young. Her obsession with her appearance and weight had finally turned gymnastics into an instrument of torture.

The narcissistic objective of today's bodybuilders is of the same nature. This time, so that they may fit the dictatorial standards of male beauty, they eat protein and lift tons of steel while their bodies inflate. Then they remove their body hair, apply spay tan to their bodies, and strike a pose in front of the audience and the jury that may give them a medal, which may improve their self-esteem.

Actually, each time someone regards sport as it really is, some people strive hard to redefine its meaning. When Pierre de Coubertin revived the Olympic Games, he aimed to promote peace and fraternity between nations. His fair wish soon became a forum where regimes mimicked war, which led to the Munich massacre. Nowadays, how many athletes want to achieve Coubertin's ideals? A few, not a lot!

Even when people deal with the beauties of sport, this attitude seems incongruous, for if gymnastics and figure skating are aesthetically pleasing, the other sports are not. Leni Riefenstahl did not really accept this view. In her *Triumph of the will* (14), she had already turned the 1934 Nazi meeting into a glamorous ceremony, and her film about the 1936 Olympic Games proves that she wanted to look on the bright side.

In the second part of her *Olympia* (15), the competition even disappears. It is neither a report on the results nor a documentary on the different sports. It is a surrealistic reverie which ends with a flight of silver birds. The way she films the men's platform diving competition glorifies geometry. The divers do not dive; they fly and create kaleidoscopic images resembling the prettiest space figures. Sport disappears; beauty spreads on film; life disappears; narcissism takes the upper hand.

Today, especially in European football, the signs of narcissism have not disappeared. Some famous football players have turned into inimitable fashion models. Each portion of their skins is digitally transformed and retextured so that the pictures may show the unrealistic ideal of the successful immature football player. Football disappears too; it gives way to pride and so much prettiness.

Sport has always deceived people: Mars has been wearing cleats since ancient times! Back then, men used to prepare for war by exercising: physical activity was aimed at killing a potential enemy. The Greeks trained their young warriors for centuries in running, fencing and wrestling. We still have to cope with this unbearable heritage, and we are quite unsuccessful.

It is a failure because the purpose of sport is to defeat an opponent. Hence, the aim is immoral and almost psychotic because challengers cannot be seen as enemies, since they are human beings who experience emotions: only insane people regard others as dangerous creatures. It is immoral because there is a loser, which shows that there is a fight which causes the consolidation of the winner's self-esteem and the weakening of that of the loser. Worst of all, from a social point of view, this demeanor is useless.

C- The psychological importance of football for the immature man.

Consequently, sport, especially football, is regarded as important by the immature men who try to mature, build their personal identity and fortify their self-esteem. Since one can easily notice that sport is characterized by immaturity, psychopathic men are attracted by stadiums, where they find a hobby they understand; they also think that they will solve their problems, but this is a big mistake.

First of all, in supporter's groups, people are in a state of perpetual childhood. The sport they used to practise when they were little boys is still their raison d'être. Football can enable boys to have a better neuromuscular coordination, but once this goal is achieved, they ought to socialize with intelligent people, whom they will not find in these organizations.

When we observe football fans (whether they are quite young or not), we are surprised by their weak verbalization skills. For instance, in 2006, a Frenchman filmed the Marseilles fans' trip to Paris (16). In the bus, they often yell simplistic songs using clumsy syntax. Their lack of socialization is apparent in their behavior: they hardly speak with one another! When they want to communicate, they sing or show a slogan on a T-shirt or a banner. One may even believe that they are illiterate. Actually, one realizes that they are stupid because they hardly speak.

On the football pitch, one meets players who are not more intelligent than their fans. During the 2010 FIFA World Cup, the French team exhibited petulance and antisocial behavior, which led Roselyne Bachelot, the minister for sport, to declare that the team consisted of "immature gang bosses who gave frightened kids orders" (17). Hence, it seems that both players and supporters are wicked, selfish little boys. It is certain that their world is not organized at the neurotic level.

Consequently, no neurotic counterpower can counterbalance their natural inclinations. Logically, from a psychological point of view, the stadium is transformed into a Roman arena where two teams are supposed to mimic war. There is no conflict between good and evil because there is no operative superego. The conflict is between "us" and "them", but "them" is a concept that is not different from how they perceive themselves. In fact, in a 2006 sociological study (18), two Belgian supporters declared that they wanted to fight with people who resembled them (19) and shared the same motivation. One of them projects his violent feelings onto others; he aims to destroy the dangerous part of himself through others. His state of mind must be a characteristic of hooliganism since the violence these men express is intense and primitive.

Truth to tell, if all of them are not unbalanced psychopaths, most of them are unintelligent and some of them are almost mad. The most violent supporters are so impulsive that they resemble the psychopathic killers we will describe in chapter 9. Two Belgian supporters even told the sociologists who interviewed them that they might kill (20). They tried to put on a brave face, but one of them declared that when riots are violent, people cannot control themselves. Some of them are so euphoric that one may presume that they sometimes regress to primary narcissism (21). The history of contemporary football shows that these brutes are involved in the major disasters, like the Heysel Stadium disaster, in 1985. On the 29th of May 1985, some English supporters assaulted the Belgian and Italian fans; 39 people died. Many people were killed or wounded because of hooliganism. The figures don't show the gloomy atmosphere: in some places, the riots are but a staging of death.

Some of them are less brutish: they brawl in order to consolidate their self-esteem; they don't want to kill anybody (22). So the riot turns into a cockfight. These cockerels go through a belated process of psychological identification (23) and do not really know what manhood is.

Many of them are aware that they brawl in order to prove themselves (24). Their pride is a key component of the group's dynamics. They are not intelligent enough to understand the concept of heterogeneity and to perceive the different personalities. They believe that they are like the other human beings, and they do not want to escape from the group in order to create an Oedipal triad and then a marital dyad, which allows the individual to understand himself and others thanks to reason and volition. Since they go through the process of identification, they need the group in order to copy its members. Their stupidity compels them to accept the decisions of the group, which acts as a kind of conscience. They don't leave the group because they fear the outside world and need to be helped. So they fight alongside their mates so that they may fortify their collective self-esteem.

In Belgium, a cultural issue makes matters worse: two peoples using different languages coexist. The political history of Belgium is characterized by conflict between the Walloons and the Flemish, which spreads across football pitches (25), along with parochialism. As a matter of fact, a man first belongs to his town or village and then to a larger space. Consequently, these immature men use the history of that country not to justify but to organize and ritualize their anger.

The most dangerous hooligans in the world might be the Poles. When the other nations must receive these people, cities and stadiums look like besieged castles. When the match takes place in Poland, the family-like atmosphere we can find in the South of Europe disappears. Children and women flee from the stadium. They do not mimic war anymore: this is war! In this connection, the Polish hooligans and supporters often exhibit Nazi insignia and xenophobia.

In Krakow, there are two groups of supporters (Cracovia and Wisla) composed of men who are aggressive and emotionally unstable (26). Interviewed by a journalist in 2007, these hooligans exhibiting antisocial traits were unable to explain why they used to brawl. They just retorted that it had always been like this, which means that they inherited the hatred of their ancestors. Like the Greeks before them, their behaviour pattern consists in killing their neighbors without knowing why. It is clear that a high unemployment rate leads difficult people to roam the streets. During the communist era, the factories operating in Nowa Huta eased social tension by supervising the most dangerous citizens. Psychopaths became robot-like workers subjugated by the production line. They kept making the same movements, which tired them and prevented them from causing trouble. Their self-esteem was even consolidated in the communist way: the most efficient Stakhanovites were decorated and enjoyed certain privileges. The mental stability they needed was guaranteed by the economic system.

After the collapse of the communist regime, the Polish economy had to deal with industry competition. Many workers were dismissed form their jobs. The less adaptable, obedient and intelligent people were the first victims of this political change. Nowadays, many immature young Polish men don't have a job, which could soothe them and be their raison d'être. The cruelty of the hooligans living in Krakow is caused by the socioeconomic factors that throw the less adaptable and more violent individuals out on the street.

D- The structural answer of unstructured minds.

The anaclitic group of football hooligans is essentially a gathering of immature men who are mentally and emotionally unstable. Nonetheless, they form a permanent group whose aim never changes: to structure their quest for pride. Their desire for murder is directed toward the outside of the group. This tactic prevents inner violence, which is why these groups don't disband. The high level of aggressiveness in football proves that there are lots of groups of hooligans, who always find suitable enemies and therefore perpetuate this phenomenon. Although the police strive hard to prevent it, they just displace the problem: hooligans do not brawl in stadiums but in suburbs or isolated places.

In order to join the group, they must follow a certain procedure. In some hooligan groups, at least in Belgium, they do not accept people who are not known by one of them or who don't know one of them (27). To propose someone allows the members to find people who think and behave like them. It also enables them to identify the police officers.

There are many ways of getting to know the candidate. The café, after the match, is a place where one can easily socialize (28). Cafés, bars and pubs are safe places since they allow them to meet people like them. When there are women, their threatening femininity dissolves thanks to asexual common interests: sport, political defamation and alcohol. These places are all the more safe because alcohol relaxes them. Alcohol is a cheap, strong painkiller (see chapter 6). Its disinhibitory effects lead people to play it cool: at last they can socialize.

Little by little they get to know each other, and the candidate can be invited to a barbecue or a family event(29), but it is his fighting skills that will move them to accept him. That being said, these organizations are not as hierarchical as obsessional institutions like freemasonry or the Catholic Church. Hence, there is no pyramid-shaped formal hierarchy; the organizational structure is horizontal, but there are some leaders. Their function is to organize the street fights and, to a certain extent, to prevent accidents.

These groups are not static: members can, at times, leave and then reintegrate into them. It depends on the vagaries of life. If a hooligan finds a job or a girlfriend, his psychological needs are satisfied in another way. When the most intelligent ones toe the line, they may end up behaving like men with Neurotic Personality Organization, but a girlfriend, a child and a job do not always enable them to solve the problem: their quest for pride compels them to stay in such groups.

Sometimes they are not that violent because they follow a few simple rules. Firstly, they try to play fair; when two supporters are among a crowd of opposing football fans, the latter intimidate them: they don't envisage killing them. A Belgian hooligan declared that two of them always fought with two members of the opposing faction(30). The Poles prefer to gather 20 or 30 supporters together and fight with the same number of people (31). Secondly, they are not armed, which proves that they do not want to kill their opponents. One of them stated (32): "... My aim is to fight, not to kill people. Our adversaries are human beings; they are not animals. ...". Death is a taboo, and the memory of the Heysel Stadium disaster (33) compels them to calm down; their leaders help them to do so (34). The most violent hooligans often beat up the others. When a man is downed, the kicks could easily kill him; the leader is there to prevent this. He acts as an external superego that allows the group to handle its desire for murder, but these men always play with fire, and thus an accident can happen.

The only problem is that belonging to a group renders people aggressive. In fact, when they gather, their fear disappears (35). The group makes them feel omnipotent. They are unarmed, but they are strong, and the strategy is simple since the winning team is always composed of the strongest men. So why should they be fearful? When they are excited and wrathful at the same time, they become really stupid: their natural inclinations prevent them from thinking. Consequently, neither their leaders nor the police can calm them down when they get together.

Their wrath is kindled by the presence of their enemies and the police. If some of them regard the police as a useful counterpower that prevents them from killing one another, some of them love fighting with them. Hence, we cannot really assign a function to them. However, one of the Belgian supporters interviewed by the sociologists (36) provided further information on the police. He stated that he enjoyed playing cat and mouse with them so that he might fight with other hooligans. Like the little boy who defies his father, this game is a way of questioning authority, the paternal superego, but not a way of integrating it into one's personality.

Hence, the function of the police varies according to the level of intelligence of the hooligans: the smartest ones regard them as useful counterpower, some others, who are less intelligent, as a superego with which they play, and the stupidest ones as an enemy they would like to defeat.

E- When the most dangerous drones escape from the hive.

Some of these immature men are really dangerous. We will examine in chapter 9 the way male psychopaths think and interact with people when they decompensate (to lose one's grip) and become mass murderers. Here, let us analyse the psychopathic rapist, a kind of Dr. Jekyll and Mr. Hyde who conceals his double life and can sometimes be seen as someone with good interpersonal skills.

The violent rapist is an enigma to society. David Bryden and Maren Grier (37) recorded in a long article what psychiatrists and psychologists wrote on him, and the result is edifying: the image is so blurred that it is impossible to link the act to a well-defined psychological state and to identify the reason why he rapes and kills. In other words, experts do not enlighten society and society overcomplicates things. For instance, the immature American feminists have been criticizing men for so many years that one wonders whether all of them must be regarded as rapists.

However, a fact emerges: rapists' mental instability. Actually, if their sanity is rarely mentioned, the mental disorders from which they suffer are never ignored. Nowadays, many people realize that the Freudian separation between Eros and Thanatos is but an illusion: when people are almost insane, sex is an act of war. Unfortunately, this does not draw a clear picture of the danger.

The rapist is not an island in a wide ocean. As an immature individual, he is the result of complex interactions between him, his parents and society. He has also an influence on society, and his behaviour tends to destroy the relations between individuals. Actually, a society is a group of persons who interact positively. Some of its members, the "outcasts", reject the social system established by the majority. If society is operative, they will form a group of opponents and try to change the rules without using violence; if it is not, they will kill. In this case, the relations between individuals are corrupted: there is no more society but death. Violent rapists, who must be regarded as outcasts, are antisocial by nature since they inflict death: social death because they debase the relations between people, mental death when they destroy the souls of the people they rape, and physical death sometimes.

Brent Brents (38) is one of them. It is clear that he didn't integrate successfully into society. When he was 12, he began attacking people and was sent to a juvenile detention center – the damage was done. In fact, the social workers did not realize how maleficent his family was. So, from his birth to the age of 12, according to Amy Herdy, he was obliged to live in a pathological ambiance and to cope with a dysfunctional family, which caused him to become a psychopath.

In the institution where he stayed, he sexually assaulted other people. In 1988, at the age of 18, he rapped a six-year-old boy and a nine-year-old girl. He was put on trial and sentenced to 20 years in prison. The judge considered that his behaviour was pathological. So he sent him first to a psychiatric hospital, where he stayed two years and four months. The response of society was classic: to isolate the danger. The originality consisted of trying a psychiatric treatment.

It proved inefficacious, and Brents's mental state remained problematic. Then, he was sent to different prisons until 2004.

His life in prison, which is another kind of anaclitic group, did not allow him to behave himself, and it's easy to understand why. In fact, he lived with people like him: unbalanced people who cannot control themselves and who are thus likely to belong to spontaneous non-societies (gangs) aimed at destroying everyone. In this connection, he describes the destructive relations between the inmates. For instance, he had an affair with a prisoner who is described as being "as fucked up in the head" as him (38), and one must admit that an individual cannot become kind and intelligent if he or she does not rub shoulders with high-minded people. Besides, the use of alcohol and drugs alters feelings and turns them into an impassable fence between them, society and reason. A good prison is a place where the inmates are educated and treated for their mental disorders. One can isolate them from the other prisoners for a while if they cannot stand each other. They must work so that they may indemnify the victims and society. They must become human beings and realize that they are not omnipotent and that the outside world they fear and want to destroy is not that dangerous. American prisons do not protect society against crime, for inmates rarely stay there forever, and they almost never enable them to be saner. Besides, the system has reached a dead end because isolation does not cure America's social ills.

Hence, sixteen years later, in July 2004, he was released from prison, and he raped again. After a manhunt, he was put on trial again and sent to another prison. Fortunately, he did not kill; Guy Georges did...

Unlike Brent Brents, social workers knew Guy Georges. Son of a GI and a Frenchwoman, he was abandoned by his parents; his grand-parents did not want to raise him either. So he was placed in a substitute family, along with many children in the same situation

(40). Nothing is known of his mental state, but his primary school teacher remembers that he was not a happy child.

At the age of 14, he began mistreating women: he tried to strangle a disabled girl. Se second time he did that, he was sent to a young offenders' institution. Guy Rouchon, a psychiatrist, met him; he stated that he was a well-mannered, kind fellow who did not know why he had attacked those girls. Other psychiatrists noticed that Guy Georges was emotionally unstable: sometimes he was kind and seemed in tune with reality, sometimes his desire for murder impelled him to kill. Many people, especially those who lived with him in different squats in Paris, were deceived by his good manners. Antisocial people behave in a simple way. When they are not too sick, they flatter people in order to manipulate them. Manipulated people are less dangerous; the manipulator can thus interact more easily with them. A person who is not manipulable is immediately rejected. Consequently, since persons with an obsessional personality display some characteristics which immature people also display, they can be manipulated, although they are more intelligent. People with Hysterical Personality Organization behave and think differently: they cannot be manipulated, but they can manipulate and persecute immature people. So we realize that the people who were fooled by him were not the crème de la crème of intelligence.

Guy Georges was not a loner. He lived like a poor worker during the day and, sometimes, at night, he went out to hunt young ladies who were not losers but radiant girls. During the trial, he explained his modus operandi, which resembles hunting. He spotted a girl in a bar, followed her to her flat, climbed the stairs silently, pushed her into the apartment, tied her hands, gagged her, cut her trousers, tortured her, put on a condom, raped her and killed her. No one noticed him in the crowd; the neighbors did not hear anything; solitude and indifference are dreadful weapons.

During his trial, he did not explain why he killed those women, which is comprehensible: he is stupid and does not understand himself. When the judge asked him if wanted to have sex or to kill, he answered that he wanted to kill. Neither the relatives of the victims, nor the police, nor the jury, nor society made out why he had raped and killed all those women. However, there was a social response: now there is a centralized database in which the genetic data on all criminals is stored. French society believes that individual freedom must not lead to secrecy: when a crime is committed, the police is allowed to collect genetic data now.

At the moment Guy Georges is still in prison; he is eligible for full parole, but he has made no application to the Parole Board. Like the Americans, the French still don't know how to regard psychopaths who rape and murder: are they mad or wicked?

However, all immature men are not serial rapists or mass murderers, but they may be dangerous. The solution they invent, the anaclitic group, leads them to believe that are in a safe environment. The absence of a superego prevents them from maturing. Their aggressiveness is directed towards the outside of the group, but if this soothes them, society is severely damaged. False solutions can lead to social suicide. In times of crisis, unbalanced, violent young men gather to form death squads that may exterminate mankind: we shall analyse this in chapter 10.

1. Western Balkan gender-based violence prevention initiative, *Exploring dimensions of masculinity and violence*, CARE, Atlanta, 2007.
2. *Op. cit.*, image 7, p. 18.
3. *Op. cit.*, image 6, p. 18.
4. *Op. cit.*, p. 36.
5. *Op. cit.*, p. 19.
6. *Op. cit.*, p. 20.

7. *Op. cit.*, p. 17.

8. *Op. cit.*, p. 23.

9. *Op. cit.*, p. 35.

10. *Op. cit.*, p. 36-37.

11. *Op. cit.*, p. 23.

12. Sueur, Laurent, "Le message medical français concernant les identités de genre (2ème moitié du XIXe s.- fin du XXe siècle", *Déviance et société*, Chêne-Bourg, 1996, vol. 20, n° 4, p. 359-375.

13. Sueur, Laurent, Le message medical..., p. 369.

14. Riefenstahl, Leni, *Triumph des Willens*, Leni Riefenstahl-Produktion/Reichspropagandaleitung der NSDAP, movie, Germany, 1935.

15. Riefenstahl, Leni, *Olympia 2: Fest der Schönheit*, Olympia Film GmbH, movie, Germany, 1938.

16. Sola, Laurent, *PSG-OM, au Coeur des supporters marseillais*, movie, Ls13.free.fr, France, 2006.

17. Platiau, Charles, "Le naufrage des Bleus devient une affaire d'Etat", *L'Express.fr*, Paris, the 23rd of June 2010.

18. SFP intérieur, *Etude du supportérisme et des manifestations de violence dans et autour des stades de football en Belgique*, Liège 2006.

19. *Op. cit.*, p. 56 and 80.

20. *Op. cit.*, p. 81.

21. *Op. cit.*, p. 74.

22. *Op. cit.*, p. 59: "People [the supporters] feel protected by all the cops. If the cops were not there, it would become dangerous. ...".

23. *Op. cit.*, p. 56: "... I do not assault anybody, I have stolen nothing. I defend my identity, that is all. ...".

24. *Op. cit.*, p. 77 and 79.

25. *Op. cit.*, p. 151.

26. Kemp, Ross, *Ross Kemp on gangs: Poland*, Tiger aspect production/LMG media company/Mongoose productions, movie, U. K., 2007.

27. *Etude du supportérisme...*, p. 48.

28. *Op. cit.*, p. 48 and 51.

29. *Op. cit.*, p. 53.

30. *Op. cit.*, p. 61.

31. *Ross Kemp on gangs...*

32. *Etude du supportérisme...*, p. 64.

33. *Op. cit.*, p. 57.

34. *Op. cit.*, p. 65.

35. *Op. cit.*, p. 86.

36. *Op. cit.*, p. 76.

37. Bryden, David, Grier, Maren, "The search for rapist's "real" motives", *The journal of criminal law and criminology*, vol. 101, n° 1, p. 171-278, Chicago, 2013.

38. Herdy, Amy, *Diary of a predator: a memoir*, Boulder, 2011. Electronic edition, pagination by kindle: l. means location.

39. *Op. cit.*, l. 467.

40. Marcoux, Philippe, *Guy Georges le tueur de l'est parisien*, 17 juin media/France 2, movie, France, 2004.

41. Dufresne, David, "Les experts jugent Guy Georges responsable de ses actes", *Libération.fr*, Paris, the 22nd of March 1999.

Chapter 6

Do not ease the pain.

Alcohol, narcotics, antidepressants and a pharmacopoeia of painkillers and natural drugs are used in order to achieve different goals. They interfere with the way neurons send, receive, and process signals via neurotransmitters; they could be regarded as magic potions that ease the pain and strengthen the brain. For the last two centuries, psychiatry and neurology have been trying to establish that mental disorders result from the alteration of the brain. During the 19th century, neurosyphilis almost proved that humans were but bodies powered by chemical reactions, which the most religious physicians attributed to the will of God, whereas the skeptics attributed them to electricity. Humans were volitionless automatons, volition being the attribute of God's conscience.

At the end of the 19th century and the beginning of the 20th century, Sigmund Freud and his followers did not completely reject the idea of the chemical reactions, but they put a special emphasis on humans' willpower. A mental illness or disorder was therefore caused by subconscious interactions that deprived individuals of their volition. They acted like brainless automatons whose subconscious compelled them to rave and misbehave.

That being said, there are people who still believe that a substance can cure a mental disorder. Uneducated persons prefer medication to psychotherapy when they have to deal with mental health. Actually, whatever the level of personality organization, people can behave in the same way and thus become addicts, which means that neither the drug addicts, nor the alcoholics, nor the analgesic addicts belong to homogeneous groups. If motivations can vary over the course of life, the aim does not change: to feel better.

A- The meaning of the figures.

So that we may distinguish the immature people from the others, we must examine the statistics, although they are imprecise.

Bergeret wrote in 1996 (1) that a 1971 report showed that 33 % of people were persons with a psychotic personality, 33% persons with a neurotic personality, and 33% immature persons. He added that, according to unidentified sources, the result was quite different: 30 % of them were persons with a psychotic personality, 50 % immature people, and 20 % persons with a neurotic personality. He did not mention the proportion of people suffering from mental disorders in each group. Fortunately, nowadays governments and international organizations provide information that is more accurate.

Unfortunately, statisticians count the people who are mentally unbalanced, not those who are in tune with reality. However, the logic of psychopathology will allow us to rectify this mistake. Moreover, statisticians and even psychiatrists do not always classify the symptoms into the right category. Anaclitic depression, for instance, is problematic since some neurotics and psychotics are sometimes categorized as depressives. We must not overestimate this phenomenon since the "mental asthenia" experienced by psychotics, because of hallucinations, cannot really deceive observers. As for the so-called nervous breakdowns of obsessives, there are so many compulsions that one cannot make mistakes all the time. Regarding the hallucinations very immature people experience, the latter don't report them, and they are quite uncommon; there may be some mistakes, but they cannot skew the results.

We know for a fact that in France 7, 8 % of people suffer from depression (2), which is a logical number when we compared it to the 7 % of the Swiss, the 3 to 5 % of the Americans and the 8 to 12 % of the British (3). We do not have any information about neurotics, but, fortunately, the British have measured the proportion of psychotics in their population (4): 4,4 % of people say that they have experienced a symptom of psychosis such as hallucinations or delusions. The first hypothesis (that on the equal quantity of individuals in each group) implies that the ratio is 4,44, which makes 19,53 % of persons with a psychotic personality (including 4,4 % of psychotics), 33,33 % of immature people (including 7,8 % of depressives), and 47,14 % of persons with a neurotic personality (including 10,61 % of neurotics). The proportion is different, and the percentage of neurotics is weird since it implies that persons with a neurotic personality go crazy more frequently than individuals who belong to the two other groups. This is illogical because the former are more stable than the latter and have a better understanding of themselves and reality than they, which enables them to cope with the outer world.

The second hypothesis is more logical. The ratio is 6, 41, which makes 28,20 % of persons with a psychotic personality (including 4,4 % of psychotics), 50 % of immature people (including 7,8 % of depressives), and 21,80 % of persons with a neurotic personality (including 3,40 % of neurotics). The proportion does not change and the percentage of insane people validates a very important fact: the persons whose personality is organized at the psychotic or neurotic level decompensate less frequently than immature people because they are more stable than they. Consequently, the hypothesis about a large percentage of immature people and of persons with a psychotic personality makes sense. However, we should gather more information in order to corroborate or refute it.

Prison population, for example, could enable us to discover the apportionment of the three levels of personality organization in a country. Some people will argue that prisons do not mirror society and that they represent the worst part of it. In fact, statistics show that 85 % of the young British inmates (5) have a personality disorder and that 10 % of them experience symptoms of psychosis.

Hence, British prisons seem to act as psychiatric hospitals where the maddest youngsters are locked up. Older inmates (6) are not saner: 72 % of men and 70 % of females suffer from at least one mental disorder. If we add the addictions, 90 % of the British prisoners cannot be regarded as sane individuals with a neurotic personality.

Besides, in the United Kingdom, the schizophrenics who have committed a crime are not automatically put in a psychiatric hospital (7). It is said that a fifth of them are sent to prison, which means that British society considers that schizophrenics, who are raving lunatics, can be held accountable for their actions. The concept of madness disappears, which therefore invalidates the concepts of sanity and reason: can't the British judges differentiate reason from madness or do they want to do so?

Nonetheless, the World Health Organization (8) is less pessimistic. According to its 2001 survey, there are only 450 million people who suffer from a mental or personality disorder, which represents 7,37 % of the world population in 2001. If we regarded mental and personality disorders as signs of psychosis and psychopathy, using the aforementioned ratio (6,41), we would consider that 47,24 % of the world population is composed of immature people and persons with a psychotic personality, which implies that there are 52, 8 % of people with a neurotic personality. However, these statistics are unreliable because, in many countries, statisticians are not competent psychologists. Let us rather acknowledge that there are lots of unbalanced people and that the most dangerous ones are in prisons and psychiatric hospitals. Those who are free must take drugs in order to cope with fear, anxiety and reality. Consequently, a high percentage of alcoholics, junkies and analgesic addicts indicates society's mental disorders.

In this connection, 26 % of British adults are "hazardous drinkers" (9). In 2011, in the United State, which is a country that has been combating addictions for a great many years, 21,9 % (10)

of youngsters were alcoholics; 23,1 % of them consumed marijuana during that year (11). If we now link these numbers to the consumption of antidepressants, we realize that Americans use a lot of substances that are normally used to treat anaclitic depression (12). Actually, antidepressants are administered to adolescents: 10,8 % of people aged between 12 and 16 take them. 15,9 % of people aged between 40 and 59 take antidepressants. These statistics are quite puzzling, for these medicines can be used to treat other diseases or prescribed when they are not required. However, these numbers and inaccurate statistics show that there are lots of unbalanced individuals and immature people.

B- Anaclitic addictions.

Are there specific interactions between narcotics, immature persons and society? Although psychopaths are not self-aware, we must examine what they say about that.

Since alcoholism is a widespread phenomenon, it seems easy to gather information about it. For instance, many famous writers were alcoholics. Unfortunately, even when they did not try to conceal it, they did not really address the issue or express their opinions. It's rather disappointing because they verbalize their feelings easily, and thus we could expect more insight and broader views. In fact, Jack London is one of the very few people who dared to speak of it, and the information he provided is valuable.

In *John Barleycorn* (13), which is quite autobiographical, the author describes the life of an American boy becoming a man during an era characterized by Christian women's struggle for temperance. We do not really know whether John/Jack wanted to behave like his father or not when he tried alcohol for the first time. However, a few pages later, the substance reappears, and he does not like its taste; he wants to feel the effects of alcohol's (14), but, according to him, it is more than just a stimulant: it's a magic potion that entices men to gather around a fireplace that warms same-sex people (15). The concept of pleasure is fundamental, and it is always associated with the absence of women. Jack London's opinion about women is unequivocal and quite psychopathic: women establish rules that must be observed, whereas the world of men is characterized by absolute freedom. Women are dangerous creatures who prohibit alcohol and the pleasure it gives (16): the awful spectre of castration looms over this novel.

However, John/Jack is a courageous kid: if he is not a person with a genital personality, his phallic character leads him to reach manhood by braving nature. In 1903, in *The call of the wild*, he had already portrayed a humanized dog that had survived winter in Klondike. The dog had adapted to the natural conditions and had preferred to cope with it rather than live with men and be enslaved. In *John Barleycorn*, the protagonist, at the age of fourteen, is a sailor who resembles Stevenson's pirates. The sea is a fantastic playground, the opposite of the suburban life in Oakland (17). On board the Annie, his ship, his mates are strong, rough and fearless; he describes them as the enemies of the law (18). When he is with them, he is not a little boy anymore but an intrepid pirate who enjoys taking part in attacks. Braving the elements, he realizes that he can dominate nature and almost enslave it; he becomes a real man and something more: a god (19)!

Naturally alcohol is an essential part of the manhood ritual. The saloon is a kind of temple where he learns how to socialize with other men (20) and where he can imitate them. One must buy a round of drinks and may expect that a "saloon mate" will buy the next round (21). Since Jack London is not a man with a genital personality, women or the image of women is not appealing. So he derives pleasure from drinking liquors: castration is circumvented by means of a drunkard's shenanigan. There is pleasure, but he has to pay the price: libido is perverted and low. Drinking with friends replaces orgasm! To make matters worse (22), he lacks willpower. He justifies his alcoholism by saying that he must be as virile as his mates: if he stopped drinking alcohol, he would lose his friends, his gender identity and his chemically induced orgasm. He is deceived by the urge to socialize. He cannot stand sobriety because he cannot live without the so-called help and supervision of substitute parents. To stop drinking implies that he will be alone, which endangers people whose personality is not organized at the neurotic level: these individuals feel abandoned, weak, vulnerable and depressed.

As for the information about drug addiction, it is inaccurate. When drug addicts speak about themselves, they spout platitudes. In fact, they are on the verge of psychosis, which is why they keep to themselves and lack intelligence and insight. However, William Burroughs (23) gives us information about that issue. He writes that when he was a child, he was subject to hallucinations (24). It is impossible to assert that his personality had been prearranged (before the end of the Oedipus complex) at the psychotic level and that he was able to mature a bit and become an immature man. Perhaps he grew up normally and met an obstacle when he was very young, which prevented him from maturing. As a matter of fact, he states that, at the age of 4 or 5, he had a strange, undiagnosed fever, which might be a trauma. He did not write that he experienced hallucinations in adulthood. However, he was emotionally unstable, which led the psychiatrists of the United States Army to regard him as a "paranoid schizophrenic" (25); they did not categorize him as a psychopath who had schizoid personality disorder.

He took drugs for terrible reasons. He remembers that a maid had once said that opium brought sweet dreams. So he declared that he would smoke opium when he was an adult (26). After this sentence, he refers to the hallucinations he experienced, which shows that he was so deranged that he already wanted to use a substance that would ease the pain. Many years later, he declares that he takes drugs in order to get out of bed, shave, have breakfast and, finally, stay alive (27). Narcotics are regarded as a stimulant by indecisive people. These automatons use this fuel to live and cope with life and reality at the same time. Of course, these painkillers are dangerous since they kill brain cells and may induce hallucinations, lead people to lose touch with reality, compel them to commit murders, and kill them. Besides, they move drug addicts to refuse to undergo psychotherapy. Most of the time, it is the police or their relatives who force them to undergo treatment, and they don't take it seriously.

As for Burroughs, he did not undergo psychotherapy to overcome his addiction but to cure his homosexuality, or rather, to lessen his anxiety over his sexuality. Hence, his whole life long, he accepted this chemical slavery, and he did not try to understand why something impelled him to take drugs. Nevertheless, he strove to discover why others began to use narcotics. They always answered that they were curious (28). As for him, he says that nothing in life interested him; then he adds that nobody really remembers why they took drug for the first time. What he wrote is inconsistent because he was not intelligent and did not understand himself. Drugs had locked him in his own body and mind and sentenced him to lifelong agony in unawareness: the mental illness from which normal people suffer!

C- The Virgin Mary will save mankind.

Modern societies have nurtured people who loathe addictions. Perhaps they are persons with neurotic personalities since they are righteous people who feel morally compelled to protect life and goodness. Nonetheless, they may underestimate the dangers of drug abuse and alcoholism and may consider that these are private matters. Besides, I have met so many drunken obsessives that I am convinced that they do not always advocate temperance. Moreover, individuals who are not too immature can do that.

Two American women became famous thanks to their crusade against alcoholism: Frances Willard and Carrie Nation dedicated their lives to this cause. I pondered what they wrote and I am unable to determine precisely their personality organization, but it is clear that they were rather sane.

Frances Willard was neither an eccentric feminist nor a religious extremist. Like many American women of the 19th century, she was a member of a church and the president of the Woman's Christian Temperance Union, which does not mean that she was a female Torquemada. Europeans readily blame the Americans for their religious practises, but they have forgotten that the British burnt myriads of witches while the Spanish and the French immolated thousands of heretics. Besides, European nations sinned a lot during the religious wars; the last one, which took place in Ireland, stopped not so long ago! Frances Willard did not burn anybody; she just regarded alcohol as a devilish substance (29). Nevertheless, she neither called the saloons houses of the devil nor considered that drinkers were lost souls. As expected, she regards drunkards as sinners (30) and one can sometimes discern exaltation in her writings. Like many religious men and women before her, she wants the Heavenly Jerusalem to become an earthly reality (31). Her mission is linked to her faith in God and in mankind: men can be saved because they are not naturally bad.

In her book, Frances explains why she dislikes alcohol and addictions. We don't know whether one of her relatives was an alcoholic, but we know that her father forbade people to drink while they were on his estates and that this parental prohibition became one of Frances' personality traits (32). When she was a little girl, she was deeply influenced by her father, who appears in her writings. It must be said that he was a man of principles, especially when he dealt with hygiene. In his house, people had to have a healthy lifestyle (33): they had to eat vegetables, fish and fowls, take exercise and go to bed early. Tight clothes were forbidden, as well as alcohol and tobacco. Children were not allowed to drink tea or coffee; they had to tell their parents the truth and to take care of them. He was a kind of Dr. Kellogg: someone who wanted his children to have a healthy body and a healthy mind.

Many years later, in his daughter's writings, the scientific justifications for temperance are so numerous that they lessen the importance of the religious motive. For example, she once examined the life insurance statistics to see what kind of person had the longest lifespan and she discovered that the total abstainer lived much longer than the moderate drinker (34). So she advocated total abstinence. She did not forget to put great emphasis on the effect of alcohol on the brain and the nervous system. She also combated nicotine, opium and any kind of drug.

The vocabulary she uses is quite "democratic": for instance, addiction is servitude, something that could have been invented by a king (35). In that regard, she does not forget to write that king alcohol has something to do with king Gambrinus, the so-called inventor of beer; combating alcoholism is also a way to fight for democracy. Nevertheless, she does not belittle European monarchies, and when she speaks of the United Kingdom, she ignores the queen in order to concentrate her mind on the parliament, which is an institution that is more democratic.

The reason why Carrie Nation crusaded against alcoholism is more tragic. Even though her parents were not alcoholics, some of her relatives were, but she is very discreet about this topic (36). In fact, her hatred of addiction has something to do with her first husband.

The young Carrie married Dr. Gloyd, although she did not know him very well. Only a few days after their wedding, he started to behave strangely. One day he came back home, threw himself on the bed, and fall asleep very rapidly without addressing her or his mother, who lived with them. Carrie was disconcerted. As she was standing in a room by her husband's bedroom, she saw a most peculiar scene through the embrasure: his mother leaned forward so that her face might be only inches from his. She waited a bit; the old women left the room; then she rushed into it, leaned forward and discovered the unspeakable truth: he smelled of alcohol! She had married an alcoholic! She started to live the distressful life of a drunkard's wife: she could not help thinking about the places he used to go in order to get drunk. Perhaps Dr. Gloyd frequented certain saloons because he met certain women there (38), which was the reason why he neglected her. He also frequented a Masonic lodge, where his friends encouraged him to booze. She did not like the masons (39), but she did not use the 19th century European clichés: atheism and the plot to establish the republic of vice. She did not know them, and she just stated that every night he was drunk, which led her to move to her father's house, along with her very young daughter. Her marriage was a disaster. Then Dr. Gloyd died; she was a heartbroken young widow, a penniless single mother full of broken dreams.

Her opinion about addiction is also linked to her morals, which are not easy to define. In this connection, she writes that when a voter casts his ballot, he should always wonder whether he did the right thing or not (40). It is self-evident that her struggle to prohibit alcohol is aimed at favoring light and purity and overcoming "the darkness of drunken bestiality" (41). However, we don't know her definition of what is morally correct, although we can make out what is bad. Actually, in her book, she says that saloons are places where all things die (42); it is a definition of morality which a person with a neurotic personality may have given.

Once she was well-off, her crusade against alcoholism turned into a biblical fight. She writes that when she attacked the first saloons, her technique was not really good, although her style was already flamboyant. She used to have a brick in her bag and would throw it against the big mirrors (43); the brick and the pieces of mirrors came down, which broke the glasses and bottles and bedazzled the onlookers. Later on, she used a hatchet instead of a brick and became very famous. Each time she attacked a saloon, she was in trouble with the authorities: she spent a lot of time in jail. Sometimes the sheriff was amused at what she had done, and the fine was not really big. On other occasions, she was seen as a lunatic (44). Her bible was always a consolation. For the sake of mankind, she tried to destroy the factor that led persons whom she called "drugged men" or "diseased men" (45) to lose themselves in a liquid that neither enabled them to mature nor helped their families.

The Christian women persuaded the American government to implement a policy on alcohol prohibition, which was ineffective. Nonetheless, this kind of activism proves that a part of society wants to safeguard people who are not mature enough to protect themselves from self-destruction. When individuals are not intelligent enough, righteous persons can act as their superegos.

D- A feeble social reaction.

Experts have always regarded addictions as mental or behavioral disorders. They strove to identify the factor that would lead people to take drugs whatever their personality organization. As usual, they were deceived by the symptom and its propensity to lead people to believe that there is always one cause, not two! It has to be said that Freud did not really help his followers to understand the phenomenon, but, as a pioneer, he discovered some facts, not all the facts, and he made lots of mistakes. In fact, he was a poor "fact-checker" and he obtained unreliable information, which prevented him from individualizing the mental illnesses. I even wonder whether he ever psychoanalyzed a neurotic; he spent his whole life meeting patients who had borderline personality disorder, and he believed that they were neurotics. Did Little Hans suffer from anxiety hysteria or was he an immature boy who had a phobia about horses? Was Dora a person with hysterical conversion or an immature woman who somatized? On the other hand, he did not really research into psychoses, which prevented him from knowing the basis of the mind. In that regard, Jacques Lacan adopted a more scientific approach, which enabled him to understand insanity and human nature much better than he.

However, if we can still find some idolaters among his followers, many of them intended to stick to the facts. They observed the symptoms, cross-checked the information and preferred the insecurity of insufficient knowledge to the false clarity of academicism.

In 1925, Sandor Rado (46) noticed that drugs addicts resembled infants, and he asserted that they often exhibited regressive oral habits. In 1933, he wrote that, in order to avoid depression, drugs were used as painkillers, which made drug addicts regress to primitive omnipotence. In 1939, Edward Glover put great emphasis on various psychological effects. For instance, when patients suffered from depression, narcotics could prevent suicide. They could also act as antipsychotics when people are severely regressed. Glover's study dealt with psychopaths' addictions; he may have been the first specialist to realize that immature people could go mad: because of depression, some of them became psychotics.

As time passed, psychiatrists and psychoanalysts enriched the clinical picture by means of symptoms of psychosis and signs of a personality disorder; neurotic traits, so far as I can judge, were ignored. Consequently, addictions continued to be seen as mental or behavioral disorders. For instance, some experts compared them to sexual perversion (paraphilia). This is logical because the substance relieves the symptoms of castration anxiety since it induces pleasure. No author dared to declare that drug addicts identified with a phallic mother, although some of them, like Francisco Hugo Freda, asserted that coitus was made possible because drugs acted as fetishes. But was this quasi-pervert a dangerous creature? No one answered. As ever, they neither suggest a policy nor a social response but the usual individual solution: psychoanalysis.

Did society need the experts' opinion to decide what to do? Americans did not follow specialists' advice when they implemented the policy on alcohol prohibition: politicians just heard the prayers of the American Christian women! Nowadays, the Mexican drug war has nothing to do with morals or mental health, for it has to do with the economy and order. Europeans also combat drug and alcohol trafficking, but the results are very much questioned, especially because some of them uses drugs and alcohol and the others don't want to finance such a policy.

Since the end of prohibition in the United States, scholars have been studying its effect on alcoholism, and the result is clear: during the 20s and 30s, Americans drank less, but they drank. However, when society decides to prohibit drugs and alcohol, it is always a positive response since it shows that people care about people. When addictions are accepted and legalized, morals are subjugated to indifference: individuals die and nobody weeps over people who supposedly chose to engage in risky behavior. Besides, although prohibition is an economic nonsense, it can be useful.

Consequently, most governments have opted for prevention policy: in schools, armies of civil servants preach sermons on health, describing the harmful effects of drugs and alcohol. A century after Frances Willard, the same arguments are set out in front of the same type of people: unintelligent individuals who cannot really behave themselves. Meanwhile, sociologists research into the phenomenon and publish statistics which show that the percentage of drug addicts and alcoholics does not change a lot. Neither prevention nor prohibition works: governments and citizens are worried.

Europeans are very upset (47) because a part of the economy relies on alcohol production. For instance, Spain, France and Italy are the world's leading wine producers, and they strive hard to sell their products. Alcohol consumption is an economic necessity. If governments agree that children must not drink, once they have reached the age of majority they must drink (a little) in order to generate wealth!

As for narcotics, the problem is much different since most of them are not produced in Europe. However, the response is also very inconsistent: the French prohibit them, whereas the Dutch don't. There are two views but a single goal: prevent drug addiction. The Dutch are more pessimistic than the French, for it is clear that they believe that addiction is a widespread habit (48). They only want to regulate the behaviour of drug addicts in order to prevent drug overdose deaths and suicides, which is why they allowed adults to buy and consume cannabis in certain "coffee shops". They wanted to separate soft drugs from hard drugs, which is questionable in the long term, but hard drugs do harm society because they enable organized crime to thrive. The Dutch are allowed to consume cannabis, but everybody knows that it is harmful (49). This policy has moved myriads of European drug addicts to go to the Netherlands in order to buy cannabis, consume it and traffic in it. In the Netherlands, the percentage of drug addicts is still high, but that policy was not aimed at solving this part of the problem: the government wanted to reduce organized crime.

Prohibition and permission are inappropriate policies because they ignore the root of the problem: the role of the psychological factors in addiction. The immature drug addict who lacks insight never agrees to undergo psychoanalysis, all the more so because he or she can find alcohol and narcotics easily. Although there are no statistics on the decompensation of immature drug addicts, I presume that many of them went mad because of drugs and alcohol. Moreover, psychopathic rapists like Guy George are often drug addicts and alcoholics. So, if they had not consumed these substances, would they have raped and murdered their victims?

1. Bergeret, Jean, *La personnalité normale et pathologique*, Paris, 1996, p. 33.
2. Ministère de la santé, de la jeunesse et des sports, *Premier bilan: "plan psychiatrie-santé mentale 2005-2008"*, Paris, 2007, p. 7.
3. Mental health foundation, *The fundamental facts, the latest facts and figures on mental health*, London, 2007, p. 9.
4. *The fundamental facts*, p. 17.
5. *The fundamental facts*, p. 31, aged from 16 to 20.
6. *The fundamental facts*, p. 30.
7. *The fundamental facts*, p. 30.
8. World health organization, *The world health report. 2001 mental health: new understanding, new hope*, Geneva, 2001, p. 3.
9. *The fundamental facts*, p. 20.
10. YRBSS, *Trends in the prevalence of alcohol use, National YRBS: 1991-2011*, Atlanta, 2012.
11. YRBSS, *Trends in the prevalence of Marijuana, cocaine, and other illegal drug use, National YRBS: 1991-2011*, Atlanta, 2012.
12. National center for health statistics, *Antidepressant use in persons aged 12 and over: United states, 2005-2008*, data brief n° 76, October 2011.
13. London, Jack, *John Barleycorn*, New York, 1913, electronic

edition, pagination by Kindle: l. means location.

14. *John Barleycorn*, l. 46.

15. *John Barleycorn*, l. 56.

16. *John Barleycorn*, l. 38.

17. *John Barleycorn*, l. 412.

18. *John Barleycorn*, l. 548.

19. *John Barleycorn*, l. 412.

20. *John Barleycorn*, l. 703.

21. *John Barleycorn*, l. 703 and 1044.

22. *John Barleycorn*, l. 1185.

23. Burroughs, William, *Junkie: confessions or an unredeemed drug addict*, New York, 1953, electronic edition, PDF pagination.

24. *Junkie*, p. 1.

25. *Junkie*, p. 3.

26. *Junkie*, p. 1.

27. *Junkie*, p. 7.

28. *Junkie*, p. 3.

29. Willard, Frances, *Women of temperance: on the work and workers of the Woman's Christian Temperance Union*, Hartford, 1883, p. 177.

30. *Women of temperance*, p. 177: "… It is clear that you have that very inconvenient sort of sin…".

31. Willard, Frances, *Glimpses of fifty years: the autobiography of an American woman*, Chicago, 1889, p. 353.

32. *Glimpses of fifty years*, p.41.

33. *Glimpses of fifty years*, p.36.

34. *Glimpses of fifty years*, p.413.

35. *Glimpses of fifty years*, p.451.

36. Nation, Carrie, *The use and need of the life of Carry A. Nation*, Topeka, 1909, p. 58.

37. *The use and need*, p. 65.

38. *The use and need*, p. 64.

39. *The use and need*, p. 65 and 66.

40. *The use and need*, p. 401.

41. *The use and need*, p. 301.

42. *The use and need*, p. 170.

43. *The use and need*, p. 134.

44. *The use and need*, p. 153.

45. *The use and need*, p. 67.

46. Pages-Berthier, Janine, "Psychanalyse et toxicomanie", Toxibase, n° 2, 1993.

47. Espad, *The 2007 Espad report*, Stockolm, 2009.

48. Trimbos instituut, *The Netherlands drug situation 2009*, Utrecht, 2010.

49. *The Netherlands drug situation*, p. 23.

Chapter 7

Anaclitic Racism.

Psychiatrists and psychologists are disconcerted by racism. They never know exactly whether it is a pathological manifestation or not. Some of them argue that extreme racism has something to do with madness, but they do not identify the mental illness. It is not a symptom of psychosis, since racists are able to write hundreds of pages, whereas psychotics cannot do so, but couldn't it be a symptom of neurosis? That's impossible because the neurotics who strive to get rid of the image of incest will try to have sex with persons whose ethnicity is much different than that of their parents. Could it be a personality trait of some people with a neurotic personality? I met many obsessives and each time I noticed that they were not that racist. As for persons with Hysterical Personality Organization, racism does not really exist: they always try to open the shell in order to discover whether there is a person of quality or not inside. Intelligence is dissected, and if the individual is stupid, they will try to understand why without considering the colour of the skin.

But what is racism? The answer is quite simple: to consider that someone is dangerous and inferior because of his or her distinctive appearance. We will soon see that different mental patterns engender such a feeling. In this chapter, I have decided not to research into Nazism because it is not a genuine invention of the Germans or the Austrians but a French concept and because Adolf Hitler and some of his followers influenced people. So I will speak of it in chapter 10.

A- Modern racism.

a- The American Civil War.

History is not helpful, for, most of the time, history is disastrous: the past is an infinite source of savagery. The turning point in racism was the American Civil War. Of course, there were racists in olden times, but most people were fascinated by exoticism, especially during the 18th century. Back then, all the continents had not been discovered: Australia was still a terra incognita. Consequently, the British and the French sailed around the world in order to find gold or spices, plant their flags on unknown islands and discover nature. The chevalier de Bougainville's adventure (1) is the best example of conflict between culture, Europe, and nature, the foreign lands. In 1766, two years before James Cook, he began a journey around the world. After many trials and tribulations, the expedition reached Tahiti in April 1768. They needed fresh food, water and wood. Bougainville's description of the island and its inhabitants does not show any preconceived idea about the natives. The myth of the noble savage living in harmony with nature may have inspired him, but it is his personality organization, his intelligence and his cultural background which really influenced him. When the first islanders approached the ship, he noticed that the women were pretty and almost naked (2). On the 6th of April 1768, *L' Étoile* and *La Boudeuse* anchor in a bay, and a most surprising event occurs (3): the islanders in their canoes encircle the two vessels and naked women described as nymphs begin to turn the French sailors on. The captain is a well-mannered aristocrat; even after six months of abstinence, certain things cannot happen. Unfortunately, despite the exhortations of Bougainville, the cook follows a woman and comes ashore. The Tahitians welcome him. They are so enthusiastic and curious that they undress him in order to see his body. He is not the first white man to reach this island, for Samuel Wallis, in June and July 1767, stayed there, but he was a bit aggressive since he opened fire on the islanders. The white cook seems friendlier. So they examine him and signals to him that he can have sex with one of the women. His is so upset that he refuses. Actually, he returns to the ship and tells the captain that he was scared to death.

A few hours later, Bougainville and his officers come ashore in order to see whether there is some water. A great many people approach them, touch them and undo the buttons of their jackets so that they may see their bodies. Bougainville is not afraid. He is the first European to describe the Tahitians. He says that there are two races. The first race is the most beautiful one(5). Men are tall and strong; he compared them to Hercules and Mars! He even asserts that they are not that different from the Europeans, even though their skin is dark. The second race is characterized by a smaller size and curly hair. He does not say that they are ugly; he just writes that they are not as beautiful as the former and adds that they are smarter.

A century later, the rapture engendered by the discovery of dark-skinned strangers disappeared. The American Civil War altered the delicate balance, achieved by the whites, between capital and work. The white Southerners believed that they could remain rich by exploiting black slaves. This certitude weakened within a few years. Thomas Dixon regretted the golden age of white supremacy. A reader whose personality is organized at the neurotic level notices immediately that the author had difficulty adapting to reality because it was changing and because his mental health depended on the outer world, which is why he needed to control it. Equality between people was an impossibility, for his immaturity compelled him to define degrees of necessity, convenience and proximity. Immature people don't know how to deal with the outer world. Unlike psychotics, they cannot regard others as persecutors they must kill, for those parental images enable them to live and mature. Their position is uncomfortable and always unstable: when they don't interact socially, they get depressed, and when they do, they feel persecuted.

In Dixon's novels, one can perceive the loss of control when he refers to economic problems. In *The leopard's spots* (6), he wrote that the end of slavery had ruined the economy. He believed that the world should have remained a cotton plantation cultivated by unpaid black slaves their masters used to whip when they did not work enough. He regarded paid work as an abomination. After the war, the planters had to pay wages and handle strikes. Dixon was furious, all the more so because some black people did not want to sign the employment contracts, which were a way to perpetuate white supremacy. Hence, so that they might manipulate them again, he figured out a religious solution. In *The clansman*, one of the characters, a white clergyman, teaches black people the new catechism and states that within six months the whites will have control over the whole race (7). Needless to say, religion is aimed at brainwashing black people into obeying the white Jesus and his white ministers.

Dixon did not accept that there were differences between people (8). From a psychological point of view, his whole life long, he regarded other humans as good people only if they resembled him. Great physical differences forbade that. Hence, he considered that blacks were dangerous because they were different from him. He dislikes their physical characteristics. His disgust has nothing to do with beauty or ugliness; it is primitive contempt. He compares them to animals. In 1902 (9), he called them donkeys and declared that they would not be as strong as horses if they mated. He added that they would become infertile mules and would remain inferior creatures. In 1905, he was even more unpleasant (10): he wrote that they behaved like apes. In his Darwinian hierarchy, apes are inferior creatures, but he did not explain why he disparaged their physique. The explanation has a lot to do with his definition of purity.

Since he was not a psychotic, he did not believe that the whites were descended from God. Nonetheless, when he depicted a gathering of white and black people, he put great emphasis on the marble statues of Robert Young Hayne and George McDuffie, saying that they were whites and that the blood of the Scottish kings flowed in their veins! These politicians were neither European aristocrats nor royals; this literary artifice is aimed at strengthening a fragile ego. It is a way to fight depression by boosting one's self-esteem, which depends on an ethnic group regarded as gratifying. One notices a symptom of hypochondria: the illusion of contamination is a long-lasting process that destroys flesh and pride. Some depressives believe that their bodies are rotting. So fighting putrefaction and looking for absolute purity are means to avoid depression. Dixon contrasts white with black, namely purity with impurity. Consequently, he cannot accept interracial unions. It is too simplistic to say that he just wants to perpetuate white supremacy, for his views are more primitive. Actually, any sexual contact between whites and blacks is considered to be "pollution" (12), and he believes that mulattoes symbolize whites' failure to remain pure (13). Hence, racial segregation will enable him and the whites to survive.

His conception of mankind is very pessimistic. His books are full of sins, unhappiness and death. If all men are not considered as dangerous, black men and women are seen as savages. Women are not as dangerous as men, for their biological inferiority cannot frighten a strong white man. Nevertheless, Dixon narrates a story about a black woman who killed her own child and burned his body "in a drunken orgy with dissolute companions" (14). He also has a bad opinion of black men, for, according to him, they are totally depraved and are often criminals. In his famous novel *The clansman*, a member of the Ku Klux Klan named Ben Cameron and a physician examine the retina of a white lady who was murdered by an unknown person. They believe that the last picture she saw will be "printed" on her retina. So, by means of a microscope, the physician examines it and beholds "the bestial figure of a negro" (15), who is the so-called murderer.

When Dixon uses oral-sadistic arguments, one notices that he regresses to the mental age of an infant. In *The Leopard's spots,* he already reported a case of cannibalism in Haiti (16). Of course, cannibalism is not an illusion. Nowadays, most of the time, it is a symptom of schizophrenia. In that book, the fear he experienced during the oral-sadistic phase impels him to portray a hypothetical black monster. Some years later, in *The clansman,* the idea reappears; he writes (17): "... He lived as his fathers lived –stole his food, worked his wife, sold his children, ate his brother, content to drink, sing, dance, and sport as the ape!" This concerns Afro-Americans, not Haitians. He has turned a supposition into a generalization and given birth to a monster that has never existed. He hated black people at a time when Europeans already disliked the Jews: racism has a lot to do with history and geography. The racial enemy is not an unreal scarecrow, for very immature people have not lost touch with reality or what is happening where they live.

However, Dixon was a racist immature man who did not display neurotic characteristics, which might have allowed him to be less hateful. His writings are desexualized, which means that he never ever considered that black women could be sexual partners. Moreover, he feared sexual contacts between whites and blacks. Consequently, he believed that Americans had to be segregationists. He was not really violent, even though he accepted the existence of a violent organization: the Ku Klux Klan. After all, he was also a Baptist minister who considered that black people were human beings created by God. Actually, extreme racism is not that American.

b- The French racists

In 1853, Arthur de Gobineau published his famous book on the inequalities between human races (18), and the date cannot be a complete coincidence. In fact, a year before, Bénédict Auguste Morel had published the first volume of his treatise on insanity (19), in which he described the degeneration of the mind and body of some inmates of the Maréville psychiatric hospital whom he tried to cure. He was the first physician to give so many details about mental retardation, but we cannot regard him as the initiator of teratology in France, since, back then, a great many French people were fascinated by monsters. However, in 1857, he systematized his approach and published a treatise on the *Degeneration of man's body, mind and morals* (20). It is clear that Gobineau did not read it, but he did not need it, for Morel had formulated his theory in his first treatise. No note or quotation shows that he read this book; the only physician quoted is Bichat, not Morel! At least we can admit that physical and mental degeneration was not an original idea back then. Hence, according to him (21), there is degeneration when there is interbreeding: the master race (the white one) changes natures when it is mixed with an inferior race (black people and Asians). He was less flamboyant than Dixon. Nevertheless, one may believe that he almost subscribed to the latter's point of view.

Gobineau is obsessed with the ideal of beauty, which may relate to his ego ideal. According to him, white is beautiful; he wrote (22): "... I have already said that among the human groups, the most beautiful one is composed of Europeans and their descendants. ..." He even hierarchizes the European ethnic groups: the Italians are prettier than the Germans (23), the Swiss, the French and the Spanish. He is not an extremist who considers that beautiful people are always fair-skinned, blue-eyed and blond. Nevertheless, he wants to believe that the ancient Greeks, the Persians and the Indians were fair-skinned and blond (24). On the other hand, he sees black as ugly. Consequently, Africans are undervalued, but less than the Melanesians (25); he wrote: "... Oceania gave birth to the most monstrous, hideous and repulsive creatures. Apparently they are a bridging species between humans and beasts. ..."

According to him, Adam is the father of the white races (26). The "Aryans" are descendants of Adam and the ancestors of the white Europeans. He believes that they dwelt in India. He writes that the etymology of the word *Aryan* comes from *Arya-varta:* the land of the honorable men (27). Hence, pride is also a part of the definition of this ethnic group.

This kind of racism is fuelled by the point of view of a loner; it is not a reaction to the presence of an ethnic group. In the 19th century, France was a multi-ethnic empire, but there was no immigration into mainland France. The first contact with foreigners occurred when the French settled in the colonies. Besides, a few black people served in the French army during World War One. In fact, the first foreigners whom the French met were the Jews who fled from Eastern Europe in the second half of the 19th century.

Edouard Drumont did not like that very much; he thought that France was invaded by them. He speculated on the number of immigrants, all the more so because official statistics were misleading. For instance, he wrote (28) that in Paris there were supposedly a little less than 15 000 Jews, but, since he saw them in lots of different places, he believed that there were between 120 000 and 150 0000 Jews in Paris and 400 000 in the rest of the country. Although he declared that they stank and were unbalanced (29), he was not that hateful. Actually, he detested their insolence (30). The clash of opposed egos provoked Drumont's reaction: first, the immature man tried to prove that they were dangerous, then he belittled them.

Some years later, during the 1889-1890 academic year, Vacher de Lapouge taught a course on the role of the Aryans in society. His lectures were published ten years later (31), during the Dreyfus affair (1894-1906); Dreyfus was a Jewish captain in the French army who had been accused of spying for the Germans. Vacher de Lapouge was a typical racist. He stated that the Jews were the only enemies of the Aryans (32), but he did not want the black and Asian populations to grow either (33)! He was so racist that he imagined a world inhabited only by white Aryans because they belonged to the master race. He did not write that the members of the other ethnic groups had to be killed, but he used the word "extermination", which proves that he lacked empathy. According to him, human beings were but animals. The solution he found (34) was systematic interbreeding: the whites would eradicate inferior races by diluting their characteristics.

He made a long list of the vices of the Jews, but he hated them because they were arrogant (35). He was unable to accept their narcissism, which threatened his. Page after page he belittled them by blaming them for a great many vices, which shows that his ego was weak. However, he did not really care about their appearance (36). Racists don't hate foreigners because their bodies are different. In fact, they recognize them thanks to them. They fear human beings because they believe that they are as dangerous as they and because they must destroy the outer world (when it does not resemble them) so that they may undergo primary narcissism, feel secure, and start to identify with role models, which will lead them to undergo secondary narcissism and turn them into persons who are less dangerous and hateful.

Like Drumont, he thought that Europe was invaded by them. He wrote (37) that during the 19th century, the Jewish population had grown from two million to ten million because of immigration and the birthrate. He was too stupid to be aware of the stagnation in population growth, but this argument justified the digressions about eugenics. Was Lapouge the instigator of the *T 4 Euthanasia Program* and the *Final Solution to the Jewish Question,* which were carried out by the Nazis? It is clear that the Germans knew his theories, for his book had been translated and published in 1939 (38), but can a book or an idea kill? This kind of primitive hatred does not need a book to surge in people, for there is no more thinking but the spontaneous expression of the desire for murder. Lapouge was the result of a dysfunctional, diseased society that wanted to immolate the so-called villains who had driven it crazy. When Philippe Pétain and the Cabinet decided to deport the Jews to extermination camps in order to please the Germans, one must admit that society went mad. When the population collaborates with the French police and the Gestapo and therefore contributes to the massacre of six million people, one must assert that humanity has disappeared, for people with a neurotic personality cannot combat this psychopathic savagery (see chapter 10).

After the war, the world discovered the atrocities committed against the Jews. In France, very few people dared to express an opinion on the matter. Fortunately, Jean-Paul Sartre (see chapter 1) gave a psychopathic answer to the psychopathic bloodbath (39). He did not understand what had happened, but he was not the only person to be in this situation. After this apocalypse, he declared that the Jews were innocent and harmless, and he did not mention the concentration camps filmed by the Americans, nor did he draw attention to the responsibility of the French and the Germans. As usual, Sartre did not comprehend reality, and he failed to fulfill his duties as an intellectual. He was just a reflection of the society in which he lived: a normal intellectual, in a normal society having committed extraordinary crimes that normal intellectuals cannot understand! Hence, this society remained ignorant and was unable to build a better future for mankind.

B- The Norwegian knight.

The root of racism is always the same: hatred of the body of persons with whom one cannot live, although there are not that different. When one does not really dislike their appearance, the problem can be the same. In 2011, Anders Breivik, who claimed that he was not a racist (he just wanted to protect his race), murdered 77 people in order to save Norway and Europe from a danger, but what kind of danger was it?

a- Paranoid schizophrenia!

The massacre shocked the Norwegians. The rest of the world was surprised since people are not used to having news of this small country of five million inhabitants, which is in the middle of nowhere. Five million inhabitants: it is the population of a city! It must be a quiet place! Racism and immigration cannot exist!

Once he had detonated a bomb outside the building housing the office of the Prime Minister in Oslo and murdered many members of the socialist party on the island of Utoya, Anders Breivik called the police in order to surrender. The judicial process began, and at the end of November 2011, the psychiatrists concluded that he suffered from paranoid schizophrenia (40). So his case could not come to trial. Was it just a mistake made by two inexpert psychiatrists or the response of a society which could not accept that murderers can be "normal people"? In fact, he was not the only immature person to be categorized as a schizophrenic; Murray had made the same mistake regarding Hitler (41). Psychopaths have always bothered psychiatrists; they used to regard them as psychotics or neurotics. The French, for example, preferred to regard them as neurotics, whereas the Germans considered that they were psychotics (Ernst Kretschmer invented relational paranoia). The Americans were much more accurate.

Those two Norwegian psychiatrists show the limits of this profession. Psychiatrists and psychologists must be intelligent, reasonable and very knowledgeable about philosophy, sociology and literature, for they keep analyzing what people tell them. This knowledge enables them to discover whether people lie, manipulate them, conceal information, simulate feelings, or rave. However, it's easy to recognize schizophrenics, for they are stiff, the way they walk and write is weird, there is paramimia (gestures are inadequate), the thinking and speech are confused, and they experience hallucinations. The two psychiatrists were deceived by the lack of empathy of the murderer. When they interrogated him, on the 9th of August 2011, they wrote that when he spoke of the Utoya massacre, he was emotionless; his vocabulary was dull; from an emotional point of view, the response was inadequate. On the 5th of September, they noticed that he was indifferent to the suffering of others. They gathered more information in order to corroborate their impression; they would have liked to find a few hallucinations. On the 10th of August 2011, they declared that they had not found any auditory hallucination. On the 25th of August, the murderer said that he had not heard voices or experienced telepathy. Besides, he pronounced words correctly and did not stop when he spoke (42). They did not forget to say that he was very rigid in his chair during the interviews.

When they met his mother, they placed much emphasis on hypochondria, which is a symptom of schizophrenia and a sign of immaturity. She told them that (43) he believed that she would infect him, which is why he did not want to talk to her and wore a face mask indoors. Actually, this may have been a symptom of depression. Besides, they noticed that he was afraid of spiders and beetles, but they did not determine whether it was a sign of psychopathy, or anxiety hysteria, or a schizophrenic hallucination. On the other hand, they did not forget to say that he kept to himself when he began playing *World of Warcraft* and that he suffered from delusions of grandeur. They inferred that he suffered from psychosis during and after the massacre.

The diagnosis satisfied neither Anders Breivik, nor the victims, nor their relatives, nor Norwegian society, nor a few psychiatrists. Hence, there was a second court-ordered evaluation, and on the 10ᵗʰ of April 2012 (44), Terje Torrissen and Agnar Aspaas issued a statement about the murderer's mental health. This time, specialists did not want to find a psychosis. At first, they gathered information about his childhood. We don't know whether they wanted to demonstrate that a trauma had caused psychopathy or just discover the process that had led to any kind of personality organization. This forensic report is not clear, all the more so because the written statements do not copy the oral ones. However, it is clear that he spoke freely, for the two psychiatrists recorded his strange political beliefs. Besides, they were not obsessed with the symptoms of psychosis: they did not want to find hallucinations, and they did not write that he was as stiff as a schizophrenic. Nonetheless, they were intrigued by his lack of empathy. So they declared that he was not moved by the massacre, although they realized that he knew that it was terrible and barbaric. This embryonic conscience prevented them from making the mistake the first experts had made. Moreover, it was a politically motivated attack. So, since he had not committed impulsive senseless murders, he could not be a schizophrenic. They were evasive about his personality organization, but since he was not a psychotic, the authorities considered that he was sane, which is why his case came to trial.

b- A man-child who does not ignore reality.

Even though the information is not accurate, one can get a clear picture of his mental peculiarities. We even have a document that describes him when he was four (45). The psychologist who met him said that he kept to himself, that he was passive and fearful, and that he gave monosyllabic answers. Thanks to other documents, we realize that his childhood shaped the strange relationship between him and women.

Actually, he is an anti-feminist, which is shown in his manifesto (46). He declares that men are now a subspecies enslaved by women. According to his mother, he accused her of being a Marxist and a feminist. He says that he has been feminized by the Norwegian feminist society (48), especially at school, where the feminist teachers try to create "beta-males", not "alpha-males" (49). Women are seen as a danger, for they are linked to his vision of sexuality, which is characterized by his rejection of the sexual liberation of the 1960s. For example, he writes that this destroyed his family and blames his mother and sister, whereas he does not say anything about his father. He loathes sexual immorality, and he blames men too. His stepfather, who is a womanizer, is labeled a primitive sex-machine (51). His half-brother added that he does not dare to make contact with girls; he thinks that he is a little afraid of them.

It is self-evident that psychological identification was difficult, and the divorce of his parents was not the only reason. The relationship between him and his mother was dysfunctional; I think that they were too close, which complicated his mental development. In fact, no man interposed himself between the child and his mother in order to show him the difference between genders and the role each of them has to play in society. Many years later, he had difficulty understanding what a man is. The biology of the human body enticed him to look like a man by building muscle;

Norse mythology taught him to kill like a man. So he became a modern knight and killed the future members of a regime which he accused of destroying the Norwegian male identity and civilization. Obviously, he is sexually incompatible with women. Some of his health worries may be unconscious reactions to his mother's noxious femininity. He wants to be a man and tries to be one, but the females who are around him tend to alter his newborn virility by means of their aggressive femaleness, which is encouraged by a feminized society. Hence, having sex with a woman prevents him from developing his gender identity.

Since he is an immature man, the main characteristic of his personality organization is narcissism, but it is impossible to separate primary from secondary narcissism. Nevertheless, he knows that narcissism is his main trait; he writes (54): "... I remember that pride and certain moral codices/principles have always been very important to me. ... Pride was more important than anything. ...". The first psychiatrists (55) noted that he was proud, and the second ones added that he believed that the Conservatives were regarded as second-class citizens. Nonetheless, his narcissism is not as demoniacal as that of a psychotic, for he knows that sometimes he needs to put it aside. For instance, when he describes the perfect Knight of Justice, he writes that his ego must be dialed down so that the plot may be kept secret and the other knights may behave themselves (57). He is not an impulsive man who will react angrily to the first disappointment; he thinks, behaves himself and observes reality. Unfortunately, his morals are rudimentary and inoperative, although he keeps saying that others are amoral, which is a classic trick aimed at belittling the enemy.

According to him, one can kill innocent people (58), and even if he believes that it is a sin, he thinks that God will forgive him (59) because Knights of Justice fight the Muslims and are often killed in action: this holy mission sanctifies anyone. In his hopeless world

(60), morality does not exist, for the aim is to survive or die, not to be good or evil. Murder is acceptable, and it becomes his raison d'être. He must kill for the sake of Norway, even though he is not a violent person. Neither his relatives, nor the psychiatrist, nor his friends said that he was violent. His manifesto does not extol mass murder. He writes (61): "... We train to kill, but that doesn't mean we love violence. We use violence only for self-defense, as pre-emptive actions and as a last option. We cannot allow our politically correct elites to sell us, their people, into Muslim slavery. ...". His violent behaviour is a response to a violent situation: a dysfunctional society that does not want to address the major problems.

Anders Breivik became a mass murderer. Was the four-year-old child violent? Did his parents and Norwegian society turn him into an aggressive adult? Not instantly, according to his acquaintances, who declared that he was not violent. Breivik said that he became really violent in 1999, when Serbia was bombed (62), but no document corroborates this. However, he spent a lot of time preparing the attack; his manifesto, even though it is, most of the time, a compilation, could not be written in a few weeks either. Everything was well-prepared and scheduled. On the other hand, he had a political objective; he used the trial as an opinion column: the opening statement and closing arguments are political declarations (63). He killed the young socialists on Utoya because they would become the future leaders of the country. He bombed some buildings in Oslo because they housed government organizations. Consequently, his wrath was aroused by a political reality: the threat might have been imaginary, but his feelings and his destructive response were not.

That being said, the attack occurred because of virtual reality (video games). Each time there is a murder, people blame violent music and video games, but are they right? If killing imaginary persons can lead people to regard life and death as abstractions, this can also enable them to sublimate their desire for murder since their ire is directed at things that do not exist. Both arguments do not apply to Anders Breivik, for he played a game called *World of Warcraft*, which is a role-playing game, not a violent video game. However, he told the first psychiatrists (64) that the shooting on Utoya island was like a game on television. So this idea may be linked to the long vacation he took in order to play that game all day.

According to his mother, he took it in 2006-2007, but an unidentified acquaintance of his declared that he took it in 2009. Whatever the year, the witnesses noticed that he avoided contact with others when he played *World of Warcraft*. He told the first psychiatrists that playing this game was a "martyrdom present". It's a plausible explanation, but did that period of virtual reality led him to lose touch with reality? It is clear that when one does not stab the enemy or hear cries of horror, war looks like a video game.

c- Light racism.

The attacks were aimed at protecting Norway against an invasion of Muslims. So was this racism or religious intolerance? Both concepts are linked, but like other racists, he emphasized the physical features of the people he wanted to protect.

According to him, white is beautiful, and he feels proud of his ethnicity (65). Actually, he is not an extremist who extols blond hair, fair skins, and blue eyes, for he does not disrespect olive-skinned, brown-haired, brown-eyed southern Europeans (66). He just fears ethnic groups that endanger his ethnicity (67). So he advocates the selective breeding of genetically pure Scandinavians, who can be found in the north of Sweden (68). The full-blooded Aryan is replaced by the full-blooded Scandinavian. The veneration he felt for the Nordic race impelled him to have plastic surgery to change the shape of his nose and to consider fixing four teeth in order to get closer to his ego ideal (69). He imagined that he was dead and wanted his body to look like that of a Scandinavian knight who gives his life for the Nordic race. Nonetheless, he does not despise the other ethnicities. For instance, he wrote that people who belonged to other ethnic groups could join in with his "army" (70) and that the only way to save the Christians in the Middle East was to form an alliance with the Jews. Hence, he is not that racist, which implies that other reasons moved him to perpetrate these crimes.

Thanks to his book, his speeches and the psychiatric reports, one realizes that he fears that Muslims may invade Europe and Norway. He believes that within ten years Oslo will become a Muslim city (72) and that within a century the Norwegians, Swedish and Danes will become ethnic minorities. Consequently, the Muslim immigrants are very dangerous, and he states that he became politically aware when he saw them mistreat the Norwegians (74). In his manifesto, he describes an ex-friend of his, a Muslim from Pakistan, who became an extremist and harassed a Norwegian. In that book, there is much information about Islam: he may have spent much time gathering it. When he refers to the demeanor of the Muslims in the schools of Northern Europe, we realize that he quoted the authors meticulously (76). The facts he compiled lead us to believe that they are dangerous psychopaths. Unlike certain racists, he has some knowledge of the Quran and Islam (77). Hence, his behaviour is not an automatic response to a mental disorder; he observes reality, which proves that Muslims have difficulty integrating themselves into Norwegian society. Of course, a person who is emotionally unstable and who strives to build his or her personal identity does not cope with ethnic tensions.

These social problems and this immature man begot a drama. On the 22nd of July 2011, he bombed buildings in Oslo and went to the island of Utoya, where young socialists were having a meeting. He wanted to murder lots of "Marxists" because he blamed them for harming the Norwegian race and Christian civilization. Many persons were killed and wounded; the citizens were shocked; the rest of the world was surprised. Anders Breivik used his trial as an opinion column. He was sentenced to twenty years in prison. Technically, he was neither a madman nor a psychopath, just an ordinary, immature guy who killed many people!

1. Bougainville, Louis-Antoine de, *Voyage autour du monde par la frégate du Roi La Boudeuse et la flûte L'Etoile; en 1766, 1767, 1768 et 1769*, Paris, 1771; Gallimard, collection Folio, Paris, 1982.

2. Op. cit., p. 224.

3. Op. cit., p. 225-227.

4. Op. cit., p. 229.

5. Op. cit., p. 252.

6. Dixon, Thomas, *The leopard's spots, a romance of the white man's burden -1865-1900*, New York, 1902, pagination of Blackmash online, p. 46.

7. Dixon, Thomas, *The clansman, an historical romance of the Ku Klux Klan*, New York, 1905, pagination of Project Gutenberg, p. 206.

8. *The clansman...*, p. 45: "I believe that there is a physical difference between the white and black races which will forever forbid their living together...". This sentence is uttered by Lincoln; of course, there is little historical accuracy.

9. *The leopard's spots...*, p. 238.

10. *The clansman...*, p. 291.

11. *The clansman...*, p. 266.

12. *The clansman...*, p. 291.

13. *The leopard's spots,* p. 127.

14. *The leopard's spots,* p. 47.

15. *The clansman...,* p. 313.

16. *The leopard's spots,* p. 127.

17. *The clansman...,* p. 292.

18. Gobineau, Arthur de, *Essai sur l'inégalité des races humaines,* Paris, 1853; complete edition: 1855. My edition: Pierre Belfond, Paris, 1967.

19. Morel, Bénédict Auguste, *Etudes cliniques. Traité théorique et pratique des maladies mentales considérées dans leur nature, leur traitement, et dans leur rapport avec la médecine légale des aliénés,* 2 vol., Nancy, 1852 and 1853; chapter 1, vol. 1: "Considérations générales sur l'état intellectual, physique et moral des simples d'esprit, imbéciles, idiots et crétins".

20. Morel, Bénédict Auguste, *Traité des dégénérescences physiques, intellectuelles et morales de l'espèce humaine et des causes qui produisent ces variétés maladives,* Paris, 1857.

21. Gobineau, p. 198; see also p. 58.

22. Gobineau, p. 152.

23. Gobineau, p. 153.

24. Gobineau, p. 312.

25. Gobineau, p. 119.

26. Gobineau, p. 129.

27. Gobineau, p. 309.

28. Drumont, Edouard, *La France juive,* vol. 1, Paris, 1886, p. 55, note 56.

29. Drumont, p. 57.

30. Drumont, p. 19.

31. Vacher de Lapouge, Georges, *L'Aryen: son rôle social,* Paris, 1899, publication of his lectures given at the university of Montpellier during the year 1889-1890.

32. Vacher de Lapouge, p. 464.

33. Vacher de Lapouge, p. 487.

34. Vacher de Lapouge, p. 490.

35. Vacher de Lapouge, p. 470: "... We think too much of the Jew who asks for something and we forget the arrogant Jew who commands. ...".

36. Vacher de Lapouge, p. 466: "... the Jews are blond, the Jews are brown, but they are always the same...".

37. Vacher de Lapouge, p. 474.

38. Vacher de Lapouge, Georges, *Der Arier und seine bedeutung für die gemeinschaft*, Frankfurt, 1939.

39. Sartre, Jean-Paul, *Réflexions sur la question juive*, Paris, 1946.

40. Husby, Torgeir, Sorheim, Synne, *Psychiatric report on Anders Breivik*, Oslo district court, the 29th of November 2011. All the documents come from the journalists of the Norwegian television TV2. They followed the whole trial and recorded it.

41. Murray, Henry, *Analysis of the personality of Adolph Hitler with predictions of his future behaviour and suggestions for dealing with him now and after Germany's surrender*, Harvard, 1943, typescript.

42. 10th of August 2011.

43. 9th of August 2011.

44. Torrissen, Terje, Aspaas, Agnar, *Psychiatric report on Anders Breivik*, Oslo district court, the 10th of April 2012.

45. Torrissen, Terje, Aspaas, Agnar, *Psychiatric report on Anders Breivik*, Oslo district court, beginning of the report, *Letter from the national center for child and adolescent psychiatry*, the 13th of February 1983.

46. Breivik, Anders, *2083: a European declaration of*

independence, electronic diffusion, 2011, p. 36.

47. Husby, Torgeir, Sorheim, Synne, *Psychiatric report on Anders Breivik*, Oslo district court.

48. Breivik, Anders, *2083...*, p. 1387.

49. Torrissen, Terje, Aspaas, Agnar, *Psychiatric report on Anders Breivik*, Oslo district court.

50. Breivik, Anders, *2083...*, p. 1174.

51. Breivik, Anders, *2083...*, p. 1387.

52. Torrissen, Terje, Aspaas, Agnar, *Psychiatric report on Anders Breivik*, Oslo district court.

53. Husby, Torgeir, Sorheim, Synne, *Psychiatric report on Anders Breivik*, Oslo district court. Breivik, Anders, *2083...*, p. 1174. He fears that he may catch the venereal disease of his mother. This is not usual health anxiety but a highly symbolic gender-related disease. Moreover, everybody noticed that he was not depressed; of course, he could have hidden his feelings.

54. Breivik, Anders, *2083...*, p. 1388.

55. Husby, Torgeir, Sorheim, Synne, *Psychiatric report on Anders Breivik*, Oslo district court.

56. Torrissen, Terje, Aspaas, Agnar, *Psychiatric report on Anders Breivik*, Oslo district court.

57. Breivik, Anders, *2083...*, p. 844.

58. Breivik, Anders, *2083...*, p. 846.

59. Breivik, Anders, *2083...*, p. 854.

60. Breivik, Anders, *2083...*, p. 846.

61. Breivik, Anders, *2083...*, p. 835.

62. Torrissen, Terje, Aspaas, Agnar, *Psychiatric report on Anders Breivik*, Oslo district court.

63. Breivik, Anders, *Opening statement*, Oslo district court, the 17th of April 2012. Breivik, Anders, *Final statement*, Oslo district court, the 22nd of June 2012.

64. Husby, Torgeir, Sorheim, Synne, *Psychiatric report on Anders Breivik*, Oslo district court.

65. Breivik, Anders, *2083...*, p. 1158.

66. Breivik, Anders, *2083...*, p. 1161.

67. Breivik, Anders, *2083...*, p. 416.

68. Breivik, Anders, *2083...*, p. 1156.

69. Husby, Torgeir, Sorheim, Synne, *Psychiatric report on Anders Breivik*, Oslo district court.

70. Breivik, Anders, *2083...*, p. 843.

71. Breivik, Anders, *2083...*, p. 454.

72. Husby, Torgeir, Sorheim, Synne, *Psychiatric report on Anders Breivik*, Oslo district court.

73. Breivik, Anders, *2083...*, p. 416.

74. Torrissen, Terje, Aspaas, Agnar, *Psychiatric report on Anders Breivik*, Oslo district court.

75. Breivik, Anders, *2083...*, p. 1377.

76. Breivik, Anders, *2083...*, p. 418.

77. Breivik, Anders, *2083...*, p. 46, 70, 75, 107.

Chapter 8

Islamic terrorism.

Anders Breivik's enemies are the Muslims. They are as immature as he. They provide religious arguments, not racist ones. He fights against Islam while Islamists fight people like him. It seems that the relations between the Middle East and the West are but a devilish anaclitic war between the crusaders and the mujaheddin. Islamists aim to conquer a space where they will build their personal identity and be able to protect it. But what is terrorism? Some dictionaries can be misleading, for they put great emphasize on the violence used by certain governments that want to remain in power. State terrorism exists, but Islamic terrorism is a more tangible reality. Hence, nowadays, most of the times, terrorists are religious persons, not states, who kill in order to achieve certain goals that are not that religious. In fact, on the 11th of September 2001, when the Twin Towers collapsed, I already wondered whether there was a religious meaning or not. My initial reaction was to compare the two skyscrapers to the tower of Babel. Mercantile pride would have been the updated sin of human nature, which is prone to challenging God's authority. Then I noticed that the other targets had nothing to do with religion. Journalists could provide explanations, I had to discover the truth.

A- Al Qaeda.

The relations between the Middle East and the West have always been tense because they were aimed at enabling a religion to spread across the world. After centuries of religious wars, persecutions and massacres, Islamic terrorism continues to harm mankind, but is its aim the same? The members of Al Qaeda and Osama Bin Laden keep saying that they follow in Muhammad's footsteps. Nevertheless, we must try to discover whether this strange conception of religion does not reflect a distortion of reality.

a- Osama Bin Laden.

Terrorism hides behind a wall of secrecy, and most of the information comes from unreliable secondary sources. However, sometimes the wall cracks and one can discover the way terrorists think. Since there is first-hand information about Osama Bin Laden, we will be able to get to know his state of mind.

First of all, his ego was weak. In 1999, Rachimullah Jusufzai described him as courteous, soft-spoken, shy and unassuming (1), and when we analyse what he said in the interviews, we realize that he considered that any trace of hostility towards him attacked his self-esteem, which he wanted to protect by being reserved. This man hated aggressive people. In a 1996 interview (2), he described a young mujaheddin named Al-Tahir and emphasized his intelligence and politeness. He feared the judgment of others and the way they behaved and looked at him. Eye contact was a serious matter, and people who did not follow decorum were deemed rude and dangerous. Politeness was a modus vivendi and a modus operandi, which proves that he was not a psychopath, since he behaved himself. It also demonstrates that he did not interact well with most people: clumsy statements and bad manners harmed his narcissism.

He was so touchy that he considered that the presence of the Americans in Saudi Arabia, during and after the Gulf War, was an insult (3). That same year, he declared that the opponents (like him) of the Saudi regime had been ridiculed and humiliated (4); intellectuals were also ridiculed by the king (5); he came to the conclusion that "Death is better than life in humiliation and shame"

(6). Some months later, the Saudi regime was regarded as arrogant (7), whereas, in Yemen, the air was "unblemished with humiliation" (8). He added that, in order to tarnish his reputation, some governments were spreading rumors that he wanted to live in the United Kingdom (9). In 1999, he asked the Americans (10) to choose a better government, which would not blemish the reputation of the other nations. In 2002, he warned them about their crusade against the Muslims and told them that, as usual, they would end up being humiliated by the mujaheddin (11).

On the other hand, he used Islam as a psychological crutch. He did not have individual conscience, and, of course, he was not an original thinker. The absence of some essential concepts compelled him to follow the preconceived ideas of others. Hence, Islam enabled him to interact, for if it did not enlighten him about all issues, at least it clarified many daily life problems. James Pennebaker and Cindy Chung (12) analyzed the data by means of a computer, and they concluded that Bin Laden used to thing in a more complicated way than Zawahiri. This does not mean that he was intelligent; it is just being between the devil and the deep blue sea! He kept quoting from the Quran, which shows that religion helped him to think. A man with a neurotic personality usually quotes his parents, especially his father (for his morals form part of his son's superego). He was unable to do so because his father, who died when he was ten, did not really raise him. The sacred book had replaced the paternal superego. So he would obey father surrogates like Muhammad and God; he stated (13): "Allah is the one who provides guidance". These father figures were dangerous, for they were linked to omnipotence: the individual had to obey or die. Sacred books do not explain; sometimes readers misinterpret what is written, which leads to manslaughter.

Thanks to Allah, he avoided sin. Although he did not know what morality was, he knew what immorality was since the Quran provided the answer. Consequently, polytheism, sorcery, usury, taking the money of orphans, alcohol, adultery, disobeying parents, perjury, slandering innocent, faithful women, fleeing combat, and murder (unless God permits it) were regarded as sins. Moreover, Bin Laden reinterpreted the Islamic concepts and expressed his opinions. For instance, when he referred to Bill Clinton's affair with Monica Lewinsky, he was aware that he had committed adultery and that he should have been punished, but he also provided a piece of information which Muhammad did not know: he said that the sexual sins committed by the Americans enabled AIDS to spread across the world, especially across poor countries. This remark shows that Bin Laden considered that sexuality was a problem since his subconscious did not prevent him from saying in an interview what a person with a neurotic personality might have concealed.

As for his opinion about war, it is devoid of morality. When people were killed by mujaheddin, he did not feel any sorrow (16). He even agreed to kill, which proves that his desire for murder was a key component of his personality and that he was amoral. Actually, he did not mind being called a murderer (18). For instance, when he described the Americans' occupation of the Grand Mosque during the Gulf war, he misinterpreted reality since the Americans, who had been invited by King Fahd, never occupied it, nor did they occupy Saudi Arabia! However, he declared that the Americans and the Jews had to be expelled and that history would decide whether he is a criminal or not.

Even when he speaks of the Palestinians, one doubts his sincerity, for his arguments are specious and may mean something else. In fact, when he spoke of the Palestine Liberation Organization and of the Palestinian authority, he stated (19) that they sympathized with the infidels. He did not say that they were traitors, but he emphasized that they had not achieved any goal because they were not violent. When the journalist told him that many Muslims disapproved of violence, he answered that fighting was a part of Islam. So people who did not fight were sinners.

Let us compare his opinion about the requirements for becoming a Jihadist with the one we find in the Al Qaeda manual. We notice that there is a similarity between Bin Laden's state of mind and that of the person who wrote it(20). The author of the handbook declares that the soldier must be calm, which shows that it was not written by a psychopath but by someone who was a bit more intelligent (21). His or her morals mirror those of Bin Laden. For instance, the justification for murdering people comes from the Quran (22), and there is no trace of emotion. Besides, many things are seen as sins, but necessity allows the Jihadist to be a sinner without being regarded as one (23). Moreover, the fight against immorality is not his main objective (24), which shows the level of intelligence of the person who wrote it: it might not be Bin Laden but someone who thought like him.

Feeling harassed was one of his personality traits. The harassers were the Jews and, above all, the Americans: he kept bashing them. This hatred had turned the shy, well-mannered man into a restless, talkative extremist. The wars in Palestine and Lebanon served as a pretext for feeling endangered by nonbelievers. Any attack on Sunnis was viewed as violence against him: the incomplete psychological identification did not enable him to differentiate between him and people whom he believed to be like him (25). Even though he spent much of his life outside Saudi Arabia, he remained an Arab: he kept talking about the corrupted regime, the wicked princes, and the arrogant king. He regarded Mecca as a kind of lighthouse, but why?

Actually, the most sacred mosques of the Arab World were so damaged that they had to be restored or even rebuilt: Osama Bin Laden's father, who was a well-known building contractor, had been asked to repair the Dome of the Rock, in Jerusalem, and to rebuild the Prophet's Mosque, in Medina, and the Grand Mosque, in Mecca, which he did. The places which the Muslims regarded as the holiest shrines meant a lot to the little Osama, who did not know his father well but admired him. According to him, this mission had been ordered by God and, to a certain extent, sanctified by him (26). He rarely spoke of his father, but when he did, he was not a grown man recalling the good moments spent with him but a believer speaking of a Saint who deserved the best place in heaven. Consequently, when the Jews and the Christians were too close to the monuments rebuilt by his father, he panicked and almost behaved like a psychotic. In fact, he displayed paranoid traits when he spoke of the United States. In 1996 (27), he had already declared that a conspiracy had been organized by the Americans and their allies, but he had not said which goal they wanted to achieve. He enumerated wars in which the Americans were supposed to take part, but this so-called plot was but a flight of fancy. In 2001 (28), the conspiracy began to take shape: according to him, the Americans wanted to conquer Saudi Arabia and the Grand Mosque. Hence, the plan had been hatched by the Christians and Bush was undoubtedly the most dangerous crusader. His idea of Christianity was so fuzzy that American Protestants became Catholic crusaders! However, he responded by giving money to the terrorist groups that massacred many people around the world. Did he personally plan some terrorist attacks? He denied having participated in any attack. Did the man who financed Islamic terrorism killed many people by himself? I doubt it. For instance, as to the September 11 attacks, the planning relied much more on Mohamed Atta than on him.

b- Mohamed Atta.

In 2012, Adam Lankford had a very good idea (29): he reclassified terrorists as "lunatics". Actually, he gathered information about Mohamed Atta and noticed that he was suicidal. Psychiatrists and psychologists are puzzled by suicide, all the more so because Freud never really studied it. Besides, depression is not a manifestation they fully understand; they use this word when they describe the mood of an obsessive, or a schizophrenic, or a psychopath, and they rarely dare to attribute it to a psychosis called melancholy, which could be placed between paranoia and schizophrenia. Adam Lankford was thorougher than they. Moreover, he knew that suicide is not an Islamic custom, and he put great emphasis on Atta's idiosyncrasies, which moved him to regard depression as a symptom of madness.

Personally, I was intrigued by his 1996 will (30), for he described how he wanted his body to be treated, although, after a suicide attack (he was planning one), the Muslim funeral rites cannot be performed, and they are not necessary. Actually, this will is rather absurd, but let's analyse it carefully.

The first oddity is his abhorrence of women, which transcends death. Once dead, sex is not a problem anymore. Since he is an immature person, his fear is intense; he wrote (31): "I don't want a pregnant woman or a person who is not clean to come and say good-bye to me...". He rejects women not because they can give birth but because they are unclean when they are pregnant. He fears that he is going to be infected, which might be a symptom of severe depression, but he adds that there will be no women during the burial, and he forbids them to visit his grave. Being a pregnant woman is defilement, and being a woman is an abomination. He does not stand them, even in the afterlife. However, this strange gender threat is also caused by men! He declares that the man who will wash his body will have to wear gloves because he does not want a man to touch his genitals without a kind of protective shield. Sex petrified him. This castration anxiety suppresses the libido (compare this case to that of Michel Foucault, in chapter one). We must not only blame his father, for he was so close to his mother that she must also be responsible for this personality disorder.

The second oddity is the parable of the ashes; he wrote (32): "You should throw the dust on my body three times while saying from the dust, we created you from dust and to dust you will return. From the dust a new person will be created. ...". The first assertion is quite common, the second one is not; it shows that he believed that he would be resurrected from the dead and that he would be transformed certainly into a more perfect man. I suspect he did not like himself very much; I also suspect he believed that there was something wrong with his body and his mind maybe. The caterpillar wanted to become a butterfly; a bad womb had borne a bad son, and only God could remake him through death.

Of course, suicide is forbidden by religion since Hell is the final destination of a Muslim who kills himself in this fashion. Hence, suicidal Muslims are bound for martyrdom. Muslim societies mitigate the population's desire for murder in this way since it is directed towards the outside of the Muslim world, which may protect the sane part of society. Nevertheless, when those persons lose touch with reality, this tactic can backfire.

As for Mohamed Atta, his suicidal behaviour depended on the eternal enemy: the United States. He wanted to die; since he did not get a medical treatment, he was bound to kill himself in a suicide attack. The information does not allow us to discern the psychological process that led him to plan the September 11 attacks and to choose to crash a plane into the North Tower (World Trade Center). Adam Lankford depicts him as a loner who was impressed by the pilgrimage he made to Mecca in 1995. After this date, he could identify his arch- enemy: once again, the Jews were regarded as devilish plotters. When he was in Hamburg, he became more antisocial: his roommates could hardly stand him. He was aware that they hated him; at least once he asked an acquaintance of his why he did not like him. In chapter 9, we will get a clear picture of an immature person who goes mad in a two-step process. Here we can only hypothesize that he was more unstable after his pilgrimage, which moved him to find an ultimate solution: he wrote his will in 1996 because he wanted to carry out a suicide attack, which he finally did five years later. Although Al Qaeda's global jihadism enabled us to see two very immature persons act, we cannot identify a trend, which is why me must study what happened in France.

B- The French Jihad.

In that country, Islam is a widespread phenomenon. Even if the collapse of the empire led to a clear separation between Muslim Algeria (which belonged to the French) and Catholic France, there are lots of Muslims in France, all the more so because immigration has not stopped.

a- Khaled Kelkal.

Khaled Kelkal epitomizes the post-colonial Algerian immigration. He was born in Mostaganem (Algeria) in 1971 and settled in Vaulx-en-Velin, near Lyon, in 1973. According to him (33), he behaved himself when he attended primary school. He began committing larceny when he attended junior high school and became a professional thief some years later. In 1990 (he was 19), he was already sentenced to six months in prison. On the 26th of August 1995, after some terrorist attacks in France, the police found his fingerprints on the adhesive tape that covered a home-made bomb. On the 29th of September 1995, he was killed by the police; he was 24. Fortunately, two years before his death, a sociologist had interviewed him. This interview was published after Kelkal's death; it gives us valuable information about his mind.

When we read Dietmar Loch's printed interview, we notice Kelkal's "suburban way of speaking", which is a kind of degraded French. For instance, he forgot the double negatives, had difficulty conjugating verbs (he had issues with the subjunctive), and chose words that did not mean exactly what he wanted to say. Maybe French was not his mother tongue, but he was also unable to speak Arabic (he learned it in prison). In fact, French was the only language he could speak, although he was not fluent in it. His vocabulary did not contain words that came from the local patois (34), which proves that Kelkal's French had nothing to do with his neighbor's culture; it was the language of the youngsters who neither want adults to understand them nor want to resemble them. His vocabulary showed that he was immature, especially when he spoke about his school, which her regarded as a fun place.

Of course, he displayed symptoms of borderline personality disorder. For instance, when he spoke of his life before his stay in prison, he described himself as impulsive and violent. His definition of robbery was even more meaningful: according to him, stealing was similar to being free and playing a game. In fact, the juvenile delinquent derives pleasure from the possibility that he could fail. If he doesn't, he feels as if he were stronger than the others, and he deceives the victim and the police, who represent the superego he does not really have.

Besides, his ego is weak, he has low self-esteem, and he belongs to an anaclitic group, which led him to formulate the concept of "unicity". According to him, it means that people look alike and interact socially, which is the definition of unity. He was quite immoral. At the end of the interview, he admitted that people had to follow rules, but he also declared that, when he was in high school, he was unprincipled; he added that he was not really able to understand what goodness was.

His religious faith may be connected to the construction of his superego. We do not know when he began to go to the Mosque and whether his father taught him the basics of Islam. Nonetheless, he declared that when he was in junior high school he used to pray, and therefore he did not have any vice and felt good and balanced. The day when he stopped praying, he got into trouble and went to jail. Hence, although his superego was quite inoperative, he had a notion of goodness and he was aware that people had to be righteous so that they might live a harmonious life without getting into trouble. This proves that he was not that immature.

Islam was also the path to what he perceived as his country: Algeria. When he was in jail, a Muslim inmate who was fluent in Arabic taught him this tongue. We do not know whether he studied divinity, but he declared that he used to watch videos showing Muslim scholars. God and religion gave meaning to his life, they clarified everything in the universe, and they put his chaotic world in order, which enabled him to build his life and identify with human beings who were Muslims; he wrote (35): "... I am neither Arab nor French: I am a Muslim. ... Whether you are Asiatic, or Black, or Red, it does not matter because if you are a Muslim, we are brothers. ...". The role models he did not find in his family, he found them in Islam.

However, he was not mature enough not to carry out the 1995 terrorist attacks, though he was not a brainless psychopath who wanted to kill everybody.

b- The suburbs are burning.

In 2005, for the first time in the history of France, the suburbs of many cities suffered violent riots, which shows that French society has changed drastically.

In the fall of 2005, during an arrest, some adolescents who lived in Clichy-sous-Bois, a suburb near Paris, tried to escape and hid themselves in a very dangerous place: an electricity-generating station. Two of them were electrocuted and died. Rumors began to circulate that the police had killed them. So violent riots broke out. During the riots, a tear bomb exploded in Clichy-sous-Bois Mosque while lots of worshipers were praying. The local issue became a national trauma: for three weeks, riots broke out all over France, even in isolated parts. The population, the intellectuals and the authorities were stupefied, all the more so because it was a widespread phenomenon. The rioters were mainly young people of foreign origin. Fortunately, the youngsters who took part in the Seine-Saint-Denis riots were studied by academics (36).

Eighty-six young persons appeared before the Bobigny court (37). All of them were boys. A third of them were less than sixteen years of age, and the age of the others ranged from sixteen to eighteen. 84 % of them had names and surnames that were not French, and 55,5 % of the boys were of North African origin. 48% of these juvenile delinquents were known to the police. It is certain that all of them were not Muslims, but the cultural background of most of them was Islamic.

This is corroborated by the fact that some of the rioters interviewed by the sociologists (38) said that the tear bomb that exploded in the Clichy-sous-Bois Mosque had moved them to riot. However, it cannot be regarded as a Muslim rebellion or a racial disturbance.

Actually, when we analyse the testimonies of some of the rioters, we realize that they were immature people and that some of them were on the verge of lunacy.

In this study, the authors chose not to publish all the data but only the best examples. The first one is about a sixteen-year-old Muslim rioter who made a statement in which his weak ego shows through: he asked for respect, he despised the police because of the way they talk to people like him, and he enjoyed fighting them in order to humiliate them. An aggressive seventeen-year-old unemployed adolescent declared that policemen often insulted him and treated him "like shit", which kindled his ire. Finally, a wrathful eighteen-year-old unemployed man said (39): "... All the guys who felt frustrated took advantage of the riots to destroy everything. Most of the guys hate the cops because they are proud; many of them are racist and treat us like shit. ... when a Jew is beaten, it is a serious matter... when it is an Arab or a Black, it is not important...". Those interesting testimonies do not prove that all the young men who rioted were very immature people, but the misunderstandings and the overreaction show that their personalities were not organized at the neurotic level. All this demonstrates that a great many French people are mentally unbalanced. Nowadays, they react violently to contempt: the desire for murder of the immature part of society causes such disasters.

c- Violence against the Jews.

We must correlate this phenomenon with other examples so that we may understand why a strange Jihadist committed certain atrocities in 2012. The crimes perpetrated against the Jews are good examples because they are not committed by white supremacists but by people who pretend to be Muslims.

If we look at the figures (40), we notice that the increase in the number of antisemitic incidents dates back to 2000: they had something to do with the problems occurring in the Middle East. Nowadays, we cannot easily correlate both trends. The statistics on assaults might be more helpful because they show an evolution of behaviors: the Jews are so disrespected that they can be beaten and even killed! Sometimes it's hard to distinguish psychotics' actions from those of immature people, but it's not a problem, for the phenomenon is so common that psychotics must be excluded. In fact, they are not intelligent enough to interact with other psychotics or behave like the rest of society. Besides, it is absurd to believe that a psychotic who has lost touch with reality is able to identify the race and religion of an individual in two shakes of a lamb's tail.

Hence, the antisemitic incidents may be attributed to immature people, and the increase in their number shows that French society is becoming psychopathic and mentally unbalanced. 83 Jews were assaulted in 2008, 57 in 2011, and 96 in 2012. In fact, France is not a safe haven for the Jews.

In 2006, a young Jew was kidnapped, tortured for three weeks, and then immolated. French historians have not recorded many acts of violence as barbaric as this one. All things considered, it was the most barbaric crime committed in France between 1946 and now, and it can be compared to what happened during World War II.

Youssouf Fofana (41) plotted to kidnap Ilan Halimi with the help of a group of his acquaintances whom the media called the gang of the barbarians. A psychopath gathered psychopaths and very immature people together in order to earn money, but misunderstanding of reality and negative social interactions turned them into monsters.

Fofana was born in Paris and lived his whole life in France, even though he sometimes went to Ivory Coast. We don't have any information about his youth, but the psychiatric report made by Françoise Toulouse-Sylvestre shows that he is a remorseless criminal, a narcissistic, uncompassionate psychopath who lacks insight and self-criticism, a predator, a manipulator, a vainglorious, paranoid man who misinterprets many things and keeps attributing the feelings he does not like in himself to people around him. In other words, she describes a psychopath who is on the verge of lunacy.

In order to earn money, he chose to kidnap Ilan Halimi, but his family could not afford to pay the ransom. Consequently, he became more and more violent as time passed. The violence he expressed was inflamed by other members of the group. If we cannot hold Emma responsible for that (the immature girl who acted as a lure to Ilan), the policemen, especially the superintendent (42), noticed that Zigo, one of the jailers, who was only seventeen, was extremely violent, for he kept beating him. He was the most impulsive, brutal and inhumane of them all. The general public was not informed of the barbarity of the acts, but the lawyers were well aware of that. Muriel Ouakine-Melki was impressed by the inhumanity of the kidnappers, who never called Ilan by his name. Caroline Toly declared that they transformed him into a thing and refused to speak to him and even to touch him: they used to wear gloves, as if they wanted to protect themselves from a disease!

Fofana claimed to be a Muslim: he used to go to the mosque and, in prison, he is described as an Islamic propagandist. Nonetheless, his crime has nothing to do with Islam or religion. It is the brutal murder of a Jew who was supposed to be rich. It reflects the moral decay of a nation that entices certain citizens to flee the country (43).

d- Mohamed Merah.

This dysfunctional, diseased society begot a drama. When one compares Khaled Kelkal in 1995 with Mohamed Merah in 2012, one realizes that the French's mental health is deteriorating.

His psychological evaluation had been performed in 2009 (he was 20) by Alain Pénin: he had already had issues with the police, and the judge had ordered psychologists to examine him in order to adapt the sentence (44).

Alain Pénin met him at the Seyne penitentiary on he 15th of January 2009. He pointed out that he was nervous and that he took sleeping pills and psychotropics in order to calm his anxiety. He had formerly tried to hang himself. He stayed in a psychiatric hospital from the 25th of December 2008 to the 8th of January 2009. This psychologist wrote that he was in tune with reality, that what he said was logical, and that his brain's processing speed was high, but he had difficulty with abstract thinking. The tests (including the Rorschach test) showed that he perceived reality as it was, which implies that he had gone through the process of psychological identification. However, the image of his mother caused him anxiety. He declared that he was quiet and liked being alone. He used to spruce himself up, but he did not flirt with girls. He was depressed and suicidal. He enjoyed reading the Quran and praying; he observed Ramadan. He neither drank alcohol, nor took drugs, nor smoke. He had committed antisocial acts and had difficulty learning from experience. Alain Pénin stated that he was an emotionally immature individual. According to him, the tests showed that he had resolved the Oedipus complex and that his personality was unstable, which is a psychoanalytic incongruity since this individual's personality was not organized at the neurotic level (45). I must add that he did not speak French very well: I noticed some misspellings and his vocabulary was limited. This psychologist realized that Merah was an immature man, but one must refute the assumptions he made about Merah's quietness and about the resolution of the Oedipus complex.

If this psychological evaluation is not excellent, Doria's documentary is irreplaceable (46), for it enables us to understand who Merah was and to determine, to a certain extent, the factors which shaped his personality.

It is self-evident that he is the product of a dysfunctional family: his mother reproached herself for having divorced his father and declared that she was unable to raise her five children because no man helped her. That being said, her husband was not a good role model: he was a drug dealer and was sentenced to five years in prison. Hence, no man separated Mohamed from his mother, or inculcated moral values in him, or helped him to interact with people, which is why he did whatever he liked. His mother was so overwhelmed that she contacted the social services. He was sent to an institution, and a document dated August 18, 1997 (he was nine) shows that, at home, the situation was problematic.

When he was fourteen, he was very aggressive: he kept insulting girls, stealing, destroying goods and assaulting people. He refused to comply with requests from adults: he was the typical psychopath. His mother stated that at an unspecified age he told her several times that there were two persons in his head. Is it a dissociative identity disorder, delusion of being controlled, or a hallucination? It is impossible to answer, but one must assume that his personality had been prearranged at the psychotic level. If after the end of the Oedipus complex he did not become a psychotic, he failed to become a person with a neurotic personality. However, he was mentally unbalanced.

At the age of sixteen, he became a bit more sociable. He already led a double life: during the day he worked in a garage and showed that he was reliable, at night he stole cars and committed robberies.

On the 18th of December 2007 he was sentenced to 18 months in prison. He went to jail for the first time, and it was a traumatic experience. We do not know exactly why, but one can assume that the other inmates bullied him, which unsettled him and ruined his self-esteem. After one year in prison, he made a rope out of bed sheets and tried to hang himself.

Then he was released. He could further his education by visiting Muslim websites. In July 2010, he went to Syria in order to meet some mujaheddin. In Islamabad, in the summer of 2011, he met Abdul Aziz Gazi, an imam who knew Bin Laden, and attended a terrorist training camp near Miranshah, in Pakistan.

On the 11th of March 2012 around 8 O'clock in the morning, in a school, he killed three young children (aged 4, 5 and 7) and a teacher: they were Jewish. The days before, he had killed three soldiers: two of them were Muslims! He declared that he wanted to kill soldiers because they had taken part in the Afghanistan War and used to kill Muslims. In a letter found in his bag, he wrote that he was an Al Qaeda soldier who fought for the sake of his Afghan brothers, but why did he kill children? In fact, he did not care about religion since he killed Muslims! Did he want to kill Jews? No, he wanted to kill children and regress to primitive omnipotence, which is characterized by oral sadism. He was so suicidal that he said to the police: "I let it be known that the man who faces you does not fear death. I like it as much as you like life." Then he did not express regret; he just said that he would have liked to kill more soldiers and children.

A dysfunctional, diseased society, immorality and lack of reason begot a dysfunctional family and an absolute monster. Islam was just a pretext for committing suicide without risking burning in Hell. The motive behind these suicide attacks is not really religious. Muslim terrorists just want to kill and die; they don't aim to conquer the world in order to establish a religion. Their Jihad is a lie of highly unstable persons. Merah was not Tariq ibn Ziyad, for there was no holiness but pure cruelty.

1. United States foreign broadcast information service report, *Compilation of Osama Bin Laden statements: 1994-January 2004*, p. 82.

2. *Op. cit.*, p. 4.

3. *Op. cit.*, p. 11.

4. *Op. cit.*, p.16.

5. *Op. cit.*, p. 17.

6. *Op. cit.*, p. 27.

7. *Op. cit.*, p. 31.

8. *Op. cit.*, p. 33.

9. *Op. cit.*, p. 34.

10. *Op. cit.*, p. 99.

11. *Op. cit.*, p. 221.

12. Pennebaker, James, Chung, Cindy, "computerized text analysis of Al Qaeda transcripts", in Krippendorf, Klaus, Bock, Mary-Angela, *The content analysis reader*, Thousand oak, 2009, p. 453-466.

13. United States foreign broadcast information service report, *Compilation of Osama Bin Laden statements: 1994-January 2004*, p. 140.

14. *Op. cit.*, p. 248.

15. *Op. cit.*, p. 218.

16. *Op. cit.*, p. 79.

17. *Op. cit.*, p. 86.

18. *Op. cit.*, p. 82.

19. *Op. cit.*, p. 86.

20. *The Al Qaeda manual*, U. S. department of Justice, electronic edition. It was seized by the British authorities when they attacked an Al Qaeda cell in Manchester in 2000.

21. *The Al Qaeda manual*, p. 16.

22. *The Al Qaeda manual*, p. 79.

23. *The Al Qaeda manual*, p. 77.

24. *The Al Qaeda manual*, p. 12.

25. United States foreign broadcast information service report, *Compilation of Osama Bin Laden statements: 1994-January 2004*, p. 11.

26. *Op. cit.*, p. 120.

27. *Op. cit.*, p. 14.

28. *Op. cit.*, p. 147.

29. Lankford, Adam, "A psychological autopsy of 9/11 ringleader Mohamed Atta", *Journal of police and criminal psychology*, 2012, vol. 27, p. 150-159.

30. Atta, Mohamed, "Im Namen Gottes, des Allmächtigen", *Der Spiegel*, the 1st of October 2001. English translation by Imad Musa (Capital communications group).

31. *Ibid.*

32. *Ibid.*

33. Loch, Dietmar, "Moi, Khaled Kelkal", Le monde, the 7th of October 1995, p. 10. In 1992, Dietmar Loch, who was writing his thesis, interviewed Khaled Kelkal.

34. The word is used in English, but it is a French idea. Since the French are obliged to speak the language spoken by the French civil servants, all the regional dialects are regarded as slang nowadays.

35. *Ibid.*

36. Delon, Aurore, Mucchielli, Laurent, "Les mineurs émeutiers jugés à Bobigny", *Claris. La revue*, n° 1, October 2006, p. 5-15.

37. Bobigny is the city where the Juvenile Court is located.

38. Mucchielli, Laurent, Aït-Omar, Abderrahim, "Les émeutiers de l'automne 2005 dans les banlieues françaises du point de vue des émeutiers", *Revue international de psycho-sociologie et de gestion des comportements*

organizationnels, Paris, 2007, n° 30, p. 137-155.

39. Les mineurs émeutiers..., p. 144.

40. Service de protection de la communauté juive, *Evolution de l'antisémitisme en France*, 2013. The information comes from the SPCJ and the French Ministry of the Interior.

41. Vigoureux, Elsa, "Youssouf Fofana, criminel narcissique et manipulateur", *Le nouvel observateur*, Paris, the 24th of June 2009.

42. Badault, Clémence, *Youssouf fofana le cerveau du gang des barbares*, France Télévisions, movie, France, 2011.

43. Belmont, Sarah, "Hausse de l'immigration juive de France vers Israël", *Le point.fr*, 17th of July 2013.

44. Penin, Alain, *Expertise psychologique de Mohamed Merah*, tribunal correctionnel, 3ème chambre, Toulouse, 2009.

45. A neurotic personality is always stable.

46. Doria, Jean-Charles, *Mohamed Merah, itinéraire d'un tueur*, Kalisté productions-France Télevisions, movie, France, 2013.

Chapter 9

The American psychopaths.

Societies influence men and women. An individual is never the direct result of his or her upbringing, for his or her parents are influenced by the beliefs and habits of their neighbors. In others words, if society is not sane enough, even a family composed of two adults with a neurotic personality will not be able to create children with a neurotic personality: the ambiance can be harmful. A sane society extols morality in order to perpetuate life. Do we find this in the United States? Not always, for liberty is the credo.

In fact, Americans idolize the French girl who splashes about in front of New York and would like to set fire to the world with her torch. Liberty is but the manifestation of a Don Juan's narcissism, who dares to state that his feelings are the measure of all things. Liberty is worse than a vice; it is a folly since man must accept his inferiority so that he may interact with the outer world. So American culture has created childish superheroes, wild cowboys and psychopathic youngsters. These rebels don't fight for a cause. Their immaturity compels them to regress to primary narcissism, which inflames their wrath. Their lives are a hopeless fight against depression, psychosis, and the outer world. Ordinary people call them psychopaths, psychologists antisocial persons, and Bergeret perverts of character. These individuals prosper, and each year they cause, at the very least, a disaster. Sometimes it is more than a personal tragedy; it is a national one.

That's what happened on the 20th of April 1999, when two students at Columbine High School killed thirteen people and committed suicide. This came as a shock because Americans discovered that "ordinary" people could be that evil. As usual, many questions were raised and no immediate answers were given.

Actually, some students realized that the two criminals were mentally unbalanced. Of course, no clear explanation was given by the murderers; there are but videotaped impressions and thousands of pages of testimonies. The police of the Jefferson County released the documents, except the psychiatric files and some videos. This is not a problem, for, thanks to the diaries of Eric Harris and Dylan Klebold, their mental disorders show through. As for the videos, some people described what they saw in them (1).

A- Trauma or interruption in the development of the ego?

We don't know why Dylan Klebold was immature; we can only note that he had failed to resolve the Oedipus complex and was mentally unbalanced. As for Eric Harris, his writings and a medical statement (2) give us important information about his mind.

Actually, we learn that on the 17th of February 1982 (he was born on the 9th of April 1981 and was therefore ten months old) his parents got a "second opinion on congenital leg problem". In his file, the last mention of the problem is dated November 10, 1982: he was nineteen months old. We also learn that he suffered from *pectus excavatum* (a depression of the chest) and underwent surgery on the 16th of December 1993. The steel strut was removed on the 9th of June 1994. Hence, the mirror stage must have been problematic, all the more so because he could compare his impaired body with that of his elder brother.

According to psychologists, the mirror stage occurs between the 6th and the 18th months. At that moment, the infant sees his reflection in the mirror, and he is a little afraid because he thinks that the person in front of him is someone else. Little by little, with the help of his parents, he realizes that it is he. This enables him to define and recognize his body and the outer world. Then he learns to like his image because his parents enjoy seeing him simper in front of the mirror, and they keep telling him that he is handsome. So he abandons primary narcissism and projects the image of his body onto other people's bodies so that he may consider that these objects are good, for they look like him. There is no sign of secondary narcissism in Eric's personality, whereas there is in Dylan's, which leads us to acknowledge that this is the reason for his immaturity. Naturally we do not know how his parents behaved back then: were they distant or did they flatter him? It is self-evident that there were worried, for the kept consulting the doctor during the mirror stage. As for the father, thanks to his diary and some of the remarks made by Eric, we realize that he was not close to his son.

A few years later, his preoccupation with his impaired body resurfaced when he referred to the flesh. He almost never alluded to his own flesh in his writings; he only did so in his text entitled *25 things that make me different* (3). Actually, the scars left by the surgery are in 13th position. We also know that he did not like his body, but there isn't an absolute correlation between this and a purely material conception of the world. In a video (4), we see him looking at a tree after a gunshot; Dylan touches the sapwood and Eric compares it to a brain. However, the most important data comes from the statements of the witnesses who were in the library during the massacre; they heard one of the two killers say to cut someone in order to see what was inside. Unfortunately, because of the stress, they did not try to discover who said that. However, Eric used to draw people who were beheaded, mutilated, covered with blood and burning, robot-like warriors whose hands were guns, bodies pierced by many bullets, and skeletons. He even did a drawing of an invulnerable warrior stepping on a sea of corpses. Eric was fascinated by the Nazi Euthanasia Program and considered that biology was the measure of the universe: matter meant everything to him and thoughts did not exist. Hence, it seems that it was he who had uttered that sentence. However, one understands his opinion about the flesh when he refers to sex.

On the 17th of November 1998, he wrote some lines (5) which show that he did not regard the body as a whole: according to him, a woman is composed of different pieces which he examines separately and can almost not put together. Nevertheless he was not a pervert, since he did not mistake females' genitalia for those of males. In fact, he had difficulty joining the different parts of a jigsaw puzzle together. Women and men were but flesh; intelligence, will and soul did not exist.

He expressed a more primitive idea in his 1998/99 diary. On Mother's Day, he quoted a line from *The tempest* by Shakespeare (act one, scene two), which reads (6): "good wombs have born bad sons". Is a quotation less meaningful than an original creation? No, it's not if it expresses exactly someone's feelings. It is an undeniable fact that he believed that some women had good wombs, which suggests that sexuality was regarded as a return to the original vagina. Did he believe that intercourse was a regression to a womb that guaranteed security and peace? Would it repair the wounded flesh of the disabled son? Was it a kind of rebirth? Whatever that may be, he did not like his body, for he had not completed the mirror phase.

On the other hand, oral sadism was his major personality trait. For example, in his diary, on the last page of the month of May 1998, there is a maxim which he changed. It's hard to read the first word; it could be humans, the humans, humanity, or the humanity. The rest is clear (7); it reads: "... are dedicated to making each day count... (8) for themselves and the people they eat (9)." Cannibalism is a sign of schizophrenia, but if schizophrenics can practice cannibalism, immature people fight against this tendency. This sentence just shows that his hatred of mankind comes from the oral-biting phase.

In his journal, there is a link between his oral sadism and his hatred of man; he wrote (10): "... I want to grab some weak little freshman and just tear them apart like a wolf, show them who is God. Strangle them, squish their head, bite their temples in the skull, rip off their jaw, rip off their collar bones, break their arms in half and twist them around, the lovely sounds of bones cracking and flesh ripping…". Honestly, it's very rare to see such violence; his journal is full of hatred; the most famous murderers were nor that wrathful. For instance, we will see in the next chapter that Joseph Stalin (oral sadism was one of his personality traits) used to compose serene poems. Hence, the devouring mouth of the wolf symbolizes his ire, which is directed at humans who are but pieces of flesh and whom he wants to dismember. This schizoid dispersal led so many psychiatrists to regard those very immature persons as schizophrenics. One must realize that he was not mature enough to think in a different way. He was a monster, but people were not aware of that because he looked contented. Since he was emotionally unstable, any aggression could increase his mental instability and provoke a hostile reaction.

Moreover, he had low self-esteem and had not gone through secondary narcissism. He did not like his body; he did not speak of the *pectus excavatum;* he just said that he was physically weak (11). In her statement, Kristi Epling (12) declares that he used to get angry when other students mocked his shortness. However, his perception of his body was based on other standards. When he said that he was weak, it meant that he was short and that he had internalized his parents' dislike of his physique, his distress at their opinion, a strong sense of inferiority because of his elder brother's athletic body and perhaps, later in life, the American beauty standards. Each time someone told him that he was not handsome this self-hatred reappeared. His body was a prison that prevented him from going through secondary narcissism, which enables the individual to like himself and to project his high opinion of himself onto people. People's reactions and his physique did not allow him to mature.

His libido did not help him because it impelled him to socialize with girls who might have been rather unenthusiastic; he wrote (13): "... The fact that I have practically no self-esteem, especially concerning girls and looks and such. Therefore people make fun of me... constantly... therefore I get no respect and therefore I get fucking pissed...". Of course, girls were not the only persons who mocked him, but we realize that a constructive relationship would have helped him to improve his self-esteem; he would have regarded others as good people since he was not as paranoid as psychotics; he would have matured. Instead, there is misogyny reinforced by zoology (14): "... women, you will always be under men. It's been seen throughout nature, males are almost always doing the dangerous shit while the women stay back. It's your animal instincts, deal with it or commit suicide, just do it quick. ...". This point of view cannot come from his bad opinion of his mother, for, in his writings and videos, there is no trace of such a thing. Moreover, the quotation from Shakespeare (the good wombs) is an allusion to his mother. Consequently, it shows that he had difficulty relating to girls.

This self-hatred prevented him from joining an anaclitic group. The psychopaths who are mentally unbalanced are in a hopeless situation: they need the others to stay alive, but their anger and the absence of secondary narcissism prevent them from socializing. Eric Harris's health and the way his relatives dealt with it might have forbidden him to mature. Unfortunately, we don't have any information about Dylan Klebold, but we know that he was almost as immature as he and had also antisocial personality disorder.

B- The signs of antisocial personality disorder.

First of all, they were not self-conscious. This is the logical result of an incomplete identification with their parents. Normally, the child must learn the differences between the sexes and build his or her personal identity with the help of the parent of the same gender. Hence, they must be close to them. Of course, children can identify with other role models, but parents remain the most efficient ones.

As for Dylan Klebold, I doubt that he was close to them. For example, in his journal, he wrote (15): "... my parents piss me off and hate me...". This is not the point of view of a toddler but that of a mentally disturbed teenager who refuses to obey people. Nonetheless, the fact that he did not like them, which shows through in other parts of his journal, demonstrates that his dislike of them was not new, which complicated the psychological identification.

As for Harris's parents, there are quite non-existent in his writings; when they appear, they are not regarded as detestable people. The image of the mother is almost indiscernible and there is only one line about his father, which reads (16): "... I had a lot of fun at that gun show, I would have loved it if you were there dad. We would have done some major bonding. ...". To say that he was not close to his father is an understatement. He did not dare to speak to him and just expressed his sorrow on a piece of paper. Thanks to Mr. Harris's diary (17), we realize that the father observed his son like an entomologist who does not understand what is happening. It is hard to believe that he had just begun to behave in that way, for Eric's mental instability and lack of insight prove the opposite.

In his essay dealing with the difficulty of defining oneself, we perceive the fragility of his self. The essay might have been empty rhetoric, but he was so concerned about this issue that he opened his heart. At first, he said that he had tried to define himself, but he had failed miserably. Actually, since he was building his personality, each new experience added up to his personality without creating a complete person who could perceive reality in a certain way. He was neither a psychotic nor a neurotic but an immature individual whose unstable personality did not allow him to form an opinion about what he saw and felt. So he kept redefining himself, not but using concept he regarded as truths, but by interacting with the hostile outer world, which perplexed him; he wrote (18): "... minds change constantly, ... I can never come up with an exact conclusion. ... when we think we know who we are when a new event happens that throw everything we knew about ourselves out the window." If the psychological identification had begun, it was just the beginning, for he did not know who he was, which led him to react instinctively to the outer world's entreaties.

Besides, they did not know what morals mean. Dylan, for instance, used to mistake good and evil; he wrote (19): "... Good things turn bad, bad things become good. ...". Moreover, he enjoyed living like a typical psychopath: when he describes his misdemeanors (drinking alcohol, smoking cigars and sabotaging the houses in the neighborhood), he is less depressed and he says that he is happy (20). He did not realize that what he did had moral implications. He was a kind of impulsive Clyde Barrow looking for a Bonnie Parker, his psychopathic female alter ego: his journal is full of heart symbols and lovesickness. However, in January 1999, there is an entry which shows that he knew what evil was (21); he declared: "... I am a criminal. I have done things that almost nobody would even thing about condoning. ...". Nevertheless, this approximation of evil does not prove that his superego was operative.

As for Harris, there is valuable information. In fact, around the 21st of September 1998 (22), he wrote a short essay entitled *Good to be bad, bad to be good*. He used to keep to himself, for he believed that his ideas would trouble many people, but his teachers were so liberal that he spoke freely. So he disclosed that he had been in trouble with the police, which had moved his parents to order him to surrender all his weapons. He was really disappointed because he had paid good money for some of them and had spent much time making the others. This text enables us to realize that he did not know what evil was: he knew that weapons were dangerous, but no superego commanded him not to use them. Instead, he declared that his parents did not trust him anymore, which had led them to punish him in this way. Consequently, he wrote that it was right, but he did not know what this word meant!

In texts he wrote for himself, his perception of good and evil is even more confused. On the 29th of July 1998, he asserted that morality was but (23) "another word". He added that it depended on the observer (24) and that the Nazis considered that they had the right to exterminate an entire race (25). None of his opinions show that he understood what god and evil were, which proves that he was amoral. Besides, he used to react violently to any kind of order or restraint; his journal is full of psychopathic hatred and mutiny, which he summarized in this way (26): "... people... telling me what to do, think, say, act makes me not want to fucking do it! That's why my fucking name is Reb!!!"

He was so immature that his ego ideal was problematic. One must not believe that it had something to do with the Nazis: he was just fascinated by the enormity of their crimes. Besides, although he loved guns, his ego ideal was not a kind of muscular GI. His passion just reflected his desire for murder and also a way to be more confident (27) and feel secure in a world he considered to be destructive. Actually, he did not have any; he stated (28): "...People are always saying they want to live in a perfect society, well utopia doesn't exist. ...". Idealism is not pathological per se. It is an incentive to keep on living when the situation is difficult. It begets hope. Eric's world was hopeless!

On the other hand, he did not accept others' narcissism and was close to viewing them as enemies he had to kill, which is quite psychotic. In his journal, violence and hatred are directed against different types of people: those he saw as inferior to him and those who dared to oppose him. In this connection, he wrote a short poem entitled *I am a gun* (29), in which he described a man who was arrogant, superficial, and who believed that he was an important personage – in other words, a self-centered man. He loathed this kind of behaviour, and he was symbolically killed in his poem. He was more explicit about that in his text entitled *You know what I hate*; he declared that he hated rude people who jumped the queue, for (30) "... if you cut, you are the following: stuck up, self-centered, selfish, lazy, impatient, rude...". He just did not stand people like him, namely people who used primary narcissism to survive, which leads us to wonder how Eric and Dylan interacted together.

Since Dylan was also a psychopath, they should have argued all the time, but he was not as mentally unbalanced as Eric. Nevertheless, he could not accept the existence of people who were smarter or more important than he. His English teacher had noticed that some weeks before the shooting: in an essay, he had described a man who was walking through a city and killing all the popular kids. However, he did not always regress to primary narcissism, for, sometimes, he used secondary narcissism to interact with people. For instance, in his journal, he described a friend of his and stressed that they were alike and behaved in the same way (32), which enabled them to coexist. If Eric was a stubborn general who barked orders, Dylan was a soldier who believed that he was like him. Consequently, he did not obey a righteous stranger but agreed to make friends with someone who resembled him and also wanted to kill.

Both of them were depressives, but Eric might have been sicker than Dylan: the autopsy report (33) revealed that there was Fluvoxamine (an antidepressant) in his blood. It is believed that this drug induced psychosis and thus had an influence on what happened, but the statements of the students and teachers and the way the attack was planned and carried out suggest that he did not experience hallucinations. Later on, we will realize that he killed the type of person he wanted to kill and saw the policemen arriving, which shows that he was aware, to a certain extent, of what he was doing. When he spoke, he expressed the opinions of a typical psychopath, not the fear of a psychotic or that of an immature individual going mad. Moreover, Klebold, who was not undergoing treatment and had not taken drugs or drunk alcohol, also killed in the same way. We always blame these medicines, but Harris had taken this drug for months without experiencing sides effects. Actually, we learn that he could not tolerate Zoloft (34), which had moved him to change medications around the middle of April 1998.

On the 24th of June 1998, he told a policeman that he was fine with Luvox. Consequently, he had taken that medicine for a year without experiencing side effects. Besides, when he died, the physicians found a small amount of Luvox. Hence, we must reject that argument.

Dylan did not take medicines, but he often said that he was depressed. On one occasion, he drew an "existence box" (35); it is a square with people inside and arrows which indicate that they will leave it and die. He did not place the representation of himself into the box but outside! He believed that he was already dead. His journal shows that he was suicidal; on the 31st of March 1997 (36), he wrote that he had thought of committing suicide, which would enable him to be in peace. He was so anxious that he kept struggling against his feelings. As for Harris, he was not self-aware enough to broach this subject. However, we realize that they felt anxious.

It is impossible to get information about their conception of the difference between life and death. Nonetheless, we realize that there was not a big difference between the two concepts, since they both believed in the afterlife. Klebold even referred to the *soul* (37), but he did not have a clear image of the hereafter: Paradise does not appear in his writings, although he described his life on earth as hell (38). He believed that, when he was dead, he would be in peace wherever he would go, whereas Eric would keep on struggling, for he thought that he would become a ghost and would haunt people (39)!

The last visible sign of psychopathy is regression to psychotic omnipotence: the individual erects an impassable barricade to protect his weak self from the outer world, and he tries to destroy it.

Two years before the killing, Klebold had already a tendency to regard himself as a God (40). Some months later, he stated that he was a god of sadness (41) exiled on earth in order to suffer. This will help us to understand his behaviour during the shooting. As for Harris, there is more information. In an essay (42), he compared himself to Zeus and declared that he enjoyed being powerful. He was not 15 and he was already on the verge of lunacy. Some time later, in a poem, he compared himself to a gun and asserted that he was God and could kill whomever he wanted (43). In spite of this, the most important document is Christopher Walker's school yearbook, which had been annotated by Eric. He had written in German (44): "Ich bin Gott". We don't know whether he wrote that when he was severely depressed, but it is very likely because depressed immature people use psychotic defenses. Hence, we realize that Eric and Dylan were almost insane.

C- Them and the others.

They were so sick that one must wonder whether they were aware of their mental disorders and tried to address them.

Eric Harris knew that he was different from the others, but he never said that he was insane. He just said that people called those who thought differently (45) unusual, weird and crazy, which led some of them to believe that he was weird. However, at the end of his life, he had to take antidepressants and consult a psychiatrist, which did not enable him to achieve greater self-awareness. As for Klebold, he knew that people believed that he was crazy (46) and that he was different from them (47), which perturbed him. As far as I can judge, he neither underwent psychoanalysis, nor consulted a psychiatrist, nor took antidepressants. Did the society in which they lived consider that their behaviour was normal? We must analyse the information in order to answer accurately.

Since they were not psychotics, we deduce that their fathers succeeded in separating them from their mothers, but they failed in the rest. Eric would have liked to be close to his father; perhaps he realized that he would have helped him to build his personal identity. I already said that in November 1998 he had been to a gun show and would have loved (48) to go there with him. In a world of primal hatred, there is nothing but peaceful sorrow. Eric was struggling to survive while his father, as a social animal, wanted to keep up appearances. Thanks to his notebook, we notice that he worried about his son's misdemeanors and that he did not believe that he was sane. He knew that Eric needed medical help and counseling, but he followed the same logic and asked him to show that he wanted to be a good son. Eric was just struggling to stay alive; each minute was a battle against his desire for murder, and every day was a victory over the threatening outer world. The father was disconcerted and disheartened (49). Did he try to understand what his son said and did? The existence of this notebook proves the opposite; so does the remark Eric made (50) about his parents' disappointment (in November 1998). Another testimony we cannot ignore because of its accuracy shows that his parents were suspicious of him; it says (51): "... Harris was upset with his dad, because his dad accused him of using LSD. ...". It is self-evident that Eric did not internalize their values.

As for Dylan, there is a white lie and a personal truth. He assured the juvenile probation officer that he got along with his parents, whereas the latter told him that it was hard to communicate with him (52). Dylan's journal shows that he believed that they manipulated (53) and hated him (54). Hence, he did not like them very much; but did he like anybody? At least he liked Eric, for he followed him everywhere. In fact, he liked a person who resembled him and with whom he used to violate the law. When he was with him, he was happy (55), which is a feeling he rarely experienced since he used to be severely depressed. Even when he believed that he had found a girlfriend, he was lovesick and sad. He admitted that he had great difficulty interacting with people, for he never knew what to say or do (56). He also realized that he scared people, that many of them did not accept him, and that he was unable to accept them (57). He was asocial, which condemned him to live alone and struggle against his mental disorders. Actually, his only friend was Eric.

Eric was in the same situation. Of course, he did not hate all the persons who frequented Columbine High School, for there were about one hundred people whom he did not want to kill and five whom he did not detest (58). People whom we will call *his acquaintances* appear in his videos and writings, but they are inconsistent. Actually, Dylan was his only "friend". From a psychological point of view, they were a lonely pair.

Some of the students gave an opinion on their behavior, and it is not the same, but most of them realized that Eric was deranged.

Patrick Kelly (59) and Kevin Larson (60) said that he was a moody student who would sit at the back of the classroom and did not participate much. Alisa Owen (61) stated that he had a dark side and kept to himself. Loni Brown (62) reported that Kate Thompson was scared by him because "I hate you" was written on his backpack. Adam Thomas (63) asserted that he had been nicknamed *Du hast* (you have), which is a song that was composed by the members of the German band Rammstein; if we add an s to it, it becomes *Du hasst (you hate)*! Kristi Epling (64) stated that he did not like to be ridiculed, but she had never seen him react aggressively. David Proctor (65), who liked him and used to play video games with him, pointed out that he was sadistic when he was playing. Kelly

Beer regarded him as a weirdo who said weird things (66). Megan Morrison (67) noticed that he was always in a hurry and angry. Christopher Walker (68), who considered him a friend of his, said that he was a nice guy, but he refused to buy him a gun because of his dark side. He noticed that he used to do weird things, like writing *I am God* or *fuck the world* on his 1997/1998 school yearbook. He had even shot an unpleasant scene in which he and Klebold had entered a cafeteria, jumped on tables and then shot at students! To summarize, although some of his classmates regarded him as a nice, normal kid, he was quite unpopular because of his dark side.

We could say the same about Dylan, even though students preferred him. For instance, Alisa Owen (69) said that he was a nice guy, whereas Eric was an introverted student with a "very dark" side. Josh Lallement, (70) who used to play with him, stated that he was a nice guy, whereas he did not talk much to Harris. The persons who can tolerate psychopaths are those whose personality is organized at the neurotic level because their egos are strong enough to withstand their narcissism and idiosyncrasies. Thanks to the police records, we realize that most students were not this kind of people but immature ones, which isolated the pair a bit more. For instance, Klebold wanted to befriend other students, but because they were immature, they did not copy the behavior of John Savage (71), who collaborated with him on various plays and who used to speak with him when students were not acting. Moreover, the wrath and antisocial behavior he exhibited did not move them to communicate with him. For example, Mandy Nichols (72) did not like Dylan's paper on the crimes committed by Charles Manson, and Nicole Ziccardi (73) was upset because he kept sneering at people and was violent when he played dodge ball. Christopher Walker declared that he had heard a student say that he had seen Dylan quarreling with someone and going crazy, which was scary (74).

Hence, although they had some acquaintances, they were loners, which prevented them from regarding people as "non-enemies".

D- The last journey.

They were very immature people who had gone through the Oedipus complex, had failed to resolve it and were neither psychotics nor neurotics. Since their personality organization was unstable, they could remain in a semblance of normality only with the help of the outer world. Unfortunately, they were confronted with a major problem in January 1998.

At the end of that month, they tried to steal some electronic equipment in a van. The police caught them, which traumatized them, especially Eric, who wrote (75): "... I do believe what happened on the last Friday night in January 1998 is the most significant event that has changed my life. ... they put me into prison-type bathroom to wait. As I waited, I cried, I hurt, and felt like hell. ... My parents lost all trust in me, and were completely disappointed beyond belief. ... I am seeing a psychologist to help me with my anger problems. ... My parents lost all respect and trust in me and I am slowly regaining it. ...". Must we consider this moment to be the point of no return? Many people have dreamed of finding the factor that leads criminals to kill. Is there one or various factors? We might find the answer here.

It is clear that his amorality impelled him to steal. Then society locked up the little bird for a short period of time, but that's not the point. The point is that his parents began to distrust him, which ruined his self-esteem. This parental rejection induced a nervous breakdown. So he received counseling and started to take antidepressants. In April 1998 he began to write his journal, which might have been suggested by the psychologist. Consequently, he could repress his desire for murder better. On the other hand, some of the students noticed that his behavior changed. Patrice Doyle (76) declared that he started wearing black cloths and boots and became a loner. Unfortunately, she did not specify the dates: she said that it occurred at the beginning of the academic year 1998-1999. Scott Rathburn (77) pointed out that in the middle of the year 1997-1998 he became introverted and did not talk with people anymore. This is a very important piece of information, for they knew each other quite well since they used to play football together. Unfortunately, we cannot say anything about Dylan's state of mind during the same period.

It is impossible to know whether Eric had already planed the massacre as early as the 30th of January 1998, when he was arrested by the police, but we notice that his mood got worse from that event until the middle of April 1999.

The first person to be alarmed by Eric's behaviour might have been Judy Brown, the mother of Brooks Brown, a student at Columbine (78). After the robbery in the van, she met Eric in a mall: he was buying a magazine. She was very upset. So she contacted the police. The date is not known, but the police officers were still investigating the robbery. Some months later, around September 1998, Eric was severely depressed, and Peggy Brown, a teacher (79), noticed that he was quieter, lonelier, and more uncommunicative and that he was always clad in black. In November 1998, he wrote in his journal that he had arms and felt stronger, more confident, and more "God-like" (80). The massacre had been scheduled for April 1999, but he specified that it was avoidable.

Around March 1999, they were extremely depressed and they longed to kill. Eric bought propane tanks in order to make bombs (81), which would be ready to use on the 20th of April 1999 (Adolf Hitler's birthday). Judy Kelly (82), an English teacher, was shocked by an essay written by Dylan, in which he described a man walking through a city and killing all the popular kids. He told her that it was just a story, but she rendezvoused with his parents, who did not panic at all; they just said that it was difficult "to understand kids today". As for Eric, the last entry in his journal is dated April 3, 1999 (83). He felt abandoned by his schoolmates; he stated that they left him out of many fun things and that they never called him; when he asked them if he could join them, they said no to the "weird looking Eric kid". After this date, some tapes show them firing their guns in a forest. The point of no return was reached on the 13th of April 1999, for, in a video (84), he asserted that this was his last week on earth and that he would be shot dead. In his diary, we can also read (85): "... suicide- point to the head with gun." As for Tyler Pearce, he declared (86) that two weeks prior to the shooting, around the 6th of April, they had shot a weird scene in which there were graveyards and skulls. They might have filmed their last will and testament (87) around the same date. However, in her statement (88), Angel Pytlinski put great emphasis on the 13th of April, for she noticed that Eric was severely depressed because his father accused him of taking LSD. As for Dylan, his mood was "very inconsistent".

On the 16th of April, Sergeant Gonzales, from the Marine Corps Recruiting Command, called Eric's parents in order to tell them that Eric could not join the Marines because of his medication (89). We do not know whether he was disappointed or not. On the same day, the owner of Black Jack Pizza appointed him as shift manager, which was good news, but nothing could change his mind (90). On the 19th of April, Eric was sitting on the floor in the hallway; he was writing something on a piece of white paper when someone asked him what he was doing; Nicholas Romanyshyn heard him reply in a normal tone of voice: "plans for tomorrow" (91). On the same day, Eric told Louis Scileppi not to go to the high school for a couple of days (92). As for Dylan, he received a phone call from Andrew Beard about an exchange of baseball players; he answered: "I don't know, I'll think about it and let you know tomorrow" (93). At last, on the morning of the 20th of April 1999, Tyler Pearce (94) noticed that Eric was present at the video production class. Everything had been organized and scheduled; he had organized and scheduled his death, which included the death of his only friend and a massacre in Columbine High School in order to leave a lasting image.

A depressive usually kills himself and his family in order to stop his anxiety and the alleged anxiety of his relatives. Here, it's a bit different, for it's more dreadful, demoniac and primitive. They planned to kill many people in their high school, and we must not overemphasize the place. They spent a lot of time at school, and they met lots of people who kept harming their narcissism. Hence, their arch-enemies were those students. Harris criticized those (95) who did not respect him or rejected him; he wanted to avenge himself (96). Primary narcissism compelled him to become what he called "a god", namely an omnipotent creature that destroys everything, which is why he wanted to destroy his childish world and his school and kill the persons he disliked. His perception of time did not allow him to imagine a larger future for himself; he lived in the present moment. He wanted to experience the joy of being the master of the universe for a while. He had "to leave a lasting image" (97). Did he want to commit suicide in order to stop his anxiety after having been in raptures over his might? Omnipotence is illogical because everything disappears but ecstasy. When he killed himself, he was under the illusion that joy would last forever.

Dylan was explicit about his intentions. Like Eric, he wanted to kill the students who harmed his narcissism, namely the popular kids (98). Then he had to kill himself because life was an unbearable fight against himself and the others (99). He suffered so much that death was the only way to stop the pain and go to a better place (100). Hence, on the 20th of April 1999, at lunchtime, they killed the people they wanted to kill. The students they liked were safe, like John Savage, who was in the library. He knew Dylan and he reported a surrealistic dialogue with Klebold, who concluded it saying: "just get out of here" (101).

The statements are not always accurate because people were stressed, which is why it's almost impossible to know who killed who and for what reason. For instance, Eric was quite racist (102), but, according to John Savage, it was Dylan who killed the black student. They killed some "fresh men", which enables us to recognize Harris's oral sadism (103). They killed pretty girls and boys who wore white caps: the popular kids whom Dylan hated. They killed a mentally retarded person; in Eric's journal we can read (104): "... kill all retards...". If they had wanted to kill any type of person, they would have killed more people without speaking to each other, and they did not do so.

During the shooting, their narcissism was perceivable. Heidi Johnson (105), who was in the library, where most people were killed, said that Dylan was quite silent and smirking. Patricia Stevens added that his eyes were weird (106). Jessica Holliday declared that they both laughed the whole time (107). Eric was frantic: Heidi Johnson noticed that he was bleeding because he had shot himself in the nose, and he kept laughing (108). It was the best day of their lives, the day when they became, at last, proud of themselves. Alas, such omnipotence turned them into crazy monsters.

1. You can read Peter Langman's book: *Why kids kill: Inside the minds of school shooters*, New York, 2009.
2. Sheriff Jefferson County, Columbine documents, *Eric Harris's medical record*, no date.
3. Sheriff Jefferson County, Columbine documents, Harris, Eric, *25 things that make me different*, no date.
4. Karim, Stéphanie, *The Columbine killers*, Doc. en stock, France-Belgium-United kingdom, film, 2007. The hand that touches the tree must be the left hand of Dylan (he was

left-handed), not Eric's.

5. Sheriff Jefferson County, Columbine documents, Harris, Eric, *Journal*, no date. There is also a transcription on Peter Langman's website: www.schoolshooters.info[1].

6. Sheriff Jefferson County, Columbine documents, Harris, Eric, *1998-1999 diary*, Mother's Day.

7. Sheriff Jefferson County, Columbine documents, Harris, Eric, *1997-1998 diary*, last days of May 1998.

8. Suspension points of the diary.

9. The printed word is replaced by *eat*.

10. Sheriff Jefferson County, Columbine documents, Harris, Eric, *Journal*, the 17th of November 1998.

11. Sheriff Jefferson County, Columbine documents, Harris, Eric, *Journal*, the 12th of November 1998.

12. Sheriff Jefferson County, Columbine documents, Epling, Kristi, *Statement*, the 20th of May 1999. She considered that she was a good friend of Eric Harris.

13. Sheriff Jefferson County, Columbine documents, Harris, Eric, *Journal*, the 12th of November 1998.

14. Sheriff Jefferson County, Columbine documents, Harris, Eric, *Journal*, the 20th of May 1998.

15. Sheriff Jefferson County, Columbine documents, Klebold, Dylan, *Journal*, the 3rd of November 1997.

16. Sheriff Jefferson County, Columbine documents, Harris, Eric, *Journal*, the 22nd of November 1998.

17. Sheriff Jefferson County, Columbine documents, Harris, Wayne, *Diary about Eric*, no date.

18. Sheriff Jefferson County, Columbine documents, Harris, Eric, *Try to define yourself*, essay, 12th of October 1998.

---

1. http://www.schoolshooters.info/

19. Sheriff Jefferson County, Columbine documents, Klebold, Dylan, *Journal*, the 21st of May 1997.
20. Sheriff Jefferson County, Columbine documents, Klebold, Dylan, *Journal*, the 23rd of July 1997.
21. Sheriff Jefferson County, Columbine documents, Klebold, Dylan, *Journal*, the 2nd of February 1998.
22. Sheriff Jefferson County, Columbine documents, Harris, Eric, *Good to be bad, bad to be good*, essay, 21st of September 1998.
23. Sheriff Jefferson County, Columbine documents, Harris, Eric, *Journal*, the 29th of July 1998.
24. Sheriff Jefferson County, Columbine documents, Harris, Eric, *Journal*, the 13th of June 1998.
25. Sheriff Jefferson County, Columbine documents, Harris, Eric, *The Nazi culture*, essay, 13th of November 1998.
26. Sheriff Jefferson County, Columbine documents, Harris, Eric, *Journal*, the 12th of April 1998.
27. Sheriff Jefferson County, Columbine documents, Harris, Eric, *Journal*, the 22nd of November 1998: "... I am fucking armed. I feel more confident, stronger, more god-like. ...".
28. Sheriff Jefferson County, Columbine documents, Harris, Eric, *Journal*, the 12th of June 1998.
29. Sheriff Jefferson County, Columbine documents, Harris, Eric, *I am a gun*, poem, no date.
30. Sheriff Jefferson County, Columbine documents, Harris, Eric, *You know what I hate*, poem, no date.
31. Sheriff Jefferson County, Columbine documents, Kelly, Judy, *Statement*, the 25th of May 1999.
32. Sheriff Jefferson County, Columbine documents, Klebold,

Dylan, *Journal*, the 23rd of July 1997.

33. Sheriff Jefferson County, Columbine documents, *Eric Harris's autopsy report*, no date. There were no drugs or alcohol in his blood, only 390ng/ml of Fluvoxamine (Luvox).

34. Sheriff Jefferson County, Columbine documents, *Eric Harris's condemnation file*, various dates (from April to August 1998).

35. Sheriff Jefferson County, Columbine documents, Klebold, Dylan, *Existence box*, drawing, no date.

36. Sheriff Jefferson County, Columbine documents, Klebold, Dylan, *Journal*, the 31st of March 1997.

37. Sheriff Jefferson County, Columbine documents, Klebold, Dylan, *Journal*, the 15th of April 1997.

38. Sheriff Jefferson County, Columbine documents, Klebold, Dylan, *Journal*, the 5th of September 1997.

39. Sheriff Jefferson County, Columbine documents, Harris, Eric, *The shit list*, no date, but he mentioned the month of April 1999.

40. Sheriff Jefferson County, Columbine documents, Klebold, Dylan, *Journal*, the 21st of May 1997.

41. Sheriff Jefferson County, Columbine documents, Klebold, Dylan, *Journal*, the 15th of September 1997.

42. Sheriff Jefferson County, Columbine documents, Harris, Eric, *The similarities between Zeus and I*, essay, 12th of February 1996.

43. Sheriff Jefferson County, Columbine documents, Harris, Eric, *I am a gun*, poem, no date.

44. Sheriff Jefferson County, Columbine documents, Walker, Christopher, *Statement*, the 29th of April 1999. He

considered that he was a friend of Eric.

45. Sheriff Jefferson County, Columbine documents, Harris, Eric, *Journal*, the 20th of May 1998.

46. Sheriff Jefferson County, Columbine documents, Klebold, Dylan, *Journal*, the 5th of September 1997: "... To some I am crazy, it is so clear. ...".

47. Sheriff Jefferson County, Columbine documents, Klebold, Dylan, *Journal*, the 31st of March 1997.

48. Sheriff Jefferson County, Columbine documents, Harris, Eric, *Journal*, the 22nd of November 1998.

49. Sheriff Jefferson County, Columbine documents, Harris, Wayne, *Diary about Eric*, the first of February 1998.

50. Sheriff Jefferson County, Columbine documents, Harris, Eric, *On a van robbery*, police file, the 19th of November 1998: "... My parents lost all respect and trust in me and I am still slowly regaining it...".

51. Sheriff Jefferson County, Columbine documents, Pithinski, Angel, *Statement*, the 3rd of May 1999. He used to work with Eric at Black Jack Pizza. He might refer to something dating back to March or April 1999.

52. Sheriff Jefferson County, Columbine documents, *Dylan Klebold condemnation file*, no date.

53. Sheriff Jefferson County, Columbine documents, Klebold, Dylan, *Journal*, the 2nd of February 1998.

54. Sheriff Jefferson County, Columbine documents, Klebold, Dylan, *Journal*, the 3rd of November 1997.

55. Sheriff Jefferson County, Columbine documents, Klebold, Dylan, *Journal*, the 23rd of July 1997.

56. Sheriff Jefferson County, Columbine documents, Klebold, Dylan, *Journal*, the 15th of April 1997.

57. Sheriff Jefferson County, Columbine documents, Klebold, Dylan, *Journal*, the 31st of March 1997.

58. Sheriff Jefferson County, Columbine documents, Harris, Eric, *Journal*, the 15th of November 1998.

59. Sheriff Jefferson County, Columbine documents, Kelly, Patrick, *Statement*, the 24th of August 1999.

60. Sheriff Jefferson County, Columbine documents, Larson, Kevin, *Statement*, the 29th of April 1999.

61. Sheriff Jefferson County, Columbine documents, Owen, Alisa, *Statement*, the 30th of April 1999.

62. Sheriff Jefferson County, Columbine documents, Brown, Loni, *Statement*, the 6th of May 1999.

63. Sheriff Jefferson County, Columbine documents, Thomas, Adam, *Statement*, the 8th of July 1999.

64. Sheriff Jefferson County, Columbine documents, Epling, Kristi, *Statement*, the 20th of May 1999.

65. Sheriff Jefferson County, Columbine documents, Proctor, David, *Statement*, the 15th of June 1999.

66. Sheriff Jefferson County, Columbine documents, Beer, Kelly, *Statement*, the 26th of May 1999.

67. Sheriff Jefferson County, Columbine documents, Morrison, Megan, *Statement*, the 28th of July 1999.

68. Sheriff Jefferson County, Columbine documents, Walker, Christopher, *Statement*, the 29th of April 1999.

69. Sheriff Jefferson County, Columbine documents, Owen, Alisa, *Statement*, the 30th of April 1999.

70. Sheriff Jefferson County, Columbine documents, Lallement, Josh, *Statement*, the 3rd of May 1999.

71. Sheriff Jefferson County, Columbine documents, Savage, John, *Statement*, no date.
72. Sheriff Jefferson County, Columbine documents, Nichols, Mandy, *Statement*, the 28th of April 1999.
73. Sheriff Jefferson County, Columbine documents, Ziccardi, Nicole, *Statement*, the 12th of May 1999.
74. Sheriff Jefferson County, Columbine documents, Walker, Christopher, *Statement*, the 29th of April 1999.
75. Sheriff Jefferson County, Columbine documents, Harris, Eric, *On a van robbery*, police file, the 19th of November 1998.
76. Sheriff Jefferson County, Columbine documents, Doyle, Patrice, *Statement*, the 4th of May 1999.
77. Sheriff Jefferson County, Columbine documents, Rathburn, Scott, *Statement*, no date.
78. Karim, Stéphanie, *The Columbine killers*, Doc. en stock, France-Belgium-United kingdom, movie, 2007.
79. Sheriff Jefferson County, Columbine documents, Dodd, Peggy, *Statement*, 3rd of May 1999.
80. Sheriff Jefferson County, Columbine documents, Harris, Eric, *Journal*, the 22nd of November 1998.
81. Sheriff Jefferson County, Columbine documents, Thornby, James, *Statement*, 5th of May 1999. The conversation took place before the 7th of March 1999.
82. Sheriff Jefferson County, Columbine documents, Kelly, Judy, *Statement*, 25th of May 1999.
83. Sheriff Jefferson County, Columbine documents, Harris, Eric, *Journal*, the 3rd of April 1999.
84. Sheriff Jefferson County, Columbine documents, *Police's*

description of a video tape by Harris and Klebold, 24th of April 1999.

85. Sheriff Jefferson County, Columbine documents, Harris, Eric, *1998-1999 diary*, written on a page that is dated April 13 and 14, 1999.

86. Sheriff Jefferson County, Columbine documents, Pearce, Tyler, *Statement*, 27th July 1999.

87. www.acolumbinesite.com[2], extract from the basement tapes.

88. Sheriff Jefferson County, Columbine documents, Pytlinski, Angel, *Statement*, 3rd of May 1999.

89. Sheriff Jefferson County, Columbine documents, Gonzales, Mark *Statement*, 28th of April 1999.

90. Sheriff Jefferson County, Columbine documents, Lau, Chris, *Statement*, 26th of April 1999.

91. Sheriff Jefferson County, Columbine documents, Romanyshyn, Nicholas, *Statement*, 13th of May 1999.

92. Sheriff Jefferson County, Columbine documents, Scileppi, Louis, *Statement*, 28th of April 1999.

93. Sheriff Jefferson County, Columbine documents, Beard, Andrew, *Statement*, 28th of May 1999.

94. Sheriff Jefferson County, Columbine documents, Pearce, Tylor, *Statement*, 23th of July 1999.

95. Sheriff Jefferson County, Columbine documents, Harris, Eric, *Journal*, the 3rd of April 1999.

96. Sheriff Jefferson County, Columbine documents, Harris, Eric, *Journal*, the 17th of November 1998.

97. Sheriff Jefferson County, Columbine documents, Harris, Eric, *The shit list*, no date.

---

2. http://www.acolumbinesite.com/

98. Sheriff Jefferson County, Columbine documents, Kelly, Judy, *Statement*, 25th of May 1999.

99. Sheriff Jefferson County, Columbine documents, Klebold, Dylan, *Journal*, the 15th of April 1997.

100. www.acolumbinesite.com[3], extract from the basement tapes.

101. Sheriff Jefferson County, Columbine documents, Savage, John, *Statement*, no date.

102. Sheriff Jefferson County, Columbine documents, Harris, Eric, *diary for the year 1998-1999*, 21st of August 1998: "nigger=darkie=rastus=loon".

103. Sheriff Jefferson County, Columbine documents, Harris, Eric, *Journal*, the 17th of November 1998.

104. Sheriff Jefferson County, Columbine documents, Harris, Eric, *Journal*, the 10th of April 1998.

105. Sheriff Jefferson County, Columbine documents, Johson, Heidi, *Statement*, 11th of June 1999.

106. Sheriff Jefferson County, Columbine documents, Stevens, Patricia, *Statement*, 26th of April 1999.

107. Sheriff Jefferson County, Columbine documents, Holliday, Jessica, *Statement*, 21st of April 1999.

108. Sheriff Jefferson County, Columbine documents, Johson, Heidi, *Statement*, 11th of June 1999.

---

3. http://www.acolumbinesite.com/

Chapter 10

Hell.

Years elapsed, resentment weakened, and memories are fading away, but the unbearable misunderstanding keeps on upsetting nations. The Second World War was hell on earth, and one must discover the psychological process that led to that apocalypse.

Years elapsed and many people strove to understand what had happened. The knowledgeable historians failed because of their complete ignorance of psychology and psychopathology. Psychologists, psychoanalysts and psychiatrists failed because they wanted to find insane culprits in order to deny that reason, or at least normalcy, can cause such a disaster. Hence, the Germans could not be responsible, since a madman and some of his followers were guilty. Honestly, can sane, righteous people agree to obey a lunatic? Can intelligent people become the obedient disciples of a monster? In order to answer those questions, one must get rid of certainties.

A- Adolf Hitler.

Fortunately, the main participant in this drama wrote a kind of autobiography when he was in prison. He published *Mein Kampf* in 1925-1926 (1). Rudolf Hess helped him and acted as a secretary. This book is so homogeneous that one realizes that only one person wrote it; Hess did not influence Hitler, all the more so because he was stupider than he and was a bad orator. Furthermore, Hitler, who was a dedicated propagandist, used to write all his speeches. Until the end, he thought in the same way: in his last will and testament, which he dictated to his secretary Traudle Junge (2), he used the same ideas, grammar and vocabulary. In Leni Riefenstahl's *Triumph des Willens* (3), his political speeches exhibit the same style and state of mind. Hence, this document is authentic.

Unlike the families of Foucault and Sartre, his was not deeply dysfunctional. Even though he does not remember his childhood very well (4), he does not criticize his parents; he wrote (5): "... I respected my father, but I loved my mother. ..." This might be true, but we know that his father was brutal. Hence, many ears later, his son does not blame him, and he does not display hatred when he speaks of him, even though Alois Hitler was not easy-going: he gave orders and Adolf had to obey them. However, as Adolf grew up, his father had less influence over him. For instance, Alois pictured his son as a civil servant, whereas Adolf wanted to become a painter. Whatever the divergence of opinion, in 1925, at the age of 36, he still wants to be as strong-willed as his father in order to be successful; he writes (6): "... I had decided to surmount these obstacles, having the picture of my father constantly before my mind, who had raised himself by his own efforts to the position of a civil servant though he was the poor son of a village shoemaker. ...". We may infer that the toughness he recommends comes from his father's attitude towards life.

Another man had an influence over the construction of Hitler's weak superego: Dr. Leopold Poetch, who was a history teacher at the Linz Realschule, where Hitler studied. In his book, he describes him, and he does not conceal his admiration for him, which is quite surprising, for, most of the time, he scorns old men; the old history teacher is portrayed in this way (7): "... An elderly gentleman with a decisive manner but a kindly heart, he was a very attractive speaker and was able to inspire us with his own enthusiasm. Even today I cannot recall without emotion that venerable personality whose enthusiastic exposition of history so often made us entirely forget the present and allow ourselves to be transported as if by magic into the past. ...". It's a pity we don't have any information about the history classes taught by Dr. Poetch, for Hitler's arguments and way of speaking might have been his.

However, the presence of a father figure does not imply a well-organized superego. Actually, the father must be virtuous and explain what good and evil are. As for Hitler, he knows what evil is, but his definition of good is either inaccurate or non-existent.

In *Mein Kampf*, evil appears when he describes his life in Vienna, and it is associated with the Jews (8). According to him, the Jews compel some white girls to prostitute themselves so that they may earn their living. So he considers that they are devils (9). A few pages further on (10), he states that interbreeding between humans is bad and that it is a sin which must be avenged.

In another part of his book, the middle class is also associated with evil (11). He says that its members are stupid and immoral when they do not accede to the legitimate requests of the working class. Hitler's moral sense is more intelligible when he talks about himself; he declared (12): "...when the waves of poison gas enveloped me and began to penetrate my eyes, the thought of becoming permanently blind unnerved me; but the voice of conscience cried out immediately: poor miserable fellow, will you start howling when there are thousands of others whose lot is a hundred times worse than yours? ...". His self is strong enough to accept the existence of others and to be quite empathic, which enables him to interact with people. It is clear that he is not a mentally disturbed psychopath.

However, his superego is quite inoperative: morality does not allow him to perceive reality as it is, nor does it facilitate social relationships. In the last chapters of *Mein Kampf* (13), one notices that he is puzzled since he writes that morality can lead a schoolboy to betray his schoolmates in order to help the teacher to find the truth (when pupils misbehave). According to him, betrayal is a serious matter that can turn a young informer into a scoundrel. He does not realize that the truth enables people to be in tune with reality.

Hitler's ego ideal was problematic too. In fact, individuals must resolve the Oedipus complex in order to realize that people who are different form themselves can be good too. Since Hitler's personality was not organized at the neurotic level, he could not comprehend that. So we must study the nature of his ego ideal so that we may understand what happened in Germany during the 1930s and 1940s.

Hitler was obsessed with the Jews. One could even believe that he was a paranoid who behaved in a paranoid way. Ernst Kretschmer had made that mistake: he thought that very immature people were paranoid, which is why he had invented a disease called relational paranoia. That being said, those people can use psychotic defenses. As for Hitler, we cannot mistake him for a paranoid because he did not feel persecuted by the Jews. In fact, when he was in Vienna (from 1908 to 1913), he did not even hate them; he wrote (14): "... In the Jew I still saw only a man who was of a different religion, and therefore, on grounds of human tolerance, I was against the idea that he should be attacked because he had a different faith. ...". One cannot perceive primary narcissism here, for there is no violence! Nevertheless, this does not show why he turned the Jews into devils who prevented him from determining his ego ideal. He even provides enigmatic information (15): "... My ideas about antisemitism changed also in the course of time, but that was the change which I found most difficult. It cost me a greater internal conflict with myself, and it was only after a struggle between reason and sentiment that victory began to be decided in favor of the former. ..." When individuals have not lost touch with reality, psychopathology cannot explain everything, and when there are quite intelligent, social, economic, cultural and political factors must be taken into consideration. Actually, Hitler's internal conflict, which is rather conscious but not really understood, is a struggle between what he thinks and feels and the point of view of Austrian society, something he wants to integrate into his self. When people are not intelligent enough, social pressure (which must be internalized so that they may become efficient members of society) can be harmful. Adolf Hitler must have had great difficulty internalizing such ideas, all the more so because at first he distrusted newspapers and anti-Semitic leaflets (16): "... the statements made were partly superficial and the proofs extraordinarily unscientific. ..." He needed science to get closer to the truth; it prevented him from losing touch with reality and enabled him to deal with it. Hence, he gathered information, spoke to many Jews and tried to discover Jewish depravities in order to justify antisemitism and then propagate it. Hitler was fascinated by language and the power of speech. He was not the typical dictator, who imposes his opinions on people, for he wanted to persuade them that he was right (17).

At the beginning of his career, he was already a dedicated propagandist. In her 1935 film about the rise of national socialism, Leni Riefenstahl (18) portrays a talented orator. She filmed some of the Nazi meetings, and one realizes that he knew how to communicate with the crowd; he even took into consideration the speed of thought of the crowd. Like the theatre actors, he used to speak loud and clear (whereas he did not in private); he knew how to mesmerize the audience. Dictators speak like marble tombs; the sentences are short, simple and definitive; they are not poets but soldiers; sentences are orders; they don't want to cajole; the answer can only be "yes, Your Excellency".

Hitler spent hours writing and repeating his speeches. He did so before some Jews, but he always failed to persuade them (19); he declared: "... a Jew can never be rescued from his fixed notions. ... within my small circle I talked to them until my throat ached and my voice grew hoarse. I believed that I could finally convince them of the danger inherent in the Marxist follies. But I only achieved the contrary result. ...". Here, as said Carl Jung (20), there is a cultural incompatibility between Wagnerian Hitler and the other cultures. Even Jung, who is not that different in that respect, is impressed by the Hitlerian ceremonies. Hitler can only be understood by the Germans; he does not understand the non-Germans.

The impossibility of persuading them leads to intolerance and hatred. His abhorrence of them is kindled by falsehood, which is an argument that immature people keep using; he writes (21): "...I do not know what amazed me the more – the abundance of their verbiage or the artful way in which they dressed up their falsehoods. I gradually came to hate them. ... How futile it was to try to win over such people with argument, seeing that their very mouths distorted the truth...".

Consequently, his ego ideal is profoundly anti-Semitic and anti-Marxist, which he regards as synonyms. The unification of the German race must be accomplished (22). According to him, the race must remain pure because, in the wild, interbreeding always leads to sterility (23), and superior species lose their leadership. The German nation needs, of course, a large territory so that people may cultivate it and produce all the food they need (24). However, he did not describe the man whom he wished to resemble: was he tall and blond, a kind of replica of the muscular statues sculpted by Arno Breker? We only know that he had to be tough and German.

This idealistic world and his idiosyncrasies are not counterbalanced by his last girlfriend's attitude of mind.

Eva Braun is not an intelligent lady. She is an immature, pretty blond girl who wants to follow her dreams: go to Hollywood and become a movie star. Unlike her famous boyfriend, she did not write lots of pages, but there are a few films about her, her family and her acquaintances (25). We also have the testimony of Frau Junger, Hitler's secretary (26).

It has to be borne in mind that such men must deal with reality so that they may remain humane and sane. Since Hitler's ego ideal endangered others, a girlfriend with a neurotic personality would have put great emphasis on morality, which would have prevented him from losing touch with reality. Unfortunately, Eva was a daydreamer, and her demeanor unsettled him a bit more.

For instance, she committed suicide in 1932, at the beginning of their love affair. He must have been shocked, all the more so because he had been traumatized by his niece's death in 1931. He offered her a dog! On the 28th of May 1935, she swallowed many sleeping pills. He offered her a house in Munich. There were not on the same wavelength: she wanted to marry him, whereas he didn't.

However, his mistress and acquaintances succeeded in creating an artificial, idealistic family life. Her movies, especially those that were shot at the Berghof, show this fairy tale in which people, children and nature are beautified. The protagonist is not he but she! So we see her picking irises in the summertime and skiing and skating in the wintertime. Sometimes he appears; he is not the Fuhrer anymore but a small, blue-eyed middle-aged man who plays with Blondi, his dog. The Battle of Stalingrad and the concentration camps are but improbabilities. Life at the Berghof is idyllic and unreal. Unfortunately, reality resurfaces and turns Eva's life into a nightmare. Thanks to Frau Junge, we almost witness her last fight against an upsetting reality.

Actually, at the end of the war, the Russians bombed Germany: it was hell on earth. In order to ignore this dreadful present, Eva organized a party. There was only one record left: they played it and danced to "Blutrote Rosen". According to Hitler's secretary, she was almost hysterically happy, it looked like the Dance of Death; it was phantasmagorical. Frau Junge felt so bad that she left the hall.

But Eva is not the only person who refuses to confront reality. Hitler's courtiers behave in the same way.

For example, his secretaries, during the Battle of Stalingrad, lunched with him and never dared to allude to it (26). Himmler himself only spoke once of the concentration camps: he extolled the way they were managed and did not refer to the massacres. The word "Jew" was never uttered, and when the Fuhrer crossed Germany, at the end of the war, the widows of his train were covered: he did not see the towns on fire or people dying.

As far as we can judge, the only person who dared to speak of the situation of the Jews is Henriette Von Schirach. Actually, she spent some time in the Netherlands and saw how they were treated; she was so shocked that she returned to the Berghof in order to tell Hitler what she had seen. He did not appreciate her "emotional" point of view. She was never invited again. Frau Junge concluded that it was impossible to discuss serious issues with him. Even at the end of the war, he was not more lucid. When he dictated his last will and testament, he kept repeating that the Jews and the communist were dangerous people. He was obsessed with his ego ideal, and the more the outer world wanted to destroy it, the more he wanted to protect it. I do not know whether his self was completely dominated by his ego ideal, but it is clear that his mind was a kind of abstraction that ignored human suffering. Technically, he was not insane, since he did not wish to redesign the outer world; he just wanted it to embody his ego ideal. He was an idealist. So reality had to comply with his volition. The ego ideal is inhumane because perfection destroys grief. Since there is no pain, there is no pity, which leads man to become a monster.

B- The courtiers.

The first circle of Hitler's courtiers is also composed of immature people (27), which is understandable: those idealists think and behave in the same way. Nonetheless, among the thousands of pages that describe the brutalities committed by the men who were put on trial in Nuremberg (28), the image of a person with an obsessional personality appears: Hjalmar Schacht, ex-Economic Secretary to the Treasury. On the other hand, two defendants, Hess and Streicher, could have been regarded as psychotics, but they were examined by psychologists and psychiatrists, who declared that they were sane, which does not mean that they were right.

As for Rudolf Hess, for instance, Gustave Gilbert, the psychologist who examined him, was biased against him (29). Besides, his complete ignorance of politics, culture and sociology prevented him from perceiving reality as it was. However, his description of Hess's mental state is accurate (30); he said: "... there is no kind of evidence of paralogism. ... the delusions, from which he suffered periodically while in England, cannot be considered as manifestations of paranoid schizophrenia, and must be recognized as the expression of a psychogenic paranoiac reaction, that is, the psychologically comprehensible reaction of an unstable (psychologically) personality to the situation (the failure of his mission, arrest and incarceration). ...". Sometimes, when people are very immature, they use psychotic defenses, especially hallucinations, which is what Hess did. Gilbert did not consider that he was a psychotic because there were no paralogisms (arguments that are unintentionally invalid), which are symptoms of a paranoia, not of paranoid schizophrenia, a sort of schizophrenia, but this is not an important mistake. Consequently, he regarded Hess as a psychopath (31).

As for Streicher, he was so stupid that Dr. Marx, his lawyer, asked for a psychiatric evaluation (32). Some days later, all the psychiatrists said that he was sane (33). Personally, I did not notice any psychotic symptom in his testimony.

Hence, it seems that Hitler's courtiers were immature people, except one.

It is noticeable that they admired the Fuhrer. Although they did not dwell on the matter, one realizes that their fascination with him led them to believe in him and to lose their objectivity.

The stupider they were, the more they were dazzled by him. Streicher's testimony is a perfect illustration of this. He met him in 1921, when the party was but a small group of agitators. At that time, very few people attended the meetings. Although there were no enthusiastic worshipers electrified by the demigod's utterances, Streicher was already mesmerized (34); he wrote: "... I saw this man shortly before midnight, after he had spoken for 3 hours, drenched, in perspiration, radiant. My neighbor said he thought he had seen a halo around his head; and I, gentlemen, experienced something that transcended the commonplace. ...".

In Joachim Von Ribbentrop's statement we find a kind of primitive, instinctual reaction to Hitler's appearance; he said (35): "... Adolf Hitler made a considerable impression on me even then. I noticed particularly his blues eyes in his generally dark appearance...". He was easily impressed by the small man, for he had a good relationship with men: he almost venerated the archetype of maleness, namely his father (36). However, he was also interested by Hitler's opinions and was impressed by his intelligence, his unshakable will and his strong personality. He believed that he could save Germany (37), a country that was in disarray because of the Treaty of Versailles.

Even Herman Goering had been impressed by the Fuhrer. Actually, he liked him because they both agreed on the same issues (38); he said: "... This conviction was spoken word for word as if from my own soul. ..."

One realizes that immature people easily regarded Hitler as the savior of the fatherland, a hero with whom all the Germans had to identify so that they might boost their self-esteem, which had been ruined by the Treaty of Versailles. Nevertheless, if we exclude people with a psychotic personality, for they are too insane to play a part in society, a high percentage of immature Germans does not explain the whole process, since societies are mainly organized by persons with an obsessional personality. Fortunately, the attitude of Schacht, who was a man with an obsessional personality, enables us to discover the interactions between reason and half-madness.

He was introduced to Hitler by Goering (39), and there were a few cultural differences. First of all, they did not really speak the same language! People with an obsessional personality speak in a certain manner: they use simple words, pronounce them correctly, and get to the point, avoiding theatricality. When they write, their prose is stark and unsentimental unless their personality contains hysterical traits, but it was not the case with Schacht, for he found Mein Kampf verbose (40) and he detested Hitler's German (41); he said: "... It is a book written in the worst kind of German...".

As a matter of fact, they had almost nothing in common: he was a Freemason (42), a cosmopolitan, a democrat, a humanitarian, a Christian, and an educated person who spent much time in the United States and who considered that Hitler was but a "half-educated man". Hence, the first meeting could have been a fiasco, but it was not (43); he declared: "... What he said concerned national questions, in which he agreed absolutely with us. No extravagant demands were stated... In social questions Hitler expressed a number of good ideas; he was especially intent on avoiding class struggle and on eliminating strikes... There was no demand for abolishing private enterprise...". He met someone who was not stupid, but there is no trace of admiration, even though he shared some of his views.

A few years later, in 1934, he agreed to assume the role of Economic Secretary to the Treasury. His opinion had already evolved. Since he was rather worried, he asked Hitler whether the Jews would get into trouble; he answered that they would remain

(44) "active in domestic economy in the same way as before". This might have been the reason why he became a member of the Cabinet. Some year had passed and the Fuhrer was not a half-educated man anymore. Schacht was surprised by his knowledge and the way he used it in debates, discussions and speeches. He even added (45): "... No doubt he was a man of genius in certain respects. He had sudden ideas of which nobody else had thought and which were at times useful in solving great problems, sometimes with astounding simplicity, sometimes, however, with equally astounding brutality. He was a mass psychologist of really diabolical genius. ...He was a man of unbending energy, of a will power which overcame all obstacles...". He, too, was impressed by him, even though he was aware of his limitations as a human being. Nonetheless, his superego told him that evil was not absent from the pact. We realize that if he did not admire him, he regarded him as an intelligent man, which moved him to compromise his principles: sometimes a sane man can be the guilty party. Schacht was the guilty party, but he changed his mind, became a partisan, opposed Hitler and the regime, ended up in a concentration camp and was captured by the Americans, who put him on trial. Many persons with an obsessional personality might have been in the same situation; mature and immature people deceived themselves in the same way!

Unlike Schacht, Hitler's colleagues acted in accordance with their ego ideals, which led to a disaster.

I wish I knew Himmler's ego ideal, for he played an important role in this tragedy. Unfortunately, he was so secretive that there is no information about it. As for Joseph Goebbles, he was much more talkative than he. So in his speeches and writings his vulnerable narcissism shows through. However, there is no tangible image of his ego ideal. There is just an animosity towards the Jews, which shows that his ego ideal was unreal, immoral, and impulsive.

There is more information about Von Schirach's anti-Semitic ego ideal. He was the head of the Hitler Youth. During the trial, he spoke about his own youth (46). His testimony shows that he was still an idealistic teenager. Very immature, but not completely antisocial, he enjoyed being with young people like him. He mentioned the existential angst of the young Germans after World War One. It is self-evident that he wanted to find his purpose in life. He emphasized that the young felt totally hopeless about the future, for, even when students had a diploma, they were doomed to become proletarians. As for the others, since they did not find an apprenticeship, they were unemployed and poor. Consequently, he read some books in order to find the hero who would save him and become a role model. He did not choose Goethe but Henry Ford (47). His hero was an American magnate whom he regarded as a paragon and the symbol of America. Hence, the young Baldur Von Schirach read the anti-Semitic books Ford published (48); he declared: "... The decisive anti-Semitic book I read at that time... was Henry Ford's book, *The international Jew*; I read it and became anti-Semitic. ...". This is really the characteristic of that period: antisemitism was so common that the upper class, which served as a model for the rest of society, was also anti-Semitic and had a bad influence on simple-minded social inferiors like Von Schirach. Social pressure brainwashed him, and he was so immature that he could not find the truth in another way.

The first circle was not only composed of aggressive anti-Semitic men. For instance, Herman Goering was an eccentric whose ego ideal was ordinary. Actually, he is a good example of the lost generation, but he was not as depressed as the characters portrayed by Fitzgerald. In fact, he struggled against the consequences of the war to recover his self-esteem (49) by means of the recovery of national pride. His ego ideal was aristocratic and peaceful: he was not a mass murderer (50) but a pilot at a time in which planes were unsafe. He was so courageous that he received the "Pour le Mérite" (this medal was awarded to Germany's highest-scoring aces). On the other hand, his ego ideal was not racist; Koern, a witness, even said that he had totally different views on the Jewish problem and that he was a moderate (51). Goering told the jury that he had never considered that a race was superior to another (52). He wanted to look like a modern aristocrat, and he hunted deer (he was Grand Huntsman), collected works of art, and helped the working class (53). According to him, the National Socialist Party was an organization that fought for ideals which he shared; it was composed of remarkable idealistic people whom he admired (54). All the Nazi leaders were not impulsive mass murderers, but most of them wanted to fortify their self-esteem.

Their superegos were embryonic. Since Schacht's personality was organized at the neurotic level, he tended towards righteousness. His superego was operative, but the world was so chaotic at the end of the 1930s that he believed that a coup d'état was necessary to get rid of a dangerous regime. The scruples he had about death disappeared and he even thought that murder was legitimate (55). Persons with an obsessional personality rarely behave in this way; at times, they consider that murder is acceptable when it is aimed at protecting innocent people.

As for Goering, contrary to Gilbert's opinion, he was not amoral (56). For instance, Bodenschatz, a liaison officer, declared that the Reichsmarschall was aware that war was awful (57), which is why he was a pacifist and did not want Germany to go to war. He was intelligent enough to realize that life is fragile. Historians emphasized the role he played in the deportation and death of the Jews, but the sources and the way he lived show us another reality. Of course, he signed documents, but he might have believed that the Jews had to leave Germany, not that they would be killed. Moreover, the tragedy was concealed by the enigmatic Himmler, who signed all the documents, who visited the camps and who appointed Hoess as commandant of Auschwitz. During the trial, Goering stated that he did not know what was occurring; so did the other defendants; they were all shocked and surprised by the documentary on this topic. Reichsmarschall Goering never visited a camp, and he clearly did not have much information; Bodenschatz declared (58): "... I never heard of the atrocities. The very first time I heard was last year, when I reported to Reich Marshal —to be exact it was the middle of March 1945... The Reich Marshal told me during the lunch that very many Jews must have perished there and that we should have to pay dearly for it. ...". Besides, before Sir David Maxwell Fyfe, Britain's chief prosecutor, he defended the Fuhrer and stated that he had no knowledge of those atrocities. Maxwell Fyfe retorted that he was very much surprised that, except Himmler and perhaps Kaltenbrunner, no politician knew what was going on. Goering repeated that Hitler didn't know anything. He himself knew that a few Jews had been mistreated, but he believed that they had been deported, which means that they had emigrated to another country (59). This argument with Maxwell Fyfe shows that he was perfectly aware of the enormity of the crime, even if he lied about the role he had played, which is not that certain. However, we perceive his superego better when he speaks of the judiciary. One may easily mistake him for a person with a neurotic personality, for he differentiated strictly men from women. It is clear that he used to protect women. In case of rape, he used to confirm the death sentence, but when a women committed a crime, he never confirmed it. His sense of justice compelled him to confirm the death sentences when the members of the German air forces mistreated the population of the occupied territories (60). Hence, Goering's superego was quite operative.

Those of Hitler's courtiers were weaker. A man like Goebbels (61) had a poor understanding of good and evil. One perceives their immaturity when they speak of their fathers, for the way they regarded them is puerile. For instance, Joachim Von Ribbentrop (62) declared that he venerated his. Even though the others did not refer to their fathers, the way they obeyed orders given by father figures such as Hitler and Himmler connotes the same psychological characteristic. In fact, since their personalities were not organized at the neurotic level, the superego of the father had not been incorporated into the psyche of the child as he was resolving the Oedipus complex. So their immaturity compelled them to look for a male external superego, all the more so because they had difficulty understanding the outer world. These two factors explain their dependence on hierarchy and why they obeyed cruel orders. Furthermore, since they were immature enough to believe that those father figures were righteous and omniscient, they did not dare to rebel.

Hence, we realize that most of the dignitaries of the Nazi Party were mentally unbalanced. All of them were not able to govern any country, although all of them were not amoral. Politicians must be sane and mature, for it is they who are to fight with the Four Horsemen of the Apocalypse.

C- The Four Horsemen of the Apocalypse.

The situation soon deteriorated. On the 9th of November 1938, during the Night of Broken Glass, the Germans vented their anger. The rest of the world began to look upon them as monster. Whatever the responsibility the German people bears for the butchery, there was so much secrecy that one must admit that some persons are guiltier than others.

The Holocaust was supervised by Himmler. The Reich Minister of the Interior signed so many documents and made so many decisions that one may doubt Hitler's culpability, even though a few witnesses stated that Himmler had said that he acted in accordance with orders given by the Fuhrer. Actually, Lammers's statement is extraordinarily important, but after so many months of trial, the judges wanted to give Goering the maximum possible sentence and were convinced that all of them were liars, which is why nobody really listened to what he said (63).

Upset by the way things turned out, he met Himmler in order to talk about the *Final Solution to the Jewish Question*. Himmler stated that it was Hitler himself who had ordered him to implement this policy, but then he added that it was Heydrich and his successor who had been ordered to do that. Then he asserted that the Jews had to be "evacuated from Germany" (64). In 1942, Lammers wrote to Hitler on the issue and received a report in which the Fuhrer declared that he had "given Himmler the order for evacuation" (65), but he did not want to have further discussions about the Jewish problem during the war. However, these evacuations were bizarre. In 1943, Lammers heard a rumor that the Jews were being killed (66). He asked Himmler whether this was true or not. Himmler denied that there were legal killings. Then he asked the Fuhrer the same question; he responded (67): "I shall later on decide where these Jews will be taken and in the meantime they are being cared for there". Then Hitler repeated what Himmler had said about the absence of legal killings. Nevertheless, Lammers believed that Himmler knew that he would come, which is why he had arranged that Hitler would say the same thing. It is clear that Himmler – who had organized the extermination of the Jews in the concentration camps – concealed everything and was the main culprit. Himmler was so manipulative and secretive that it seems that Hitler often repeated what he told him without being aware of what was going on. Hitler was obsessed with the destruction of communism, not with the rest. His attitude toward France proves that his hatred was not that primitive: he was able to restrain his desire for murder, and he did not destroy the country that had almost destroyed his!

Bodenschatz's statement corroborates this impression. He asserted that neither Hitler nor Goering spoke of the concentration camps in his presence, whereas Himmler, according to the information the defendants who knew him very well gave him, alluded to this issue and kept saying that the Jews were not exterminated (68). Hitler never denied this fact, for he never spoke of it! If he knew about it, it seems incredible that he never made a slip of the tongue while he was talking to his colleagues, all the more so because he hated the Jews. Even a person with Hysterical Personality Organization cannot lie so well about such an atrocity. Hitler was but an immature man: he could not control his emotions that well (which is why he had clashed with Henriette Von Schirach). As for Himmler, who was an immature man too, each time he had to face the truth, which was disturbing, he rejected it.

Hoess, the commandant of Auschwitz, helped Himmler to exterminate the Jews. He was very obtuse. Gustave Gilbert (69) wrote that he was quite matter-of-fact and apathetic and that he kept to himself. In the past, he had already shown that he could be violent, for, in 1923, he had been involved in a political crime (70). In his memoirs (71), he admitted that he knew what hatred was and that he had already experienced it. Since he regarded Himmler as a holy man (72), he obeyed him slavishly: he was as silent as the grave. Himmler had even ordered him to conceal the information from Glücks (73), his superior. However, his wife was in the know. His conception of morality was absurd: he ordered soldiers to kill thousands of people but considered that robbery was a sin (74). He put emphasis on the immorality of the gypsies, who could not admit that they had to be punished for having misbehaved. Hence, his superego was weak and inoperative. Actually, what he regarded as bad served as a catalyst for hatred and justified murder. Since he was on the verge of lunacy, he kept projecting his violent feelings onto others in order to remain the good guy who destroys the outer world, which is seen as evil. It was primary narcissism that shaped his personality: he described barbarous acts without exhibiting emotion. He justified his demeanor by saying that the only way to bear such a burden was to stifle emotions. This immature man probably used psychotic defenses to prevent psychosis. He might have been extremely depressed (75). Technically, he was not insane, but he had lost touch with reality.

The fierce physicians who were tried at Nuremberg provided more information about the factors that led them to consider that human beings were but flesh. It is self-evident that biologists and physicians study physical and chemical manifestations, but this does not prevent them from regarding man as a creature that thinks. During the war, they carried out experiments that were not always aimed at preserving life, and they killed many inmates in a most barbaric way. All of them said that they only experimented on criminals who had been sentenced to death, but we know that most of them had not (76). They also stated that they had volunteered; can we consider that an inmate who knows that he or she may die volunteers? They were terribly insincere and crueler than Hoess or Himmler. Consequently, most of them were certainly very immature people who used psychotic defenses. Unfortunately, the quality of the information is poor and there is none about Mengele, who was the main culprit. However, Kurt Brandt provided important information.

Along with Morel, he was Hitler's physician. He had been appointed as head of the euthanasia program. He had to organize the murder of people who were not accepted by Nazi society, namely the mentally disabled. In his final statement, like the others, he tried to prove his innocence by blaming the hierarchy: he had but obeyed orders. Then he declared (78): "... I did so with the deepest conviction, just as it is my conviction today, that it was right. Death can mean deliverance. Death is life –just as much as birth. It was never meant to be murder. ..." He was amoral, for he believed that it was right and proper to kill someone without his or her consent. He did not realize that the jury would be horrified by what he said. Moreover, he did not know the difference between life and death! The resolution of the Oedipus complex allows the individual to fully understand how life is precious; since immature people failed, they cannot really comprehend that. According to him, death could mean deliverance! It sounds like a fascination for death, which depressed people have. Kurt Brand was hanged in 1948.

Were the members of the Einsatzgruppen, the death squads, as immature as he? There is no information about the soldiers, but there is some about the officers, which is interesting because they planned and carried out the massacres according to their political believes. Their involvement in the butchery is total: they caused bloodshed in Russia and Europe.

More than in any other part of the Nazi state, we find obedient immature people here. For example, Blodel, who was not really talkative, just declared that he obeyed the orders of the General (79). So did Naumann (80), who was overwhelmingly dependent on General Von Schenckendorff. Unable to distinguish good from evil, he regarded him as a substitute father he obeyed slavishly. His statement is very important because he was aware that he was the little one, the child, whereas Von Schenckendorff was the adult (81). He was a successful immature man since he had found a father figure that enabled him to mature. Moreover, in the army, he found the adequate remedy for his self-esteem: each time he fulfilled his duty, his superiors congratulated him and gave him a medal sometimes. He did not care about the people he killed; he just wanted to obey the commands given by the Fuhrer.

As for Ohlendorf, whose superego was also inoperative (82), he had perfectly understood how to take away the responsibility from the soldiers so that they might perpetrate the crimes without being traumatized (83); he said: "... the aim was that the individual leaders and men should be able to carry out the executions in a military manner acting on orders and should not have to make a decision of their own; it was, to all intents and purposes, an order which they were to carry out. ...". Once again the leader was the father who told his son to obey unconditionally. In that anaclitic society, this was an efficient method, for people wanted that, all the more so because they were not intelligent enough to fully understand themselves and others: obedience destroys the whys and wherefores.

It is clear that each member of German society did not kill Jews or partisans. However, the Germans were so stupid that they voted for the Nazis; their idealism and expectations enabled those politicians to perpetrate the most dreadful crimes ever committed. After the war, people like Hannah Arendt were amazed to find out that these criminals were ordinary people. They did not realize that normalcy is neither reason nor humanity. It is a kind of average of people's behavior. It can never be extremely psychotic because psychosis is too different from reality, which is why it cannot handle it. It cannot be neurotic, for there are not so many people whose personalities are organized at the neurotic level. Hence, normalcy is anaclitic. Hanna Arendt did not realize that normal people committed extraordinary crimes because normalcy is dangerous.

D- Primal violence.

The more they fought, the more ruthless they became. When the Germans invaded Russia, barbarity spread and conscience was defeated. It seems that they all became schizophrenics: they opened Pandora's Box in order to release death and insanity, which turned the soldiers into automatons that dismembered the Russians. Almost half of the persons who died during World War II were killed on the Eastern Front. The combatants regressed to the lowest level of humanity: a struggle for survival, a psychotic battle between the good inside and the harmful outside. Although most soldiers were not psychotics, they used the same defenses because persecution is the logical response to mass destruction.

Joseph Stalin, who was an immature man, decided on military strategy and supervised all the important battles between Russia and Nazi Germany. Unfortunately, his writings do not enable us to explain the psychogenesis of his immaturity. An acquaintance of his described his attitude of mind, but we cannot say that Trotsky is a reliable source! However, when Iosif Vissarionovich Dzhugashvili was 17 (in 1895), he published some poems. Although the language is quite artificial, once translated into English, we discover his mental state. In the poem entitled *Morning*, he tells the story of a man who returns to his village to tell the truth, which Stalin calls reason. The inhabitants don't want to listen to him or accept what he has to reveal; they poison him in order to destroy this annoying reality, saying (84): "Damn you! Drink! Drain it to the bottom, your song is strange to us, your truth we do not need". A person with a neurotic personality would have written the opposite. Moreover, these lines sounded like a prophecy: his whole life long, he killed the men who tried to tell him that the regime was objectively dysfunctional. The most famous one was Leon Trotsky, who was killed by a Russian secret agent when he was in Mexico. On the other hand, in the same poem, there is a direct link between telling the truth and self-respect. In fact, the poor unfortunate is supposed to be treated as a hero, but the confrontation with reality infuriates the villagers, who kill him. At the age of seventeen, Stalin had failed to resolve the Oedipus complex. No Oedipal characteristic could make him realize how precious life is. In his writings, we only find a problematic self-esteem and poetical violence when the outer world tries to tell him the truth. Nonetheless, there are no hallucinations or persecutory delusions, which proves that he was not a psychotic.

Nevertheless, some documents show that he was on the verge of lunacy. For instance, there is a speech in which he calls Hitler a cannibal (85), which makes the audience laugh. Was it a joke? I am not so sure, for the idea reappears in a humorless letter (86) which reads: "... National and racial chauvinism is a vestige of the misanthropic customs of the period of cannibalism. Antisemitism, as an extreme form of racial chauvinism, is the most dangerous vestige of cannibalism. ...". Oral sadism is a characteristic of schizophrenia which manifests itself in acts, not in words. Here a man whose personality organization is less primitive exhibits a fear which may be the most important part of his mentality. The extreme violence that comes from the oral-biting phase, and violence in general, characterized Stalin's behavior, especially in wartime, when the war turned into a psychotic explosion which unleashed primal violence. Stalin's primitive wrath is visible in the speeches he delivered during the war; on the 1st of May 1942, he said (87): "... The men have become more embittered and more ruthless. They have learned to hate the German fascist invader in earnest. They have realized that you cannot defeat an enemy without having learned to hate him form the bottom of your heart. ...". This echoes the opinion about the necessity of hatred that Hitler expressed while he was speaking to Henriette Von Schirach. Like him, he was not a psychotic because his anger was kindled by a genuine attack and he wanted to kill only the aggressors, not everybody (88).

He was more obsessed with self-respect than Hitler, which moved him to harm everybody's narcissism. Hence, he kept calling the Germans scoundrels, villains, butchers (89) and wild beasts; he wrote (90): "... these men, destitute of conscience and honor, these men with the morals of beasts, have the insolence to call for extermination of the great Russian nation. ....". If we perceive primary narcissism, there is no trace of secondary narcissism: he was the archetype of the misanthropist. Besides, he was too immature to know what conscience and morals meant: political murder and concentration camps epitomized his amorality. Conscience and morals were words he used to belittle the Germans, not to describe something he understood.

Moreover, like a classic immature man, he used to act in accordance with his ego ideal. In his speeches and writings, glory is everywhere (91), and it is not really difficult to picture what he regarded as a hero; he wrote (92): "... Today the world wants to know who are these people who accomplished such a heroic deed and saved mankind. ... they [the Soviet soldiers] were the best of us —noble, pure dedicated and selfless fighters of socialism, for happiness of their people. ...It is necessary to continue with this tradition. Create such literary hero fighters of communism with whom Soviet people would equate and whom they would imitate. ...". In fact, Marx's theories became Lenin's obsessions and a dream come true for Stalin. Communism was his ideal of society, but its concretization did not mean that the Russians had to destroy a nation or all capitalist countries. Unlike Trotsky, he did not want to turn the planet into a communist world. His ego ideal was not as dangerous as Hitler's. However, because of the circumstances, his amorality, the misconceptions about life and death he had, and the violence of his anger, his reaction to the German invasion was appropriate but disastrous for the world. He was not insane, which is why he defended his country, but he did not try to protect the population. He even aroused the military and nation's ire, which moved the Einsatzgruppen to cover Russia with blood and despair. Ordinary people used psychotic defenses and turned reality into Dante's Inferno.

It is not a psychopath who unleashed the atomic primal violence but Harry Truman, who thus defied humanity, history and eternity.

His memoirs are very interesting, but one must admit that it is almost impossible to understand what he wrote if one does not have the same personality organization, all the more so because he was secretive. First of all, it must be said that he was so moralistic that he looked like a person with an obsessional personality. Actually, he was too moralistic to be one, and his attitude towards his old mother shows something else; he wrote (93): "... I was deeply devoted to her, and we were very close. She was a wonderful mother. At ninety-two she was still keen and alert and saw things in their true perspective, even at a time like this. ...". A man with an obsessional personality is not that close to his mother, and when he goes mad, he does criticize her. An immature man could have written this, but all father figures would be depicted as enemies since they would be seen as intruders that want to separate the child from his mother. It was not the attitude of mind of Truman, who used to obey his father and did not hate the male members of his family. Moreover, his family was functional.

It is self-evident that his personality was organized at the neurotic level and that his superego was strong. Was he a person with Hysterical Personality Organization? Since in his speeches and writings there isn't any sign of phobia, one must assume that he was. Actually, a few pieces of information support this theory. The first one has to do with his attitude towards sex. In his memoirs, he describes his life in France during World War One. At the end of 1918, he stayed three days in Paris. On the 7th of December 1918, he went to the *Folies Bergère* to see a show in which the girls were almost naked. He found this "disgusting" (94). Men like him are fond of beauteous blue-eyed ladies who resemble his fiancée, but the ladies whom they marry must also display moral, intellectual, domestic and human qualities. Prudery is the norm for people like him, which is why he got married at the age of 35!

His flowery writing style suggests his personality organization. The best example is the message he sent to General Eisenhower on the 8th of May 1945 (95), which reads: "In recognition of the unconditional and abject surrender of the Nazi barbarians, please accept the fervent congratulations and appreciation of myself and of the American people to the heroic achievements of your Allied Army, Navy and Air Forces. By their sacrifices and courage they have saved and exalted the cause of freedom throughout the world. All of us owe to you and to your men of many nations a debt beyond appraisal for their high contribution to the conquest of Nazism. ...". The other messages he sent on that day are inspired by this one. The meaning of the original is corrupted by empty rhetoric, which is aimed at flattering people, flattery being a trick persons with Hysterical Personality Organization often use.

His conception of morality is more sophisticated than that of people with an obsessional personality since the law is not an end in itself. The goal is to discover the truth through reason. He is as Voltairian as Voltaire: thanks to reason, he achieves wisdom. In his 1952 address, he declared (96): "... Free government is based not only on morality, it is also based on reason. ... in democracy, everyone engaged in politics has a duty – a moral duty – to try to keep public debate reasonable and based on a fair discussion of the issues. ...". This extract is interesting because we can see the obsessional foundations of a personality that is organized at the hysterical level: morality is an important trait, but it is aimed at achieving a higher level of conscience, which enables the individual to perceive reality as it is, deal with it, and accept mankind's imperfections (97). This is a religious emotion; man realizes that all things are fragile and that life must be preserved. Needless to say, this level of intelligence and humanity is very rare. I have been looking for such a personality for more than thirty years, and it is the first time I have met one.

Harry Truman is the only man who dared to use atomic bombs to kill people, and it must have been a very difficult decision to make, but he wanted to hasten the end of the war and save the lives of many American soldiers. In 1945, when the Americans revealed the atrocities committed by the Axis powers, most people wanted to stop this apocalypse as soon as possible. Truman, who had no knowledge of physics and who did not have a college degree, asked Stimson, the Secretary of War, about the atomic bomb (98). He listened attentively to what he told him, for he considered that he was a man of great wisdom and foresight. He also consulted with Churchill, who was in favor of the atomic bomb because he wanted to conclude the war (99). By means of the Postdam declaration, he asked the Japanese to surrender. On the 25th of July, he wrote in his diary that the bomb was a dreadful weapon and that he did not want to use it to kill civilians, especially children and women (100). On the 6th of August, the first bomb exploded over Hiroshima; on the 9th of August, another one exploded over Nagasaki. Around 220 000 people were killed and the Emperor agreed to surrender. In a world drenched in rage, reason stopped the war: a humane, reasonable and sane man acted as the superego of insane humanity. He did not punish it but killed a part of it in order to protect the other part. He played the role which his personality organization had compelled him to play. Unlike psychotics, he used violence and death to protect life, not to destroy everything. A personality organization that venerates life was obliged to kill!

1. Hitler, Adolf, *Mein Kampf,* Munich, 1925 and 1926. English translation by James Murphy, Hurst and Blackett

ltd., London, 1939. Electronic edition: Project Gutenberg Australia.

2. Heller, André, Schniderer, Othmar, *Im Toten Winkel: Hitlers Sekretärin*, film, Dor film Produktionsgesellschaft, Austria, 2002.

3. Rienfenstahl Leni, *Triumph des Willens*, movie, Reichsparteitagsfilm, Germany, 1935.

4. *Mein Kampf,* p. 18-19.

5. *Mein Kampf,* p. 40.

6. *Mein Kampf,* p. 43.

7. *Mein Kampf,* p. 34.

8. *Mein Kampf,* p. 101.

9. *Mein Kampf,* p. 106.

10. *Mein Kampf,* p. 439.

11. *Mein Kampf,* p. 80.

12. *Mein Kampf,* p. 321.

13. *Mein Kampf,* p. 636.

14. *Mein Kampf,* p. 91.

15. *Mein Kampf,* p. 94.

16. *Mein Kampf,* p. 96.

17. *Mein Kampf,* p. 104.

18. Riefenstahl, Leni, *Triumph des Willens...*

19. *Mein Kampf,* p. 105.

20. "Is tomorrow Hitler's?", *Omnibook magazine*, New York, February 1942, p. 142; interview with Carl Jung about his opinion of Hitler.

21. *Mein Kampf,* p. 106.

22. *Mein Kampf,* p. 435 and 437.

23. *Mein Kampf,* p. 486.

24. *Mein Kampf,* p. 220.

25. Clarke, Isabelle, Costelle, Daniel, *Eva Braun dans l'intimité d'Hitler*, movie, production CC et C Louis Vaudeville,

France, 2007.

26. Heller, André, Schmiderer, Othmar, *Im Toten Winkel: Hitlers Sekretärin*...

27. The Nuremberg trials are a valuable source of information. Actually, witnesses and defendants are so stressed that they cannot conceal their traits. Since many colleagues of Hitler were interrogated, and thanks to other documents, we have a clear idea of the personality of the persons who rubbed shoulders with Hitler.

28. *Trial of the major war criminals before the international military tribunal*, Nuremberg, 1947.

29. Gilbert, Gustave, *Nuremberg diary*, New York, 1947; *The Psychology of Dictatorship: Based on an Examination of the Leaders of Nazi Germany*, New York, 1950.

30. *Trial of the major...*, vol. 1, p.162.

31. *Op. cit.*, vol. 1, p. 159.

32. *Op. cit.*, vol. 2, p. 22.

33. *Op. cit.*, vol. 2, p. 156.

34. *Op. cit.*, vol. 12, p. 309.

35. *Op. cit.*, vol. 10, p. 227.

36. *Op. cit.*, vol. 10, p. 224: "... I had a great veneration for him. ..."

37. *Op. cit.*, vol. 10, p. 228.

38. *Op. cit.*, vol. 9, p. 237.

39. *Op. cit.*, vol. 12, p. 419 and f.

40. *Op. cit.*, vol. 12, p. 422.

41. *Op. cit.*, vol. 12, p. 422.

42. *Op. cit.*, vol. 12, p. 419.

43. *Op. cit.*, vol. 12, p. 420.

44. *Op. cit.*, vol. 12, p. 450.

45. *Op. cit.*, vol. 12, p. 450, 451.

46. *Op. cit.*, vol. 14, p. 364-369.

47. *Op. cit.*, vol. 14, p. 368.

48. *Op. cit.*, vol. 14, p. 368.

49. *Op. cit.*, vol. 9, p. 237: "... the defeat of the fatherland, and that one could not let it rest with that. ...".

50. *Op. cit.*, vol. 9, p. 12. Bodenschatz, a liaison officer, declared that they used to speak of the war, but Goering kept saying that he was against it and that he wanted to end it.

51. *Op. cit.*, vol. 9, p. 164.

52. *Op. cit.*, vol. 9, p. 651; see also p. 277 (it deals with his hostility to Goebbels's "utterances").

53. *Op. cit.*, vol. 9, p. 14.

54. *Op. cit.*, vol. 9, p. 242.

55. *Op. cit.*, vol. 12, p. 453.

56. Gilbert, Gustave, *Nuremberg diary*, New York, 1947.

57. *Op. cit.*, vol. 9, p. 12.

58. *Op. cit.*, vol. 9, p. 15.

59. *Op. cit.*, vol. 9, p. 614.

60. *Op. cit.*, vol. 9, p. 361.

61. Goebbles, Joseph, "Mehr moral, aber weniger moralin", Wetter leuchten, Munich, 1939, p. 382-385. Translation by Randall Bytwerk.

62. *Op. cit.*, vol. 10, p. 224.

63. *Op. cit.*, vol. 11, p. 51-53.

64. *Op. cit.*, vol. 11, p. 51.

65. *Op. cit.*, vol. 11, p. 51.

66. *Op. cit.*, vol. 11, p. 52.

67. *Op. cit.*, vol. 11, p. 53.

68. *Op. cit.*, vol. 9, p. 15.

69. Gilbert, *op. cit.*, p. 149-160.

70. *Op. cit.*, vol. 11, p. 397.

71. Hoess, Rudolph, *Death dealer: the memoirs of the SS commandant at Auschwitz*, New York, 1992, p. 142.

72. *Op. cit.*, vol. 11, p. 153.

73. *Op. cit.*, vol. 11, p. 398.

74. Hoess, *Op. cit.*, p. 138.

75. *Op. cit.*, vol. 11, p. 401. He does not understand the behavior of others; when Dr. Kauffmann asks him if he ever felt pity for the victims, he utters a crepuscular yes. This apathy is a classic symptom of depression.

76. *Trials of war criminals before the Nuremberg military tribunals under control council Law n° 10*, Nuremberg, vol. 1, p. 101.

77. *Op. cit.*, p.138-139.

78. *Op. cit.*, p. 139.

79. *Op. cit.*, p.397.

80. *Op. cit.*, p.392.

81. *Op. cit.*, p.393.

82. *Op. cit.*, p.383-386.

83. *Trial of the major...*, vol.4, p.324.

84. Stalin, J. V., *Staline, Izbrannye sochinemya v 3-kh fomakh, Tom 1, Izdatelstvo gazety "Patriot"*, Moscow, 1999, p. 1-4. Translated by Shubhra Nagalia.

85. Stalin, J. V., *On the great patriotic war of the soviet union*, Moscow, 1946, p.77.

86. Stalin, J. V., *Works*, vol. 13., Moscow 1954, p. 30, letter dated January 12, 1931.

87. Stalin, J. V., *On the great...*, p. 58.

88. Op. cit., p. 47.

89. Op. cit., p. 79.

90. Op. cit., p. 30.

91. Op. cit., p. 79.

92. Stalin, J. V., "Discussion in the meeting with the creative intellectuals", *Pravda*, 1946, in Zhukhrai, V., *Stalin: Pravda i lozh*, Moscow, 1996, p. 245-251. Translated by Sumana

Jha.

93. Truman, Harry, *Memoirs by Harry S. Truman: year of decisions*, New York, 1955, p. 58.

94. Op. cit., p. 149.

95. Truman, Harry, *Messages to allied leaders and to general Einsenhower on the surrender of Germany*, the 8th of May 1945.

96. Truman, Harry, *Address before the national conference of citizenship*, the 17th of September 1952.

97. See also: Truman, Harry, *Address in San Francisco at the closing session of the United Nations conference*, the 26th of June 1945; *Address to the United Nations conference in San Francisco*, the 25th of April 1945.

98. Truman, Harry, *Memoirs...*, p. 104.

99. Op. cit., p. 462.

100. Truman, Harry, *Diary*, the 25th of July 1945, Truman library.

Conclusion.

Hell must not be man's destiny. It is clear that societies are dysfunctional because they are composed of individuals who are rarely reasonable, which is why they perpetuate violence and anarchy. Societies are not separate entities. When they try to kill themselves or nations, this does not mean that there are more psychotics, for it takes a lot of time to change the proportion of the three groups of personality organizations. Consequently, insane people are never the cause of the massacres, since they are always sudden. As for the persons with a neurotic personality, they cannot exhibit the rage which characterizes such events: they are doomed to feel the pain, shout and pray. The very immature people are the monsters that misbehave when societies are diseased. The history of mankind is but a sinusoid that goes up when reasonable people are in power or more numerous and down when immature people get the upper hand, which is logical since there are lots of psychopaths.

However, the main issue is that there are unbalanced people who keep misinterpreting reality, which moves them to to destroy the outer world, namely society, as if they were real psychotics, but they are more efficient than they, for they have not lost touch with reality. That being said, all immature people are not mass murderers. Some of them are neither that immature nor that unbalanced. People like Albert Camus are humane and reasonable. I do question the psychiatrists' definition of madness: according to them, the dividing line between sanity and insanity is between the paranoiacs and the psychopaths, whereas I consider that half-madness (psychopathy) is real madness. They believe that since psychopaths do not experience hallucinations (which is not that true), they are not mad. Honestly, re-creation of reality is not a good definition of madness. A person with Hysterical Personality Organization like me puts great emphasis on the necessity of telling the truth and accepting the truth, which implies that 99% of humans are insane! Let us adopt a more moderate approach to that problem. In fact, each time reality is perceived as a danger, the individual misunderstands it. The outer world says something; the immature individual understands something else. This is not reason anymore but unreality. Reality is distorted so that it may fit into the observer's preconceived ideas: this is madness.

Moreover, individual become dangerous when they do not understand certain concepts, the most important one being the meaning of life. I don't know whether very immature people are fascinated by death, but I know that they do not understand what life is. For instance, Véronique Courjault considered that her babies were but pieces of flesh: outgrowths of her body. As for Karl Brandt, the Nazi physician, he was just unable to distinguish life from death. Consequently, Himmler and Hoess could exterminate all the earthlings; they strove to kill the persons whom they regarded as dangerous wooden puppets: old little boys and girls are always monsters! Of course, psychopaths are not always mass murderers, for they don't always decompensate, and there are not always retarded. Some of them are more intelligent, which enables them to mature and be inoffensive. Others are more unstable: they crash their planes into skyscrapers or kill students in American High Schools, for they are on the verge of lunacy.

Decompensation is the real danger indeed, but why do immature people decompensate? Since they are emotionally unstable, we suppose that it is caused by a misinterpretation of realty, which leads them to act inappropriately, which turns the outer world into a persecutor that makes them lose their mental balance. If neurotics and psychotics need a big shock to go mad, psychopaths need a small one, which is why people must support them constantly. We have seen that Harris was alarmed by his father twice. He was supposed to be a good role model and a supportive adult, but he proved to be the opposite. The acquaintances of the mentally unbalanced Eric

Harris did not enable him to be saner: Klebold's desire for murder exacerbated his and the other students did not prevent him from yielding to madness and barbarity. Harris declared that things could have been different. Yes, they could, and one must admit that interpersonal relationships have a lot to do with personal tragedies and social catastrophes.

Unfortunately, societies tend to perpetuate the behaviors that lead to failure. Hence it seems that immaturity is the destiny of mankind. It is self-evident that most immature parents create immature children. Are their children always psychopaths? We don't know, but we can assume that there is a high risk of a further worsening of social dysfunctions. In the case of Isabelle Caro, death was the end of the road. I will not oversimplify the problem, but I do not think that two immature parents often create children with neurotic personalities. Caro is the product of her mother's idiosyncrasies. His father was unable to oppose his wife's crazy ideas. She compelled her daughter to live in a world of morbid illusions, and nothing or no one could enable Isabelle to be more humane, intelligent and efficient. If she had gone to school, the result might have been different. However, if the teachers or the director had been immature people, she would not have been much more intelligent or saner. In fact, the children who attend Summerhill School are also condemned to a lifetime of mental and educational inferiority. Laziness and self-indulgence do not allow children to mature. Happiness is but the harmful projection of an immature adult's feelings and dreams onto a child regarded as an idealized self-image. True happiness is the direct result of the resolution of the Oedipus complex. In fact, when the son realizes that the old man he is going to sacrifice on the altar of his own barbarity represents mankind, he lets go of his dagger. His desire for murder evaporates. The father can set the scintillating crown of civilization upon the head of his son. The boy is a man now; he is not a potential murderer anymore. Humanity can survive and prosper. Happiness can spread.

Nevertheless, society is not always completely stupid. We have seen that literature and filmmaking are not really optimistic about childhood, or youth, or immaturity, but viewers do not take them seriously, for they are not supposed to educate people. Thinkers, I mean philosophers, do this. They are the conscience of brainless nations. Unfortunately, some of them are not reasonable people. For instance, in post-war France, Michel Foucault and Jean-Paul Sartre were very immature persons. What they expressed in their books is a kind of sepulchral unreality. They were the tip of the French iceberg. Actually, the society in which they lived was so dysfunctional that it was impossible to distinguish reason from half-madness. Hence, it could not be saved. When sane people are not at the top of the "mind pyramid", society disintegrates, and reason and intelligence disappear.

Immature people strive to find "solutions". Some of them use substances that kill them sometimes. Others join a group of football supporters and try to mature, but since their leaders are not good role models, they fail miserably and remain little boys.

Actually, if society does not address this issue, it drifts into anarchy. The process is always the same. The first factor is economic depression. People who are mentally and emotionally unstable are traumatized. The situation becomes problematic when persons with an obsessional personality (like Jérôme Kerviel and Hjalmar Schacht) collaborate with immature people, for those with Hysterical Personality Organization cannot enlighten society anymore. In fact, when persons with an obsessional personality, who represent the majority of people with a neurotic personality, do not want or cannot play fair, it's hell on earth.

The second factor is generalized regression to fear of others. Two planes crashing into the World Trade Center, a young Jihadist killing

French soldiers, and a southern novelist insulting black people may be regarded as unusual crimes, but they are not. When many people begin to fear differences between religions or races, one must realize that they are not sane anymore and that society is unable to deal with its psychopaths.

When there is a national trauma, reason and humanity give way to carnage. Frau Junge once said that Hitler stole the conscience of the Germans. Hitler did not steal what they did not have anymore! By means of the Treaty of Versailles, the French had ruined the Germans' self-esteem, which is why they became bloodthirsty killers. Besides, almost all Hitler's courtiers were immature people, which means that there were not enough persons with a neurotic personality to prevent the administration from losing touch with reality.

Schacht was probably the only Secretary of State with a neurotic personality. He was absolved of all wrongdoing! When sane people choose to collaborate with monsters, one must admit that reason is guilty. Unfortunately, when the world is in disarray, pure raison is unhelpful. Harry Truman, a man with Hysterical Personality Organization, had to kill the last enemy. Truth compelled him to protect the good. Then he contributed to the establishment of the United Nations in order to avoid further bloodshed. However, if governments and international governmental organizations must bring peace to the world, individuals must also act to increase people's level of awareness.

For the sake of mankind, whatever the regime, societies must be organized in a very different way. First of all, intelligent, sane people must be social leaders. There is no salvation without the help of persons with Hysterical Personality Organization, for it is they who define truth and reason. They must be assisted by the other persons whose personalities are organized at the neurotic level and by people who are not too immature. This group is the sane part of society, which can deal with very immature people and psychotics. In fact, madness and psychopathy must obey reason so that the system may work.

Moreover, culture and science must play a more significant role in society because they enable leaders and citizens to be more objective. Nonetheless, the most important factor is counterpower. Montesquieu was right: we must tame the most dangerous members of society. Personally, I would establish lots of local counterpowers, and destroy empires, central administrations, multinationals, academicism and monolithic learning. You see, the overcrowded planet cannot survive any major error. Individuals must mature so that societies may be sane. Normalcy leads to perdition because it combines the wildest fears with the wildest dreams. Reason is the key to survival. Hell must not be man's destiny, for man's nature is not essentially evil.

No man is an island,
Entire of itself,
Every man is a piece of the continent,
A part of the main.
If a clod be washed away by the sea,
Europe is the less.
As well as if a promontory were.
As well as if a manor of thy friend's
Or of thine own were:
Any man's death diminishes me,
Because I am involved in mankind,
And therefore never send to know for
whom the bell tolls;
It tolls for thee.

John Donne.